Somatic Psychology

Somatic Psychology

Body, Mind and Meaning

LINDA HARTLEY MA, SRDMT, RMT, UKCP

Practitioner and Teacher of Body–Mind Centering®,
Senior Registered Dance Movement Therapist and
Transpersonal and Body-oriented Psychotherapist

W

WHURR PUBLISHERS
LONDON AND PHILADELPHIA

© 2004 Linda Hartley

First published 2004 by
Whurr Publishers Ltd
19b Compton Terrace, London N1 2UN, England and
325 Chestnut Street, Philadelphia PA 19106, USA

British Library Cataloguing in Publication data

A catalogue record for this book is available from the British
Library.

ISBN 1 86156 430 9

Contents

Dedicated to all those who work to relieve the suffering of others,
and those who seek their help.

Foreword

The direct experience of the human body has had a difficult time gaining a hearing for its unique voice as the field of psychology developed since the late 19th Century. The tenaciousness of Cartesian dualism, which provided the unquestioned foundation for modern scientific thought, keeps interfering with the original insights into the crucial importance of bodily experience articulated by Sigmund Freud, C. G. Jung, and Wilhelm Reich. Mental and verbal processes took over as the primary focus of psychotherapy. In addition, the brilliant proliferation of the empirical biomedical sciences created the illusion that we were on the threshold of uncovering the biomechanics of what traditionally had been thought to be the special preserves of subjectivity: emotion, feeling, character, value.

Working parallel with academic psychologists since the late 1900s has been a very large number of teachers and practitioners whose work has focused on intricate, specific, highly nuanced, and publicly shareable explorations of the meaning inherent in experiences of breathing, moving, touching, and awareness focused on specific regions of the body. Because these innovators worked largely outside the university and medical clinic, they wrote little. Like women of an earlier era, their wisdom was transmitted primarily through craft, direct contact, and oral transmission. Only slowly has the enormous importance of their work for health-care, psychology, and education reached the general public.

In this book, Linda Hartley joins her important voice to the growing number of philosophers, biomedical scientists, and psychologists who are bringing these works into the mainstream dialogue. Her writing deals with two essential areas. For the necessary work of theory construction, she turns to such important figures as the developmental psychologist Daniel Stern, and the earlier analytic theories of Jung and Reich. At the level of practice, she analyzes the experiential methods of Mary Whitehouse, Janet Adler, and Bonnie Bainbridge Cohen. This is a particularly welcome text at a time when the human body is jeopardized on every side, from political and personal violence, to the degradation of the physical environment necessary for bodily wellbeing.

Don Hanlon Johnson
San Fransisco, CA
April 2004

In 1983 Don Hanlon Johnson, PhD, created the first graduate studies program in Somatic Psychology, fully accredited and licensed by the State of California, located at The California Institute of Integral Studies, where he is a professor. He is the author of several books and articles in the field, and a contributing editor of the journal *Somatics*.

Acknowledgements

My thanks go to the many people who have guided, encouraged, and inspired my learning over the years. I am indebted to all of the teachers who have patiently tutored me in the arts of dance, creative writing, movement practice, bodywork, counselling, psychotherapy, meditation, and the art of living mindfully.

And to all of those who have studied with me, or been clients in therapy. Without their trust, courage, and willingness to face the challenges of growth, my own work could not have evolved. I am deeply grateful for the experiences we have shared and for the privilege of witnessing a part of their learning and healing journeys.

In particular, I thank those students and clients who have contributed material for this book, or given permission for their stories to be included.

I wish to thank Bernd Eiden, Roz Carroll, Gill Westland, Susie King, Janet Adler, Deirdre Gordon, Fran Lavendel, Lucy Liddell, and Karen Packwood for reading the text, or parts of it, at various stages of completion. Their comments have been invaluable in helping to clarify the text and bring the book to its present form.

I am especially grateful to Cordelia Grimwood who acted as my academic supervisor while I wrote the dissertation that formed the basis of this book. Her enthusiasm for the project and her good humour kept me going through many a difficult time.

I am also deeply grateful to Deirdre Gordon, my clinical supervisor. Her constant compassionate support together with her clarity and good sense helped me enormously in the development and articulation of my work.

The presence of friendship in my life during the many years in which I have been researching and writing this book has been crucial. I thank all of the friends who have enriched my life and supported my work.

Figures 2.1 and 2.3 are reproduced with the permission of the Zero Balancing Association and Fritz Frederick Smith. Figure 2.2 is reproduced with the permission of The Theosophical Publishing House, India and C.W. Leadbeater.

Material from Jung & Reich: *The Body as Shadow* by John P. Conger, published by North Atlantic Books ©1988 by John P. Conger is reprinted by permission of the publisher.

Material from *Interpersonal World of the Infant: A View from Psychoanalysis and Developmental Psychology* published by the Perseus Books Group and is reproduced with permission of the publisher, with permission conveyed through Copyright Clearance Center, Inc.

Material from *Organic Transference* by Jacob Stattman, is reproduced with the permission of Internationales Institut für Biosyntheses.

Introduction

In ancient times it would have been unthinkable to separate body, soul, spirit, and the natural world, as modern Western science, religion, philosophy, and medicine have done. When individual or collective sickness or misfortune befell, the shaman, as healer, priest, artist, visionary, and ritual master, was called in to help. Today we take our sick bodies to the doctor, our feelings to the psychotherapist, our thirst for knowledge to all sorts of educators, gurus, and books, and when our spirit ails us we may turn to religion, or to alcohol, drugs, sex, and other addictive behaviours in an attempt to alleviate our suffering.

Through the influences of Eastern philosophy, the discoveries of new physics, and a growing recognition of the urgent need to reclaim our sense of wholeness, we are now understanding once again that not only are body, mind, soul, and spirit intrinsically related but that we are also interdependently connected to each other and to the whole of life. This calls for a revision of the way in which we address sickness in the individual, as well as the imbalances and conflicts prevalent in our social, political, and ecological environment.

This study is part of a growing movement concerned with the development of a holistic approach to therapy and healing that embraces body, mind, and spirit within a changing social, cultural, and spiritual context. From the holistic viewpoint the traditional medical model, in its relentless quest to eliminate the symptoms of disease, is limited. Freedom from symptoms is not necessarily a sign of wellbeing and health from the holistic perspective; nor does the presence of symptoms necessarily constitute a problem for the individual. People who have learned to work with and grow from their problems may consider the emergence of a symptom to be part of a welcome healing process, a guide on the path towards greater integration and wholeness.

The heart of this work seeks the cultivation of conscious awareness in the individual, which can lead to greater health and wellbeing, creativity, choice, and responsibility. Through developing awareness, the often hidden sources of inner knowledge, creativity, intuitive wisdom, and healing can be contacted. Most of us need help in contacting and learning to trust our inner mentors and healers; few of us have been encouraged to do this in the past. I

1

see the primary role of the holistic educator, healer, and therapist as facilitating another in the process of discovering their innate wisdom and potential for healing, growth, and creativity; and beyond that, supporting them as they learn to trust, use wisely, and celebrate those innate powers.

The holistic view, which embraces the spiritual, as well as physiological, psychological, and social dimensions of human existence, is reflected in the work of many healers and therapists today, as discoveries in the field of new physics and the views of ancient spiritual and philosophical traditions impress themselves upon our experience and beliefs about human existence and consciousness. These views inform therapeutic work with the fundamental belief that the deepest, the ultimate nature of each individual is essentially loving, wise, compassionate, and full of joy. For example, M. Scott Peck describes his view of the relationship between individual consciousness and the spiritual dimension, ordinarily beyond conscious awareness, in this way:

> In my vision the collective unconscious is God; the conscious is man as individual; and the personal unconscious is the interface between them. Being this interface, it is inevitable that the personal unconscious should be a place of some turmoil, the scene of some struggle between God's will and the will of the individual . . . I believe that the conscious is the seat of psychopathology and that mental disorders are disorders of consciousness. It is because our conscious self resists our unconscious wisdom that we become ill. (Peck, 1978: 282)

Similarly, according to the Buddhist view, the ultimate nature of our mind is pure awareness, beyond duality and the creation of spatial and temporal limits. Mental disorders and the symptoms arising from them are likened to temporary obscurations, resistances within the ego-mind to fully experiencing the deeper nature of the mind; a source of wisdom, healing, and enlightened awareness is discovered to be at the very core of our experience when the ego-mind becomes still and we deepen to this level.

From this we can come to understand that what we need in order to transform our sickness into health, and our confusion into wisdom, lies essentially within us, and not in the hands of the doctor, therapist, priest, or healer. Wholeness and intrinsic good health are the conditions at the core of human nature, and the way to healing lies in contacting and supporting the innate wisdom and inner healing process of the client, which often lie hidden and unrecognized within us.

In a culture that is primarily oriented towards mental and verbal processing and communication, as ours is, bringing awareness to the subtleties of bodily processes, sensations, physical symptoms, and unconscious movement patterns offers a particularly powerful way into accessing the lost or hidden messages of the unconscious. Lost memory, information from the unconscious about our psychological, physical, and spiritual needs, and the body's own innate intelligence and healing powers, can all be accessed through deep bodywork and somatic movement processes.

Of course, movement and bodily processes are not the only ways by which we can access inner knowledge and healing; dreams and images, creative process, relationship difficulties, accidents, illness, and extreme states of consciousness are some of the ways in which unconscious messages attempt to reach our awareness. However, working with the body is an effective approach for many people. This is especially so in our modern culture where historically the body has been repressed and disavowed. Aspects of our nature that are repressed or regarded as inferior by the individual and the culture are the places where our unconscious process, and hence also the seeds of healing, wisdom, and further growth, can be most directly contacted.

In recent years many new approaches to bodywork, somatic movement therapy, and body psychotherapy have been evolving as effective means of addressing unconscious patterns held within the body. Experience shows that these patterns can affect functioning at all levels - physiological, psychological, social, and spiritual. Research into this area is still relatively new, but in this study I will present some examples which I hope will offer the reader a glimpse into some of the potential benefits of somatic movement therapy and body psychotherapy.

Somatic process

Originally trained as a dancer, movement therapist, and bodywork practitioner, I continue to use movement and somatic process as an important foundation for my own work. Later training in dance movement therapy, the transpersonal psychotherapy of psychosynthesis, and process-oriented psychology has deepened and broadened my awareness of the relationships between psyche, soma, and spirit, and of the need to respond to all levels of experience in therapeutic work.

For healing and growth to be deep, enduring, and meaningful to the client, all aspects of his or her being must be engaged. A primarily mental and verbal approach to therapy requires that attention also be given to bodily and energetic processes; psyche and soma are inextricably connected, and movement at one level necessitates awareness of change at others too, so that consciousness can be grounded in living reality. Similarly, somatic therapy alone may not enable the client to access the insight necessary to integrate feelings and changes happening at the somatic level; consciousness needs to be brought to bear, in order to understand the *meanings* of bodily experiences, and integrate psychological levels of the process. Bodily processes and altered states of consciousness are also closely related, and explorations through movement and bodywork sometimes lead to experiences of a perinatal, transpersonal, or spiritual nature (Grof, 1985: Chapter 2). The holistic therapist holds all of these dimensions in awareness in order that the client may be helped to access and integrate them.

I base my own practice of somatic movement therapy upon the principles and techniques of body-mind centering®, an approach to somatic movement therapy and education originated by Bonnie Bainbridge Cohen (USA). It involves a study of the relationship between body and mind in movement, through a detailed and subtle exploration of human anatomy, physiology, infant development, movement, and perception. Essentially what we study is the mind as it is reflected in movement and postural expressions. In the introduction to her book *Sensing, Feeling, and Action,* Cohen writes:

> The mind is like the wind and the body like the sand; if you want to know how the wind is blowing, you can look at the sand.
> Our body moves as our mind moves. The qualities of any movement are a manifestation of how mind is expressing through the body at that moment. (Cohen, 1993: 1)

This work is part of a growing area of study and practice called *somatics.* The term somatics was introduced in 1976 by Thomas Hanna, and the name has come to represent a whole field of enquiry concerned with the experiential study of the body. In traditional studies of medicine, movement education, physiotherapy, and so on, the body has been approached as object and studied as something external and separate from self. In the various approaches within the field of somatics, the body is studied as subject, experienced from within rather than observed from without. When we study the body pervaded with conscious life, rather than observing static images derived from lifeless cadavers, there emerge new insights into the functioning of the body and a radical new perspective on what we call body and mind, and the relationship between them.

We recognize body and mind as having distinct functions, and yet through experiencing the body from within we come to see that they are also integrally connected aspects of a greater whole. We see that both the physical body, and the thoughts, feelings, and images which constantly flow through our awareness are but different expressions of that quintessential something which underlies the flow of our individual lives – what we might perhaps call the life-stream, pure mind or consciousness, inner self, soul, or spirit, manifesting in constantly changing forms through the veil of our individual and collective karmic tendencies. Body, like mind, is continually in flux, changing from moment to moment in response to the underlying process of which it is an expression: cells are born and die; breath, food, and fluids enter the body, are incorporated into our tissues and cells, becoming momentarily a part of us, then are released again as waste once they have served their purpose; sensory impressions from both inner and outer worlds constantly assail our nervous system and the deepest cellular recesses of the body. Only through the miracle of complex interdependence does our bodymind appear to go on continuously being.

Somatic therapies attend to this subtle flux within the bodymind and through various techniques including touch, tissue manipulations, sensory awareness, body imagery, and movement, bring awareness to unconscious patterns, introduce new sensations and choices of response, and support changes towards greater integration, health, and wellbeing.

Healing the split

The bodymind is the aware, intelligent body, the body that we not only perceive and learn about, but which we also perceive with and learn through. The young infant lives and learns through its bodily existence, body and mind not yet separated. But in the process of development, out of the essential unity of psyche and soma the infant begins to differentiate body sensation, emotion, and thought. This is a natural and necessary process, but if it becomes extreme we experience the unnatural splitting of those areas of experience from each other. The experience of being thus divided within ourselves is a very common one in modern society, in part an outcome of religious and cultural values and conditioning, and in part due to personal history and trauma. As we painstakingly heal the wounds of early life and dismantle the belief systems and rigid identities we have formed that keep us separated from our authentic feeling self, we can begin to experience the integrated bodymind again, in full consciousness. Ken Wilber describes this as *centauric consciousness,* the bodymind once more integrated and whole within itself, available to the fullness of life and accessible to transpersonal and spiritual realms of consciousness. Wilber writes of the split within the self, and the reintegration of the centauric level of existence, quoting Alexander Lowen:

> The body is reduced from self to property, something which is 'mine' but not 'me'. The body, in short, becomes an object or a projection, in just the same way the shadow did. A boundary is erected upon the total organism so that the body is projected as not-self. This boundary is a split, a fissure, or, in the words of Lowen, a block.
>
> 'The block also operates to separate and isolate the psychic realm from the somatic realm. Our consciousness tells us that each acts upon the other, but because of the block it does not extend deep enough for us to sense the underlying unity. In effect the block creates a split in the unity of the personality. Not only does it dissociate the psyche from the soma, but it also separates surface phenomena from their roots in the depths of the organism.' . . . To come back to the centaur is to realize that mental and physical well-being already circulate within the total psychophysical organism . . . Whereas the ego lives in time, with its neck outstretched to future gains and its heart lamenting past losses, the centaur always lives in the nunc fluens, the passing and concrete present, the lively present which neither clings to yesterday nor screams for tomorrow, but finds its fulfilment in the bounties of this moment. (Wilber, 1979: 106, 118)

It is to this process of reintegrating psyche and soma that the many approaches to bodywork, somatic movement therapy, and body psychotherapy address themselves. Some may have other specific goals, but all have this in common. Awakening awareness in the body where sensation has been split off from consciousness helps to dissolve the blocks created through trauma, pain, or conditioning; this reconnects us to the organic feeling life and wisdom of the body, and can help heal the split between body and mind, soma and psyche.

The body in psychotherapy

Reflecting the split between body and mind which is endemic in the modern Western world, twentieth-century psychology has divided up the person, assigning mind and feelings to the psychotherapist or analyst, and body to the bodywork practitioner or movement therapist. However, to offer to a client *only* psychotherapy, or *only* bodywork can subtly or directly reinforce the body-mind split from which so many of us suffer; in some cases this will be a reinforcement of a dilemma central to the client's problems. To address this problem many somatic therapists are recognizing the need to develop counselling skills and techniques to help their clients process emotional material; and at the same time there is a growing interest amongst psychotherapists in the inclusion of the body in the therapeutic process. This interface of psychotherapy and psychological theory with the somatic practices of bodywork and movement therapy is the subject of this book.

The exclusion of the body from psychotherapeutic practice ostensibly has its source in ethical concerns about the abuse of clients, particularly sexual abuse, when touch is involved. However, it is now becoming clear that abuse of power is a problem related to the therapist and not the technique; therapeutic touch can be ethical in the right hands, just as a no-touch approach can lead to unethical behaviour in the wrong ones.

As Bernd Eiden points out, another underlying reason for the exclusion of touch may be connected to people's preconceptions, based on their relationship to their own body:

> They reflect our culture's ambiguous attitude to the body, which is a mixture of fear, fascination and narcissistic attachment. Individual and collective projections into the body are strongly split between the body as an idealised object on the one hand, and as a source of fear, pain and threat to the ego on the other.
> (Eiden, 1998: 12–14)

The field of body psychotherapy has recognized the need to address these issues directly, for the exclusion of the body from psychotherapy will inevitably leave important areas of a client's process untouched. Eiden (1998) continues:

In exclusively verbal work, mainly oriented towards mental functioning, the body easily becomes the vehicle for everything that is unresolved and uncontained. This is why we can speak of mental and psychological conflicts becoming 'somatised'. In Western culture the body lives a shadow existence, and its pain, dysfunctions and symptoms acquire emotional significance in relation to everything in the psyche that is repressed, unlived, neglected. The field of counselling and psychotherapy can no longer afford to collude with this neglect of the body.

Somatic psychology and psychotherapy

The practices of body psychotherapy and transpersonal psychotherapy have begun to build bridges between the once-separated processes of psyche, soma, and spirit. Today the newly emerging field of *somatic psychology* is also beginning to contribute a subtle differentiation of bodymind process to the expanded field of psychology, developed through almost a century-and-a-half of research and practice in somatic therapy and education. I refer to the integration of somatic psychology and practice into a body-oriented approach to psychotherapy as *somatic psychotherapy*, a specific approach existing within the broader field of body psychotherapy. This book represents an attempt to articulate that integration.

(I am using the term *somatic psychotherapy* here to denote the specific integration of somatic therapy and psychotherapy. It should be noted that the term has occasionally been used interchangeably with the term *body psychotherapy*. However, the latter is now in common and official usage, and the use of *somatic psychotherapy* as a general term to denote *body psychotherapy* is relatively rare.)

I hope firstly to introduce the reader unfamiliar with this field to the great richness and potential inherent within the interface between somatic and psychotherapeutic theory and practice. Secondly, I argue that both disciplines need the other in order to realize more fully the potentials within their own areas of expertise, as well as to address more holistically the needs of clients seeking help.

The first section of the book begins the exploration of psyche, soma, and movement by introducing some trends in the fields of psychology, somatic therapy, and movement process, with a focus on the body-mind interface. We move from the general, in an overview of the field, towards the specific, with a discussion of a practice that explores the embodied expression of mind, soul, spirit, and community, and the essence of therapeutic practice in the embodied relationship between therapist and client.

Chapter 1 makes a very brief survey of some of the main developments in twentieth-century psychology, with respect to the place that some of its main protagonists have given to the body. It would take several volumes to do this subject justice, but my aim here is simply to indicate some general developments within the field, and hope that the interested reader will explore further.

The theory and practice of somatic therapy are then introduced, and the body-mind connection explored. Chapter 3 describes the disciplines of dance movement therapy and authentic movement as approaches that facilitate embodied expression of mind and spirit in a therapeutic context, and that also take us beyond into ritual and mystical practice.

The second section of the book explores the process of human development from the perspective of the body. In Chapter 4, Ken Wilber's evolutionary map of spectrum psychology will provide a theoretical context for these explorations. The work of Daniel Stern and other psychologists will be presented to affirm the central importance of movement and bodily process in early childhood development, their fundamental role in the emergence of a sense of self, and the need to address preverbal levels of development in therapy through attention to somatic process.

Chapters 5 and 6 describe the process of infant movement development and explore the psychological implications of the basic neurological patterns at the root of this process. This work contributes a theory of infant development grounded in the body, in movement and somatic process.

In the final section, the application of a specific somatic psychology to psychotherapeutic practice will be introduced. A *language of the body* based upon body-mind centering® theory and practice is first presented. Psychological meanings held in the body tissues, and the integration of the body into the psychotherapeutic process are then explored. The last chapter gives an in-depth description of a case study, which I hope will offer the reader a window into one approach within this new and growing field.

Case material is offered throughout the book to elucidate theoretical sections; this includes first-hand accounts from students. To simplify the text I have chosen to use the female pronoun throughout; both genders are intended in all cases, unless referring to a particular person or single-gender group.

This study offers a description of one approach to somatic psychology in practice, based on my personal quest to develop an integrated and holistic approach to human growth and healing. It embraces both the reparative and healing potentials of bodywork and movement therapy, and also their potential to facilitate entry into a psychotherapeutic process and dialogue with the unconscious.

The meeting ground between the disciplines of somatics, psychology, and psychotherapy is vast, rich, and deep and, in a book of this sort, I cannot possibly do justice to the work of all the pioneers forging this new field. This is a small offering – one tip of the proverbial iceberg. I hope that readers interested in the practice of both somatics and psychotherapy will join in my enthusiasm at their prospective 'marriage', and find something of interest in this humble attempt to bring that marriage a little closer to realization.

PART I

Towards a holistic approach

CHAPTER 1

Psychology and the body

Historical and cultural roots of somatic psychology

The term *somatics* was first introduced into modern psychology by Thomas Hanna with his book *Bodies in Revolt*. The Greek word *soma* is defined as 'the body experienced from within' and reflects the efforts of modern bodywork practitioners and somatic movement therapists to move away from the dualistic splitting of mind from body, towards a model of integrated functioning of the whole person, psyche and soma. 'The science of somatology . . . sees the human spirit as transparently embodied and sees the human body as transparently inspired. *Somatology* is the holistic science of human experience and behaviour' (Hanna, 1994: 4).

Hanna goes on to recount how the science of somatology is not in fact new; the term was first used during the late sixteenth century when the study of the human being was divided into psychology and somatology. In the late nineteenth century somatology was further divided into the separate studies of anatomy and physiology, structure and function becoming unnaturally divorced from each other, and the split between mind and body was thoroughly entrenched into scientific thinking. Hanna reintroduced the naming of the science of somatics into modern thinking in the 1970s, as a development within the field of humanistic psychology. However, as Johnson claims, somatic approaches being practised today all have roots that go back to a few individual researchers and practitioners of the mid-1800s (Johnson, 1995: xii).

The holistic approach of somatology of course goes back much further than sixteenth-century Western science. It shares common origins with ancient healing, yoga, meditation, and shamanic practices from every part of the world, and every period of pre-modern civilization that we know of. These ancient traditions took the experience of the embodied self, the integrated bodymind, as fundamental to the practice of healing and disciplines of psychospiritual development. To go back to the roots of Western culture, the view of an integrated bodymind or psyche-soma was prevalent in the philosophy and healing practices of the ancient Greeks. In

11

describing the ancient practice of 'incubation as a therapeutic method', C.A.
Meier writes:

> Studying the sources, we see at once that incubation is for the cure of bodily
> illnesses alone. You might then ask what it has to do with psychotherapy. In the
> first place, the sources constantly emphasise that Asclepius cares for *soma kai
> psyche,* both body and mind – 'body and soul' is the corresponding Christian term;
> and second, bodily sickness and psychic defect were for the ancient world an
> inseparable unity. The saying *mens sana in corpore sano,* which is often misun-
> derstood today, is a later formulation of this idea.
>   Thus in antiquity the 'symptom' is an expression of the *sympatheia,* the
> *consensus,* the *cognatio* or *coniunctio naturae,* the point of correspondence
> between the outer and the inner. (Meier, 1989: iv)

Many ancient practices of healing and psychospiritual development have
been revived as part of the 'growth movement' that began in the 1960s, and
both specific and general aspects of their theory and methodology have
significantly influenced the development of new approaches to therapy,
healing, and education.

New approaches

Now there is a multitude of techniques for working with and through the
body, but also several different approaches with different aims. In *Touching –
Body Therapy and Depth Psychology,* Deldon Anne Mcneely succinctly
outlines some of the major differences:

> There are many approaches to working with the body whose aim is simply to
> improve physical and mental well-being, without necessarily involving the goal of
> increasing awareness of the interior life, for example the physical therapies,
> aerobic exercise, massage, faith healing. Additionally there are approaches to
> working with the body which acknowledge the need for harmony between
> interior and exterior worlds, and which seek to promote that, such as T'ai Chi
> Ch'uan, the martial arts and the techniques of Moshe Feldenkrais. In these
> approaches there is concern for self-actualization through centring awareness in
> the somatic sphere, but there is no intention to expose psychic contents or to
> create a dialogue between conscious and unconscious.
>   . . . Body therapy refers to any approach that focuses on the somatic expres-
> sion of complexes, with the intention to reveal and transform the complex and so
> to extend the ego-Self interaction. (Mcneely, 1987: 14)

The second approach mentioned here is the area of *somatics,* or *somatology,*
and includes many methods of somatic movement therapy and education
which seek to increase the sense of the embodied self, 'the body experienced
from within', and to cultivate awareness and harmony within the body-mind-
spirit continuum. As well as the practices mentioned by Mcneely, others such
as the Alexander technique, body-mind centering, eutony, ideokinesis,
sensory awareness and yoga are included within this field (Johnson, 1995).

We might also include bodywork practices where the client is less actively involved, but may nevertheless develop somatic awareness through the sensitive application of touch and movement by the practitioner; practices such as craniosacral therapy or cranial osteopathy, postural integration, rolfing, therapeutic massage, and zero balancing could be included here, if practised with the intention of cultivating awareness within the body. (For the sake of simplicity I will use the term 'somatic therapy' when referring to approaches which include somatic movement therapy and hands-on bodywork, which seek to cultivate this inner awareness and body-mind integration.)

Body psychotherapy, or body therapy as Mcneely defines it here, explores the bodily expression of psychoemotional complexes in order to support the client's psychological development, and facilitate her ability to relate to self and others in meaningful and rewarding ways. The somatic therapist who has experienced personal psychotherapy herself will invariably offer her clients a space for their psychoemotional process to be held, through the presence she embodies. However, a defining feature of body psychotherapy is the conscious attention given to the relationship between client and therapist, and its relevance to the client's on-going psychological development.

Somatic psychology offers a bridge, an interface between psychotherapy and somatic therapy; it addresses the psychological implications and meaning of bodily expressions and symptoms. Searching for an integrated and cohesive psychology based on authentic body process and experience is not an easy task. The small but growing number of people involved in this field are working against centuries of dualistic thinking that has split asunder mind and body, spirit and matter, function and structure; we are working in the shadow of mainstream culture, and the integration we seek will take time to evolve as we work to heal the fundamental split within ourselves and deep within the cultural mind.

This form of dualism has given such precedence to 'objective' scientific data over 'subjective' embodied experience that the individual has been disempowered in the hands of 'experts' in the fields of mental and physical health. Somatics and somatic psychology seek to re-empower individuals by validating their own subjective experience and the knowledge accessed through bringing awareness to bodymind processes. Hanna (1994: 6) speaks of the 'bi-modal perception' that somatic therapies use:

> . . . If it happens that our subject of observation is a human individual, we suddenly confront the fact that there is not simply one way of observing a human subject but rather two: *there is the scientist's third-person, detached perception of that individual, and there is that individual's own first-person observation of himself.* This is the fact of human bi-modal perception, inescapable if we are finally to develop an authentic humanistic science.

I would add that there is at least one more way of perceiving, within the therapeutic context, and that is the scientist's (here read psychologist's or therapist's) own first-hand experience. This touches on the realm of countertransference and the kind of empathic resonance that the bodyworker and somatic therapist develop. We ourselves become a central tool in therapeutic work when we understand how the client's process reverberates through our own bodymind, creating energetic, sensory, and emotional changes which yield valuable information and insight into the client's process, her feelings, and projections.

A difficulty that can be encountered in developing a somatic psychology is that most schools of psychology and many of the various somatic approaches have developed quite separately, each addressing partial aspects of human experience and behaviour, and operating within different frameworks and paradigms which do not always sit easily together. The development of the study of the human being has grown out of the overriding scientific paradigm, as well as philosophical and religious beliefs that have dominated modern Western thought; a major emphasis has been on the split between mind and body, and the desire for mind to control and maintain superiority *over* the body and nature. Reverberations of this clash are still felt within the field of psychology and psychotherapy where adequate attention to bodily experience is often not given, and in the field of somatics where psychological development and issues such as transference and countertransference are often not understood or addressed. Each expresses just a piece of the total picture. To work therapeutically with the whole person, we can but benefit from the integration of both perspectives.

Modern psychology's roots grew out of the ground of the biological and dualistic medical model of nineteenth-century psychiatry. Mental illness was viewed as originating in organic disorders and treatable through physical and chemical therapies. It is interesting to note that somatic therapists also affirm that bodily states and changes in these can affect mental states profoundly; however, this is not seen as a purely causal principle, but rather that mind and body are expressions of a unified whole, and changes at any level will affect all others. Change can be approached through the body, mental processes, emotional feelings, or imagination. Somatic therapy could be seen to reflect a return to old ground from a new perspective, a turn of the spiral, where mind and body are not viewed as opposing or separate aspects of the individual, but more like different points on a continuum of being. Instead of viewing the relationship between mind and body as causal, it is viewed within a holistic paradigm that sees mental and physical symptoms as different but integrally related expressions of the individual's process and her whole being.

Early pioneers

Although there are differences in the philosophical ground out of which traditional psychoanalysis and body-oriented therapies have grown, Mcneely (1987: 27) considers that body psychotherapy was pioneered by Freud,

Ferenczi, Adler, Groddeck, Reich and Jung. Although not all of them worked with the body directly, they all contributed to or made possible the development of several body-oriented approaches to therapy, and were concerned with the distribution of psychic energy within the body.

Freud's work grew out of the collective attitudes towards the body that were prevalent in the nineteenth century, but in his development from physiology, to neuropathy, to hypnosis, and finally to psychoanalysis, Freud was a pioneer in the 'movement from mechanistic therapy to depth analysis'. His message was that psychic energy could be misdirected and somatized into bodily symptoms: 'a sick or disturbed body indicates a disturbed psyche that needs healing' (Mcneely, 1987: 28).

As Mcneely declares, this was not a popular message. Nor was Freud's insistence on the primacy of the sexual drive in the development of the personality and neuroses. Later on, emphasis shifted to the life (sexual) and death (aggressive) instincts, Eros and Thanatos, and to the relation between the id, ego and superego. The ego was the seat of conflicts between the chaotic emotions of the id, based in bodily experience, and the superego, which reflected parental and societal morality, judgements, and the necessities of external reality. 'Freud described the ego as a "body ego", but his conceptualization of resistances was entirely in the realm of mental defence mechanisms, which have never been clearly translated into physiological terms' (Mcneely, 1987: 31).

Ferenczi took a more interactive approach than Freud, encouraging the patient to re-enact memories and fantasies, with the analyst engaging actively in the dramas. His emphasis on countertransference, the acting out of the parent-child relationship with the analyst, and his active engagement with the client's process set the ground for the development of psychodrama.

Adler's work explored the bodily expression of character traits and encouraged the use of expressive movement, a precursor of dance movement therapy. Also based on the instinct theory, Adler's focus was on the will to power and the aggressive drive in personality formation. He writes of the relationship between physical disorders and psychological states: 'The refusal of normal functions may be an expression of jealousy and desire; insomnia, of ambition; over-sensitivity, anxiety, and nervous organic disorders, of craving for power.' He describes how mental tension affects both the central and autonomic nervous systems; autonomic stimulation causes functional changes in respiration, circulation, and the muscles, endocrine glands, and organs of the whole body:

> As temporary phenomena the changes are natural and only show themselves differently according to the style of life of the person concerned. If they persist, one speaks of functional organ neuroses. These, like the psychoneuroses, owe their origin to a style of life which, in the case of failure, shows an inclination to retreat from the problem at hand and to safeguard this retreat by clinging to the bodily and psychological shock symptoms which have arisen. This is the way the

psychological process reflects itself in the body. (Alfred Adler, from Ansbacher and Ansbacher, 1956: 223)

The work of Groddeck also has considerable bearing on the development of body-oriented therapies. He proposed that, parallel to the unconscious of the thinking brain, each cell, tissue, and organ of the body has its own unconscious. All of these parts are connected and in communication, and thus analysis of the unconscious brain can have beneficial effects on the unconscious of the other organs and cells. Like Adler's perspective, this has direct relevance for the bodyworker and somatic movement therapist. However, what Groddeck did not do was to reverse the process and explore how change to the unconscious of the body tissues at a cellular and organic level might affect the unconscious of the thinking brain. It is exactly in this area that somatic therapies operate. For example, body-mind centering works specifically with the dialogue between the conscious and the unconscious processes through the cells, tissues, and organs of the body; this allows us to access and potentially influence the unconscious organization of the brain and its perceptual and thinking processes. The Feldenkrais method also focuses on the repatterning of the nervous system and neural responses through somatic movement therapy, which influences how we perceive, think, and feel, as well as move.

Reich was one of the most influential of the psychoanalysts who ventured far into the territory of the body. Like Freud, he saw sexual energy as primary, and viewed the blocking of this energy in the body as the source of all neuroses, social ills, and character traits. In the early days Freud had used massage with his patients to help free the blocked libido, but later free association became his primary method, and contact was excluded from this approach. Reich, however, continued to use physical interventions, working directly with the body through contact and movement exercises, to release the dammed up sexual energy. Reich was excluded from psychoanalytic circles during the 1930s, but whether the reason for this was on theoretical or political grounds, or for some other reason, is not clear; certainly Reich's views were way ahead of his time, for he brought to his work a social conscience which led him to take his ideas about psychoanalysis, sexuality, and vegetative therapy to the people. His work has been of prime importance in the field of body psychotherapy, the neo-Reichian and Bioenergetic schools being the main developments of his original work.

Jung has also contributed to and made possible several developments in the field of body-oriented therapies, and in particular has influenced the work of a number of dance movement therapists. The body was not a primary focus for Jung, and although he would at times encourage clients to express themselves in creative movement, he has written relatively little about the body. Some would claim that the Jungian approach can lead to a transcendence of the body, and this may be so, depending on the approach of the analyst. However, as Mcneely points out: 'His psychology has furnished a container in which his followers have been able to develop many facets and directions, including body therapy and dance movement' (McNeely, 1987: 39).

What Jung did, of course, was reintroduce into Western psychology the place of the transpersonal. The contribution of Jung and some of his followers to the field of body psychotherapy and somatic psychology, as well as to the relationship between the body and spiritual dimensions of experience, will be revisited later.

The body-mind split

An exploration of modern psychology must, of course, begin with Freud, but we must remember that his own roots were in nineteenth-century psychiatric medicine and the dominant patriarchal, dualistic, and materialistic culture of the day. The theories of new physics, feminism, and other sources now challenge some of the ideas at the root of classical psychoanalysis. However, Freud's basic discoveries about the power of the unconscious over conscious thought and behaviour form the basis of further developments in twentieth-century psychology, and modern psychology has grown out of the ground of Freudian thought and psychoanalytic practice. Some may criticize much Freudian thinking today, but fair due must be given to the 'father' of modern psychology.

Nevertheless, one blatant problem appears: although the issue of mothering takes a central place in psychotherapy, and many see 're-mothering' as an essential part of practice, modern psychology does not have a 'mother', only a 'father'. In discussing the power of the analyst, Frosh writes:

> In general it is not the explicit figure of a father that hovers over the analyst, but the implicit patriarchy involved in the manifestations of power present in the therapeutic setting. The way in which this infiltrates the classical notion of the analyst as a distant, neutral interpreter of psychic conflicts has already been described; the law-making paternal role provides an unarticulated substratum to this mode of practice. (Frosh, 1987: 264)

Unless power dynamics are questioned, psychoanalysis and psychotherapy can reinforce patriarchal structures and values. However, as Frosh points out, Freud was the first to face directly the issue of the power of the doctor/analyst, and despite appearing to reinforce such power dynamics, psychoanalysis does potentially offer methods to evaluate and change them. The focus on the relationship between the two parties within the psychoanalytic encounter emphasizes the power relations inherent in therapy, but it also offers tools with which to address them. Thus, writes Frosh, 'the apparent authoritarianism of analysis can turn out to be more progressive and "subversive" of internalised authority than do the more apparently egalitarian efforts of many of Freud's opponents' (Frosh, 1987: 81).

This power dynamic includes the dominant view of male supremacy in society, as well as the tendency of patriarchal philosophy and religious aspiration towards transcendence. One basic tenet of classical psychoanalysis, the mastery and control of repressed instincts by the ego through mental analysis, is a way towards transcendence of bodily function by the mind. Although Freud was opposed to religion, his work does nevertheless grow out of the androcentric thinking that was interwoven into the fabric of a male-God oriented religion. The body and its instinctual energies are viewed as base and inferior - through analysis of them we can gain some degree of control and thus transcendence over our 'animal' nature. By implication, an embodied and intuitive approach to therapy, which values direct personal experience, is also inferior to a rational and analytical approach.

Jean Hardy traces the development of the split between spirit and matter in Western thinking, with reference to the schism which has been created between science and mysticism over the last 400 years. She quotes Francis Bacon (1561-1626), noting his significant use of gender pronouns:

'The new man of science must not think that the "inquisition of nature is in any part interdicted or forbidden". Nature must be "bound into service" and made a "slave", put "in constraint" and "moulded" by the mechanical arts. The "searchers and the spies of nature" are to discover her plots and secrets.'
The transcendental God was still believed in by such scientists of the seventeenth century, but the immanent God present in all things had vanished. Instead, natural things were seen as being legitimately subjectable to the forces and language of the Inquisition. (Hardy, 1987: 103)

Bacon's view of the relationship of the dominant masculine to the feminine, and the association of the feminine with nature, has had obvious disastrous consequences for women, for the natural environment, and for our relationship to the human body too. This dualistic way of thinking was further developed by Descartes, with his belief in the ultimate truth of reason and analytical thinking.

He rejected the idea of the unconscious. He believed in a complete split between mind and body: 'there is nothing included in the concept of body that belongs to the mind; and nothing in that of the mind that belongs to the body' . . . [Descartes] believed, with Bacon, that the purpose of science was to gain control over nature. This split between mind and body was of radical significance to subsequent thought, and one that broke from the picture of the body as a symbol of the soul. (Hardy, 1987: 104)

These views were further developed and established as the dominant scientific paradigm through the work of Newton, and later Darwin, and it was in such a climate of thought that Freud developed his work. Freud's work was certainly revolutionary for its time, but it is based on scientific premises, a paradigm, which are now outdated. A paradigm is an accepted picture of reality from which all scientists of the time work, a commonly understood and accepted set of models and principles about the nature of life and the world. Hardy (1987: 98) writes: 'Eventually, the practitioners will begin to discover more and more anomalies and exceptions, and gradually the paradigm will be questioned – often against the considerable opposition not only of the scientific community but of the society at large.'

The new paradigm of the twentieth century has been described in works such as those of Capra and Bohm (Capra, 1975, 1982; Bohm, 1980). The profound changes in the world of physics since the beginning of the twentieth century have uprooted the old mechanistic and dualistic world view of the Newtonian-Cartesian paradigm, creating a radically new perspective and understanding. However, as Stanislav Grof (1985: 17) points out, psychology has been slow to catch up with the discoveries of the new physics:

> In the course of this extraordinary transformation, it has become quite complex, esoteric, and incomprehensible for most scientists outside the realm of physics. As a result, disciplines like medicine, psychology, and psychiatry have failed to adjust to these rapid changes and to assimilate them into their way of thinking. The world view long outdated in modern physics continues to be considered scientific in many other fields, to the detriment of future progress.

The work of the holistic and body-oriented therapist is based upon the view that the spiritual, as well as physical, psychological, and social dimensions of human existence are intrinsically connected. We are both individual and unique human beings of physical matter and form, and also beings of conscious spirit connected in mysterious ways to the whole of existence. In Grof's (1985: 344–6) view, symptoms of mental and psychosomatic illness can be expressions of a lack of balance and integration between these dual aspects of our nature:

> Human beings show a peculiar ambiguity which somewhat resembles the particle-wave dichotomy of light and subatomic matter. In some situations, they can be successfully described as separate material objects and biological machines, whereas in others they manifest the properties of vast fields of consciousness that transcend the limitations of space, time, and linear causality. There seems to be a fundamental dynamic tension between these two aspects of human nature, which reflects the ambiguity between the part and the whole that exists all through the cosmos on different levels of reality . . .
>
> In the broadest sense, what is presented as psychiatric symptom can be seen as an interface conflict between two different modes in which humans can experience themselves. The first of these modes can be called 'hylotropic consciousness' (matter oriented); it involves the experience of oneself as a solid physical entity with definite boundaries and a limited sensory range, living in three-dimensional space and linear time in the world of material objects . . .

The other experiential mode can be termed 'holotropic consciousness' (aiming for wholeness or totality); it involves identification with a field of consciousness with no definite boundaries which has unlimited experiential access to different aspects of reality without the mediation of the senses . . . Experiences in the holotropic mode systematically support a set of assumptions diametrically different from that characterising the hylotropic mode.

Grof offers a new perspective that reflects the paradigm shift of new physics from the purely hylotropic view, which is essentially materialistic, mechanistic, and dualistic, to a view that also encompasses the expanded holotropic consciousness. In treating sickness and mental health problems, levels of experience, and the interface at which they meet, must be embraced. Human consciousness has reached this level of understanding of reality and so it is to such a reality that we must now attune ourselves; the old model is too limited and limiting to our further growth.

The integration of the findings of new physics into the field of psychology is fundamental to the development of an integrated and holistic psychology – a psychology that includes matter, body, mind, soul, and spirit, and is concerned with the relationship of the individual to the universal. Within the context of an imperative to align psychology with the new paradigm of modern physics, the fields of humanistic, transpersonal, and body psychotherapies have been evolving.

Reich and Jung: towards a holistic approach

The Freudian and post-Freudian classical approaches, whilst considering processes rooted in the instinctual life of the body to be a basis of neuroses, do not usually deal directly with the body in therapy; and they have tended to consider religious involvement or spiritual aspiration to be a sign of pathology, not a genuine quest to develop the spiritual dimension of life. Classical analysis primarily addresses the verbal and Oedipal stages of development; Klein, Winnicott, and others have addressed more specifically the earlier pre-verbal phases but adult psychoanalysis is still primarily conducted through the verbal channel. This of course can be an effective approach in many cases; but in others it may be a significant limitation. Of all of Freud's followers, it was Reich and Jung who delved most deeply into the areas of body and spirit, and paved the way for many new developments in the fields of humanistic, transpersonal, and body psychotherapy.

As Jung himself was aware, each psychological theory reflects the psychological tendencies of the theoretician; thus the analyst's own psychological makeup will influence the approach, and the probable outcome of the analysis or therapy. (In my own experience, each approach to therapy also has its own shadow side, its particular blind spots, related to the standpoint it takes; training in more than one approach is helpful, in order to recognize and integrate the shadow of each chosen path.) In this view, Jung reflects the discovery of new physics that the observer affects that which is being observed. In discussing the different theories of Freud and Adler, Jung (1972: para. 2) wrote:

> . . . Owing to his psychological peculiarity, each investigator most readily sees that factor in the neurosis which corresponds to his peculiarity. It cannot be assumed that the cases of neurosis seen by Adler are totally different from those seen by Freud. Both are obviously working with the same material; but because of personal peculiarities they each see things from a different angle, and thus they evolve fundamentally different views and theories.

The same is true of Jung and Reich, two who left the Freudian fold to develop in radically different directions. Yet, as Conger shows in his book, *Jung and Reich: The Body as Shadow*, despite their different approaches these two men had much in common, and much to complement and complete the other's perspective in terms of developing a holistic approach to the human condition.

Treating the whole person

Both Jung and Reich held the view that, living in a sick society as we do, adaptation to this society through analysis does not necessarily constitute health. Both sought to free individuals from the bonds and constraints of the collective norm, and to help them to realize their potential for a creative and uniquely fulfilling life. Although the approaches to therapy of Jung and Reich, and the theories they based this upon, differed widely, each in the end and in his own way came to a common understanding about life, and about man and woman's place in the universe. Conger writes:

> Coming from different directions and in different styles, Jung and Reich both stepped through the layers of personality, the 'shadow' and 'character defence', the 'secondary layer' and 'personal unconscious', to experience the wider collective world of nature, which has its own functional logic. From their rigid particularity, they both stepped into an experience where, as Jung says, 'Man is no longer a distinct individual, but his mind widens out and merges into the mind of mankind – not the conscious mind but the unconscious mind of mankind where we are all the same.'
>
> The psychological systems of both Reich and Jung took them 'down to the very foundations of life'. (Conger, 1988: 5–6)

For Jung, these foundations were the collective unconscious, and for Reich, the experience of orgone energy at the core of the individual and the universe. Each, through his unique approach, and deep personal experience, realized the movement from ego-consciousness to a deeper awareness of self, rooted in the world of archetypes and nature. Jung came to the realization that archetypes are an aspect of instinct, inherited by each individual, as are the biological instincts; and Reich (1973: 283) came, towards the end of his work, to recognize the mystical dimension of orgone energy as 'God', an 'objective functional logic in the universe', which pervaded all life.

Both recognized the need to treat the whole person, not just the symptoms, which is the basis of holistic therapy. Jung (1933: 117) writes: 'We have come to understand that psychic suffering is not a definitely localized, sharply delimited phenomenon, but rather the symptom of a wrong attitude assumed by the total personality. We can therefore not hope for a thorough cure to result from a treatment restricted to the trouble itself, but only from a treatment of the personality as a whole.'

Reich's idea of *character* parallels this statement by Jung. For Reich, character was a total bodily attitude, expressed through and maintained by muscular body armouring. This holistic approach is generally found in body psychotherapies and somatic practices, where the total body expression is seen as a reflection of the whole person; attention is paid to the symptoms within the context of the healthy functioning of the whole person, and not as isolated phenomena.

Reich's focus was on the body and the healing of the body-mind split. Like Freud, sexuality was central to his theory: 'He believed that all neurosis was caused by an unholy alliance between a psychic conflict and dammed-up sexual energy, that the blocking of the life force in the very tissue of the body was the cause of the misery in the psyche of man and his world' (Conger, 1988: 32).

Muscular armouring locked this energy into the body tissues, inhibiting the individual's free and spontaneous expression of her life force in full orgasm, which Reich believed was the one factor central to psychic health. He formulated a method of character analysis based on his work with body armouring, and came to view chronic muscular tension and attitudes of character as functionally identical and inseparable. As Myron Sharaf (in Boadella, 1976: 10-11) points out, Reich's understanding of character structure and the need to address the whole personality in therapy, not just the symptoms, was later incorporated into psychoanalytic theory and practice. He developed a method called vegetotherapy, based on breath and the flow of energy through the body. The aim of this approach was to dissolve neurotic conflicts through the breaking down and releasing of chronic energy blockages in the body. He writes: 'From now on, I was able to make practical use of this unity. When a character inhibition would fail to respond to psychic influencing, I would work at the corresponding somatic attitude. Conversely, when a disturbing muscular attitude proved difficult of access, I would work on its characterological expression and thus loosen it up' (Reich, 1970: 241-2).

Reich observed that a change in psychic functioning led to somatic change; and somatic change also produced a corresponding psychic change. This two-way interaction between psychic and somatic interventions is fundamental to body psychotherapy; in this it differs from verbal psychotherapy that works primarily through verbal interventions, or from somatic therapy that uses touch and movement but generally does not address the psychological context directly.

Reich was also the first to introduce and articulate the concept of *somatic resonance*, a crucial tool in all body psychotherapies, whereby the therapist feels something of the client's somatic experience within her own body. Sensations within her body are evoked by, or resonate with, the client's psychic and somatic experience in the moment; recognition by the therapist of her own somatic experience, evoked by the client's process, facilitates the awakening of awareness in the client, and the release or transformation of energy.

The spiritual dimension

Reich did not, in the early days, believe in the mystical dimension, but was firmly rooted in the view of biological causation, of sexual energy as the driving principle behind psychic life, so he did not find allegiance with Jung. It was only later in his career that Reich was able to embrace the spiritual dimension, coming to it as a scientist with the discovery of the cosmic orgone ocean, an energy he showed to be observable and measurable. This direction in his work enabled him to perceive the 'objective functional logic in the natural functions beyond [one's] personal being' (Reich, 1973: 283), and to see that we seek to know that we participate in the whole of nature, as microcosm to macrocosm.

Jung's primary contribution was the search to heal the split in the psyche of modern man and woman that alienates us from the deeper roots in soul, in the archetypal realms, in the spiritual dimension of being, and in our connectedness to the whole of life. For Jung, neurosis had its roots only partially in the patient's past, and was always triggered by present circumstances. He viewed sickness, both psychological and physical, as an attempt to heal some imbalance; a neurosis indicates that a new psychological adjustment is required, and its appearance can stimulate significant growth experiences. Jung viewed the psyche as a self-regulating system that always seeks to maintain equilibrium, as the body does. The principle of compensation is important here; symptoms and dreams are seen as attempts by the unconscious to compensate for an imbalanced conscious attitude, and attention to them can bring about the necessary changes. Thus the personal unconscious is viewed not just as a repository for repressed and disowned childhood affects and rejected remnants of experience but as a source of healing, containing the seeds of new life and potentials yet to unfold. The collective unconscious is the realm of archetypes, our ancestral heritage, which is shared by all beings, human and animal, and the true basis of the individual psyche, according to Jung.

Jung was primarily interested in issues that concerned the person in mid-life; his orientation was towards the future and the unfolding of unexpressed potential, as opposed to Freud's retrospective approach, which focused solely on past events as sources of neurosis. Jung discovered that creative and sensitive people needed more than adaptation to the norm in order to be psychologically healthy, and sickness often arose when creative potential, seeking expression, was blocked. Such a person often has special tasks to fulfil in life, and will not find balance and wellbeing until this is realized. The search for meaning and purpose in life is a search that Jungian and transpersonal therapies address; it is thought to be of particular relevance to the mid-life period, also described by Wilber as the *centauric* phase of development, although these issues may come to the forefront at any age.

Mind and matter

For Jung, the self represents the whole psyche, conscious and unconscious, whilst the ego 'is only the point of reference for consciousness' (Jung, 1968: para. 17). He saw mind and body as

> simply different aspects of a single reality as viewed through different frames of reference . . . Jung's belief in the ultimate unity of all existence led him to suppose that physical and mental, as well as spatial and temporal, were human categories imposed upon reality which did not accurately reflect it. Human beings, because of the nature of language, are bound to categorise things as opposites . . . But these opposites may, in fact, be facets of the same reality. (Storr, 1983: 25)

Closely attuned to the ideas of new physics, Jung was an early spokesperson for the revival of the holistic perspective more prevalent today, which was also at the root of ancient healing practices. He broke away from the materialism of the nineteenth century, which proclaimed psyche to be derived from physiological processes, recognizing that 'the psyche is living body, and the living body is animated matter' (Jung, 1976: para. 961). Jung, however, gave sovereignty to the psyche, in contrast to Freud who essentially gave sovereignty to the physical constitution (Jung, 1976: para. 967-8). Many therapists and practitioners today still fall into one or other camp; others, myself included, believe that either and both can be true, that illness can have both physical and psychological causes, but that the overall process of the human being, individually and collectively, is guided by more complex and subtle forces than dualistic thinking can conceive. Jung was well aware of this but consciously chose his standpoint in order to study the psyche in depth (Jung, 1976: para. 968-9). Because of this, he has sometimes been accused of developing a psychology that transcends the embodied experience (Goldenberg, 1989: 244-5), but as Mcneely points out, Jung's work had an openness of application that has led to the development of creative and body-based therapies, such as dance movement therapy. Some of his followers, notably Marion Woodman, are now doing very interesting work in the area of the body in analysis (Woodman, 1982, 1985).

Jung had recognized how body and psyche interact, through his work with galvanic skin tests and association tests, and he was also well aware of how psychological trauma is incorporated into and affects the overall functioning of the body. He related this to the activation of complexes, and to the breakdown of the ego-complex in neurotic and psychotic episodes (Conger, 1988: 64).

The body as shadow

Both Jung and Reich were aware of the body as shadow, as holding the unacknowledged and unexpressed aspects of the self. Conger (1988: 64) writes:

> Indeed, the body *is* the shadow insofar as it contains the tragic history of how the spontaneous surging of life energy is murdered and rejected in a hundred ways until the body becomes a deadened object. The victory of an overrationalized life is promoted at the expense of the more primitive and natural vitality. For those who can read the body, it holds the record of our rejected side, revealing what we dare not speak, expressing our current and past fears. The body as shadow is predominantly the body as 'character', the body as bound energy that is unrecognized and untapped, unacknowledged and unavailable.

Conger goes on to point out that Jung's concept of the 'shadow' and Reich's 'secondary layer' of biopsychic structure both equate more or less with Freud's 'unconscious'. Reich worked directly on this secondary layer as manifested in chronic muscular armouring, which defends the person from inner and outer assaults, and shuts down the free flow of energy. Whilst Reich's own belief was that this armouring should be completely dissolved, in order to free the inner person who is essentially good and loving, therapists today have come to recognize that a certain amount of body armouring is necessary; now the goals of therapy focus more on flexibility of choice around opening and defending, and a holding of the creative tension of the opposites. It is understood that the layer of armouring, the *shadow* held in the body, holds the vital life force and power which has been disowned, and needs to be integrated and related to, not dissolved away.

Using active imagination and the creative arts, Jung worked on the shadow through dream images and symbols, which he believed to originate within the body:

> For Jung, the so-called mystic, the greatest of mysteries were present in the body itself. From his studies of Eastern yogic practices, he knew of the production of the 'diamond body', the development of something eternal and durable in the laboratory of one's life. And he knew that the alchemy he sought involved similar bodily changes. The creation of the philosopher's stone, a durable self in a world of change and decay, and even the formation of symbolic images from the unconscious, is reflected in the body. 'The formation of symbols', Jung wrote, 'is frequently associated with physical disorders of a psychic origin, which in some cases are felt as decidedly "real".' He continued: 'The symbols of

the self arise in the depths of the body, and they express its materiality every bit
as much as the structure of the perceiving consciousness. The symbol is thus a
living body, *corpus et anima*'.

The Eastern mind feels that thought itself has substance. Man as a living being,
said Jung, outwardly appears as a material body, which inwardly manifests itself as
'a series of images of the vital activities taking place within it. They are two sides of
the same coin.' Rather than working directly on the body, Jung chose to work with
the symbols, knowing that they had a materiality of their own, and profoundly
shifted the energy of the body. (Conger, 1988: 185, quoting Jung, 1980: 173 and
Jung, 1969: 326)

This understanding of the relationship between body and symbol was also
used by Assagioli in his development of psychosynthesis; like Jungian
practice, psychosynthesis mainly works on the body through exploration of
the symbols that arise from its depths, using guided imagery and other
techniques. In my own practice I combine this approach with movement and
bodywork, where we discover that bodily changes also affect the images and
symbols directly.

Jung and Reich both deviated from Freud's view of neurosis as rooted in
the past, and saw it as being recreated every day through the patient's current
attitudes – an ongoing living process manifesting through body function and
symptoms, dream images and symbols. Jung's primary concern was with the
second half of the life cycle, but he recognized the connection between
transformation at this level and regressive processes rooted deeply in bodily
and intrauterine experience. The alchemical vessel that was the symbolic
container for transformatory psychic processes was also the womb of
infantile regression and death-rebirth experiences:

Regression goes back, said Jung, to a deeper level than the sexual, to a nutritive
and digestive function, and then the libido withdraws into an intrauterine,
prenatal condition, past the personal layer, into the collective psyche in a journey
of the underworld. While the libido, immersed in the unconscious, triggers infantile reactions and fantasies, it also enlivens archetypal images that can have healing
value. (Conger, 1988: 73)

The body, like the dream, holds the seeds of healing and growth, and through
exploring the body, its chronic contractions, pains, and symptoms of disease,
we may access this healing source. The healing is already held within the
symptom. The hope is that, as the body as shadow is acknowledged, owned,
understood, and its processes integrated into consciousness, the body
becomes a guide and teacher in our development, indicating where we are
out of balance, where we have strayed too far from our path, where we have
overstepped our limitations or not met our basic needs, and where wrong
attitudes are keeping us stuck and immobilized. Or, as Conger says, 'Physical
illness, rather than representing blatant failure, may be a sign of how far we
have evolved as we are tested once more in the fire at the core of our lives'
(Conger, 1988: 200). The body can reveal all of this, and much more, when

we learn to listen to it, just as the dream image that emerges from our night sleep or day reveries can catalyse insight, healing, and change. Then bringing awareness to the body need no longer be fraught with fear, anxiety, guilt, shame, or disbelief, but may become an adventure of courage and curiosity, the hero and heroine's journey embodied within.

> The body is our school, our lesson, our protagonist, our beloved enemy, our shadow and anima/us, the deep friend of our soul. Our bodies, so much the stuff of the world, so sensitive to our inner images, are more changeable than we think, more fluid and spiritual, more infused with light than we guess. Our bodies finally become the jumping-off place into the higher realms, and may accompany us in some higher form into other worlds. We may not be buried with our spears, servants, and favored animals, but if our life continues at the death of the body, some fabric of body may dress us still in a primal and gracious form. (Conger, 1988: 189)

CHAPTER 2

Somatic practices

A multitude of therapeutic approaches within the transpersonal and humanistic fields have developed in the wake of Jung and Reich, all seeking holistic ways to heal the body-mind-spirit split that so threatens us today. Body psychotherapy has recently been defined as a development within the humanistic and transpersonal movement, although the work has been evolving since the time of Reich. It is within the field of body psychotherapy, where the expression of psychoemotional issues through the body are explored, that the integration of psyche and soma in therapy has been most directly and dynamically addressed.

In distinction to body psychotherapy, somatic therapies do not always or primarily focus on emotional expression, and psychological issues may not be explicitly addressed. However, somatic work does touch upon deep emotional and psychological processes, and change can be effected at many levels even when conscious integration of psychoemotional issues is not an explicit focus of therapy.

There are many interfaces between somatics and psychology, many meeting places where each can complement and enrich the other. The field of somatic psychology reflects this meeting place. In general, psychology can bring to somatic therapy an understanding of the psychological context within which a client's process unfolds and thus help to orientate and guide the work appropriately. The development of skills to help process psychoemotional issues arising during somatic work, and an understanding of transference and countertransference issues are some of the ways in which psychology can contribute to the development of the field of somatics. Somatic therapy returns us to the body as the ground from which to explore our experience, and offers a foundation for the development of a psychology based on somatic process. Where psychology is founded largely upon clinical observation, somatics is grounded in direct experience. This alternative perspective can enrich greatly and deepen the understanding of psychology and the practice of psychotherapy through the insight gained from a highly subtle and differentiated exploration of bodymind processes.

A wide range of practices comes under the general category of somatics and includes both therapeutic and educational approaches. Their common factor is that they address the body directly through combinations of touch, physical manipulations, movement and sensory awareness. All aim to develop the sense of 'the body experienced from within'; beyond this, each approach may differ quite widely from the others in its specific aims and objectives, although in general they all seek to cultivate more efficient movement and postural patterns and a healthy sense of self through the integration of the bodymind. Included are techniques of primarily passive manipulation, such as massage, rolfing, structural integration, craniosacral therapy, and zero balancing, as mentioned in Chapter 1. Many somatic practices place more emphasis upon the student's or client's active participation; some approaches involve learning about oneself through enhancing subtle awareness of the breath, as in the work of Elsa Gindler, Ilse Middendorf, and their followers. Many somatic approaches involve movement, often combined with sensory awareness, touch, physical manipulations, visual imagery, and breath work; the Feldenkrais method, the Alexander technique, body-mind centering, eutony, yoga, martial arts, and dance movement therapy are examples.

In his introduction to *Bone, Breath, and Gesture,* a collection of essays by and interviews with some of the foremost practitioners in the field of somatics, Johnson notes the long history of the development of somatic practices in the West, all of which go back to a few innovators working in the nineteenth century. Johnson notes that the skilful and brilliant work of these practitioners has rarely been acknowledged by academic scholars, medical researchers, educators, or funders, which is indicative of the dominant mind-over-body split of Western culture (Johnson, 1995: xii). In speaking of the diverse community of somatic practitioners and practices, Johnson (1995: xvi) writes:

> Underlying the various techniques and schools, one finds a desire to regain an intimate connection with bodily processes: breath, movement impulses, balance and sensibility. In that shared impulse, this community is best understood within a much broader movement of resistance to the West's long history of denigrating the value of the human body and the natural environment.

Traditional Reichian and bioenergetic body psychotherapy had a basis in third-person observation. Of course skilled practitioners develop keen intuitive and sensory skills, but theory was based primarily on observed bodily structure rather than felt inner experience. Observation, analysis of character types, exercises and techniques to break down muscular armouring and thus improve the psychosomatic wellbeing of the individual were fundamental to early body psychotherapy practice, which tended to be very much directed by the therapist. Skilled observation is, of course, an invaluable tool, but to individuals who are sensitive to their own subjective meanings, another's interpretations of their unique somatic expression may be felt to be judgemental or intrusive if not offered with great sensitivity. Newer developments in body psychotherapy, such as biosynthesis, hakomi, and core process psychotherapy, are sensitive to such issues, and favour a client-directed approach that is guided by the client's inner experience.

Janet Adler's fine articulation of the process of witnessing is most helpful in this regard (see Chapter 3); the therapist's perceptions can be offered to a client, but owned for what they are – her own interpretations, judgements and projections. This creates space for recognition or rejection on the client's part, which empowers the client and enables her to constantly test out her own reality against that of another. Transference issues tend to dissolve over time when this approach is used; countertransference is constantly monitored as the therapist witnesses her own process in the presence of the client, owning her own experiences, judgements, interpretations, and projections.

Many somatic therapies tend to place greater emphasis on the first-hand direct experience of the client, in terms of the content, meaning, and direction of the process; this information, together with the first-hand experience and third-hand observation of the practitioner, informs and guides the therapeutic work. Thus, somatic therapy focuses on the direct embodied experience of the client, and the development of self-knowledge gained through insight and intuitive perception as the client explores the subtleties of inner bodymind processes. The great depth and subtlety of differentiation that somatic work accesses can greatly enrich the perspectives of a body-oriented psychotherapy. A focus upon 'the body experienced from within' may also potentially help avoid the pitfall of objectifying the body; as Michael Soth has pointed out, this problem can arise in body psychotherapy when the therapist's concept of the 'rightness' of bodily expression over mental repression of somatically held feeling creates conflict between bodily process and the ego position, thus perpetuating the body-mind split (Soth, 1999b). Of course the somatic practitioner also observes body structure, breath, movement patterning, and flow of energy, and uses this information to assess and guide the work, but in general authority is given to the client as 'the expert of their own experience' (this phrase is credited to Janet Adler, dance therapist and teacher of authentic movement).

The information gained from this kind of work is not as easy to define, categorize, or research as that gained from a more objective stance. As Middendorf describes, the experience of each person is very individual, and the simplest practice, pursued with awareness, can yield years of new learning and insight (Elizabeth Beringer, 'Interview with Ilse Middendorf' in Johnson, 1995: 67–73). In this, many somatic practices can be likened to meditation disciplines. It is this very quality of somatic work that has perhaps led to its being relatively little written about. Thus it has not been taken very seriously within the medical and psychological communities, until recent times.

It is interesting to note that whilst the majority of psychological theorists, including the innovators of body psychotherapy, are men, there has been a predominance of women innovators in the somatics field, with a few very notable exceptions such as Moshe Feldenkrais, F.M. Alexander, and Rudolf Laban. This seems to reflect the direction of movement of the feminine principle, which is a deepening to the inner knowledge and power accessed within, in contrast to the masculine way of ascent and acquisition of what lies beyond – a process of immanence rather than transcendence, which implies spirit embodied in matter. Deepening to the infinite world contained within the boundaries of our skin, a microcosm of the world without, is the way of somatic practices.

Amongst somatic practitioners we find a great range of perspectives on the relationship between body, mind, and spirit; they adhere to no single ideology, except perhaps to rescue the body from its denigrated position as inferior and base, and quite separate from mind and spirit. Some practitioners work explicitly with psychoemotional issues, whereas others do not; many work within a spiritual context but this is not necessarily integral to every somatic approach. The varying approaches seem to cross the boundaries of the many distinct somatic therapies, and tend to be personal orientations rather than group ideologies.

When we work directly with the body, using somatic experience as the ground of our practice and theory, we do need to be wary of straying too far towards the other extreme of the mind-body split. There is a risk in taking the reclamation of the body too far, so that a new kind of materialism creeps in, or a worship of the body as the ultimate source of all knowledge and experience. This danger can occasionally be observed when somatic therapists claim that everything can be reduced to bodily functioning, that psychological and even spiritual experiences are the result of somatic processes alone, or when practice limits itself to physical integration without attention to the psychoemotional or spiritual levels of the work. This view may not be held consciously amongst many practitioners, but it is an attitude that is sometimes implied. The middle way between the extreme viewpoints of mind-over-body and body-over-mind can be a broad path, but at times it narrows to a fine knife-edge when we unconsciously imply that every experience and phenomenon is a result of somatic causes. It is not so much a question of whether this is right or wrong; it is simply a limited point of view that excludes other possibilities. The causes of experience are multifaceted; personally I prefer to look at matter, body, mind, soul, and spirit as different but complexly interacting aspects of our individual and collective process.

The body-mind connection

The effect that the mind – our positive and negative thought patterns, emotions, images, beliefs, expectations, and so on – has upon the body is now quite widely accepted, and the healing potential of this connection has been researched and applied in medicine and various therapeutic methods. The Simontons were among the first to research into the use of mental imagery with cancer patients, and such methods have yielded many positive results (Simonton, Mathews-Simonton and Creighton, 1980).

Drawing upon extensive scientific research spanning several decades, Paul Martin demonstrates how illness and health are affected by both physiological and psychological factors; the old belief that illness has either a physical or a mental cause has been shown to be not only untrue but an obstacle to better understanding and treating many diseases. The studies to which Martin refers show that our state of bodily health and our susceptibility to disease can be influenced by our perceptions, our behaviour, and our personality, as well as biological factors. He persuasively argues:

> That our mental state and physical health are inexorably intertwined. That stress, depression and other psychological factors can alter our vulnerability to many diseases, including bacterial and viral infections, heart disease and cancer. That the relationship between mind and health is mediated both by our behaviour and by biological connections between the brain and the immune system. That these connections work in both directions, so our physical health can influence our mental state. That all illnesses have psychological and emotional consequences as well as causes. That there is nothing shameful or weak about the intrusion of thoughts and emotions into illness. That our social relationships with other people are central to health. And that our dualist habit of contrasting mind and body, as though they were two fundamentally different entities, is deeply misleading. (Martin, 1998: 314).

Emotion, memory, and the brain

Joseph LeDoux, in *The Emotional Brain,* describes the history of brain research, which has led to the undoubted conclusion that systems in the brain mediate and enable the integration of perceptual processes, cognition, memory, and emotion with associated bodily responses. He shows that much processing, both cognitive and emotional, occurs unconsciously and outside of the verbal realm, and thus may be impossible to access accurately through language alone (LeDoux, 1998: 71). Language and consciousness are relatively new in evolutionary terms but the non-verbal, visceral intelligence of the bodymind has been functioning since the beginnings of time to ensure our biological survival. The systems that supported survival in primitive species still function in the human brain and bodymind, underlying cognitive and verbal processing.

Focusing on the study of the emotion of fear, LeDoux describes how a structure in the brain called the *amygdala* mediates what he calls 'implicit emotional memory' (LeDoux, 1998: 202). The amygdala system triggers a whole set of physiological events that impel the body to prepare to freeze, fight or flee a perceived danger. The processing of the emotional stimulus through this system is very fast and not conscious. Simultaneously, perceptions of the threatening situation are also processed by a system involving the *hippocampus* and related cortical pathways, which form 'explicit memory about the emotional situation', or conscious memory. These two distinct systems within the brain function in parallel, enabling us to respond immediately to a perceived life-threatening situation before we are consciously aware of what threatens us; the cognitive perception, processed a split second later, enables us to modulate our response according to how the threat is now consciously perceived. Memory of a fearful event may also be unconsciously aroused at a later time, but even though unconscious it will nevertheless result in the same bodily and emotional responses that constitute the state of fear. This unconscious processing of emotion, and the accompanying physiological arousal are considered to be at the root of many anxiety disorders and post-traumatic stress. Studies such as those that LeDoux describes have given us a neurological mapping that forms the basis for understanding how body, emotions, and mind interact with each other.

Psychoneuroimmunology

Research in the fields of psychoneuroimmunology and psychobiology is now also showing us a great deal about how the mind actually affects the body, through intricate intercommunications between the nervous, endocrine, immune, and neuropeptide systems, as the work of Rossi demonstrates (Rossi, 1986). By bringing together findings from these different fields of enquiry, Rossi has greatly contributed to our understanding of the mind-body connection.

He describes how information passes between the cerebral cortex (seat of cognitive functions), the limbic system (emotional processing area of the brain), and the hypothalamus. The limbic-hypothalamic system mediates messages to the autonomic nervous system, the endocrine system, and the immune system, and thus to all the cells of the body. As Rossi writes:

> Under 'mental' stress, the limbic-hypothalamic system in the brain converts the neural messages of mind into the neurohormonal 'messenger molecules' of the body. These, in turn, can direct the endocrine system to produce steroid hormones that can reach into the nucleus of different cells of the body to modulate the expression of genes. These genes then direct the cells to produce the various molecules that will regulate metabolism, growth, activity level, sexuality, and the immune response in sickness and health. There really is a mind-gene connection! Mind ultimately does modulate the creation and expression of the molecules of life! (Rossi, 1986: xiv)

Drawing upon Milton Erickson's approach to hypnotherapy, Rossi shows how accessing unconscious information encoded within the limbic-hypothalamic system can effect changes in psychobiological function. His approach does not use hypnotic suggestion, but seeks to support the client's own natural processes of healing by accessing the positive encodements that he believes are inherent within the limbic-hypothalamic system, patterns that will ensure our greatest wellbeing and survival potential:

> We may suppose that encoded in the limbic-hypothalamic system are experiential modes for optimal functioning, as well as the problematic patterns we have discussed. These optimal patterns are undoubtedly associated with happy memories of health, wellbeing, joyful experiences, creative work, and effective coping. They are the *raw material or inner repertory of resources* that our accessing formulas seek to utilise in healing. The fundamental task for each individual is to learn how to access and utilise his or her own unique repertory of psychobiological resources that can ultimately modulate biochemical processes within the cell. (Rossi, 1986: 148)

The neuropeptide system

Recent research is showing what the somatic practitioner, the complementary therapist, the meditator, and the intuitive mover know by experience: that mind, emotions, and bodily processes are not separate and that each influences the other through extremely subtle and complex interactions. In fact mutually interactive neurochemical processes inextricably link them. Candace Pert, former chief of brain biochemistry at the National Institute of Mental Health (USA) has been at the forefront of research that is changing the dualistic paradigm that has dominated scientific medical thinking for centuries. Pert's (1999) exploration into neuropeptides and their receptor sites has revealed that mind and body influence each other in a two-way process of communication.

Peptides are chemical messenger molecules produced by cells, which communicate information from one cell to another by attaching to receptor sites on the cellular membrane of the receiving cell; specific peptides, and also drugs and other chemicals that mimic their molecular structure, attach to specific receptor sites. This causes changes in the cell's activity. Neuropeptides also create alterations in mood, or emotion, and their receptor sites are found in abundance in the emotional centres of the brain. Peptide research has revealed that neuropeptides, originally thought to be produced and received only in the brain, also communicate with the cells of other body systems; and they are also produced, stored and secreted from other cells of the body, including the cells of the immune system (Pert, 1999: 82–3). Similarly, receptor sites for peptides produced in the cells of the immune and other body systems have been located in the brain as well as other parts of the body. This means that there is a multidirectional flow of information between the brain, the immune, endocrine, gastrointestinal, and other body systems and tissues. Neuropeptides and their receptor sites, located throughout the brain and other parts of the body, form a network of communication linking the brain and nervous system, the endocrine system, the immune system, the digestive organs, and other tissues of the body, a 'psychosomatic network' of information communication. It is thought that the central and autonomic nervous systems, the endocrine system, and the immune system may all be channels that carry the messenger molecules of the neuropeptide system (Rossi, 1986: 182-3); the blood, lymph, cerebrospinal, and interstitial fluids may also be mediums of transport. The implications of this concept of a network of interconnecting systems are paradigm-breaking, claims Pert. Connections between brain and body have traditionally been thought of as 'the power of mind over body', but her research has led her to the view that:

> Mind doesn't dominate body, it *becomes* body – body and mind are one ... the flow of information throughout the whole organism, [i]s evidence that the body is the actual outward manifestation, in physical space, of the mind.

Her research also led her to see emotions as the link between mind and body, mediated by the neuropeptide system. This research has important implications for understanding the relationship between thought, emotion, and the body in the development and healing of disease. Pert's research leads her to the conclusion that neuropeptides actually produce emotional states. Furthermore:

> '[W]hat we experience as an emotion or a feeling is also a mechanism for activating a particular neuronal circuit – *simultaneously throughout the brain and body* – which generates a behaviour involving the whole creature, with all the necessary physiological changes that behaviour would require.'

Pert has shown how neuropeptides and their receptor sites are fundamental to the interconnectedness of mind and body, and to the process by which emotions are experienced throughout the body, along with associated physiological changes. From this perspective, the traditional view of a discrete mind distinct from the body no longer serves; a functionally integrated 'body-mind' becomes a more accurate description of the reality that is revealed as more is learnt about the neuropeptide system. '[N]europeptides', writes Pert, 'provide the physiological basis for the emotions.'

Her conclusions led her to the understanding that consciousness is not located in the head, a common Western assumption, but can be projected into different areas of the body. She speculates that: '[W]hat the mind is is the flow of information as it moves among the cells, organs, and systems of the body.' Much of this flow of information happens beneath the threshold of conscious awareness, manifesting through the activity of the autonomic, or involuntary, processes of the body.

> The mind as we experience it is immaterial, yet it has a physical substrate, which is both the body and the brain. It may also be said to have a nonmaterial, nonphysical substrate that has to do with the flow of that information. The mind, then, is that which holds the network together, often acting below our consciousness, linking and coordinating the major systems and their organs and cells in an intelligently orchestrated symphony of life. Thus, we might refer to the whole system as a psychosomatic information network, linking psyche, which comprises all that is of

an ostensibly nonmaterial nature, such as mind, emotion, and soul, to soma, which is the material world of molecules, cells, and organs. Mind and body, psyche and soma. (Pert, 1999: 185)

Pert's ground-breaking work has not always been immediately accepted within mainstream scientific circles, and her holistic approach to the science of human experience, consciousness, and behaviour has been at times scorned by those who would keep the various disciplines of scientific enquiry quite separate. However, her approach has led to important discoveries that promise to yield new ways of treating diseases such as AIDS and cancer. The spirit of her work is in tune with the times, with the discoveries of new physics, and with the beliefs of complementary practitioners who have welcomed her scientific research as validation of their own views and practice. The field of psychoneuroimmunology is showing without a scientific doubt that mind, body, and emotions all play a role in the development of mental and physical illness, and the creation of health.

Effects of movement and sensation on the mind

While Rossi's approach to healing, and that of others in the field, focuses upon the effect of the mind upon the body, the other side of this equation has been less well researched and documented – that bodily processes affect mind, spirit, and psychoemotional states. Of course this view forms a basis of psychiatric medicine, but the healing potential of natural methods such as touch, physical manipulation, and movement upon the mind has not yet been fully embraced by the medical establishment or medical researchers. In his seminal book *Touching: The Human Significance of the Skin*, Montagu explores the importance of touch for physical and psychological wellbeing, citing many examples of research studies that demonstrate the importance of touch for well-balanced psychological development, as well as mental and physical health. He writes:

> The psychosomatic approach constitutes an invaluable contribution to our under-standing concerning the influence of the mind upon the body . . . and of the extra-ordinary sensitivity of the skin in reacting to centrally originating nervous disturbances . . . The psychosomatic approach to the study of the skin may be regarded as centrifugal; that is, it proceeds from the mind outwards to the integu-ment. What we shall be concerned with in the present book is the opposite approach, namely from the skin to the mind; in other words, the centripetal approach. (Montagu, 1971: 19)

Somatic therapy uses the centripetal approach, accessing the brain and central nervous system through focused contact with the skin and cells of all the body tissues. The flow of information between the nervous, endocrine, immune, and neuropeptide systems is a multidirectional, cyclical flow; information from cells is also sent to the brain via the various channels of the psychosomatic network. So we can hypothesize that changes at the cellular level also affect emotional and cognitive functioning. If the cells of the body are stressed, or if they are comforted by touch and relaxation, different kinds of information will be sent to the brain. Somatic work seeks to touch the cells and tissues directly; sometimes it involves the cognitive aspect too, where a mental image, direction, or particular focus in the body may be used, thus engaging fully the cyclical flow of information between cell, limbic-hypothalamic system, and cortex.

In his book *Job's Body*, Deane Juhan gives a convincing account of *how* bodywork effects change, not only at the physical level, but also mentally and emotionally. He describes in subtle detail, right down to molecular formations, how the various tissues of the body are structured and function in relation to each other and to the organism as a whole, and shows how therapeutic touch and tissue manipulations affect the various tissue levels. Touch and movement are the first senses through which we learn and form ourselves, beginning in utero, and continuing throughout life (Cohen, 1993: 115; Juhan, 1987: 29). Both are essential to the full development of the nervous system and the immune response, and are thus powerful mediums of creative change when something goes wrong. Stimuli, in the form of movement and sensations, are essential food for the nervous system, without which a range of problems can result, from minor sensory-motor disturbances, to loss of ego boundaries, and even death in extreme cases. Juhan writes: 'Not only is it true that the nervous system stimulates the body to move in specific ways as a result of specific sensations; it is also the case that all movements flood the nervous system with sensations regarding the structures and functions of the body. Movement is the unifying bond between the mind and the body, and sensations are the substance of that bond (Juhan, 1987: xxvi).

We perceive ourselves, and organize our internal and external muscular responses through the proprioceptive sensory information constantly flowing to our brain: touch to the skin, pressure on deeper tissues, contraction of muscles, and distortion of tissues as we move our joints, all inform our sense of our body-self:

> As we develop and mature, most of us build up and reinforce a reliably consistent sense of ourselves by carefully selecting and maintaining a specific repertoire of movement habits – which generate a specific repertoire of sensations – and by surrounding ourselves with a stable environment with which to interact. This careful process of selection is largely unconscious, and so as long as we are comfortable we are rarely aware of any limitations or potential dangers our culti-vated habits may entail. (Juhan, 1987: xxvi)

Juhan goes on to describe how this cycle of interaction between habitual behaviour patterns and the chronic conditions of the body tissues can be interrupted by skilfully applied touch. As new movements, new pressures, new relationships between the body parts are experienced, the nervous system is flooded with new sensory information which can alert us to what we have been doing to create our aches and pains. The flood of new sensations can open up the possibility of choosing new responses, and as more healthful patterns are selected and reinforced, a healthier, more expanded sense of self can develop. 'In other words, just as the mind organises the rest of the body's tissues into a life process, sensations to a large degree organise the mind. They do not simply give the mind material to organise; they are themselves a major organising principle' (Juhan, 1987: xxvi).

Somatic therapy, by skilfully introducing new sensory experiences, can effect changes in neuromuscular patterning and, because emotional and mental patterns are so inherently embedded within the behavioural habits of the individual, these too can be positively influenced. As new possibilities are experienced, new choices can be made as we recognize that we are not permanently bound to the restrictions of our limited habitual ways. Painful and traumatic experiences stored within the body tissues can be a source of such limited functioning; defensive postural, movement, and behavioural patterns are established to protect from further injury, and some degree of numbing of feeling or dissociation from bodily experience usually occurs. Bodywork is particularly effective in reawakening feeling in numbed areas of the body, returning consciousness to places that have been abandoned, and introducing positive sensory stimuli upon which a fuller sense of self can be built.

Through skilled manipulation of the body tissues, bodywork can reverse this kind of patterning; by recreating sensations of softening, lengthening, pleasure, and relaxation, the reduced muscle tone that normally accompanies such feelings can be evoked. Reduction in muscle tone can relieve pressure on proprioceptive nerves throughout the body, further increasing sensations of relaxation and ease; circulation is increased in formerly constricted and numb or painful areas, so that metabolism in those areas is improved, and energy is felt to flow; tissues lengthen and soften, increasing movement range and comfort in formerly uncomfortable positions. All of this helps to restore the free flow of sensory information that organizes body and mind.

> Even though structural changes are to be expected, the crux of the therapy is not *material*, but has to do with the sensory evocation of *feeling states*. It is art, not science in the strict sense of the term, and it is aimed towards shifts in mental response, not mere physical adjustments. This is why it must always be subjective and intuitive, in addition to being well-informed. (Juhan, 1987: 275-6)

As well as influencing the neuromuscular system, the movements, pressures, heat, and friction generated by bodywork and somatic movement therapy have an important influence upon other body systems. In particular the connective tissue of the body, which wraps in sheaths around every cell, vessel, organ, gland, muscle, bone, and nerve, is directly affected. Connective tissue, as well as differentiating and holding together the different tissues and structures of the body, provides a medium for the passage of fluid to and from the cells; the condition of the connective tissue greatly influences the flow of nutrients and oxygen to the cells, and the disposal of toxic wastes. Bodywork and movement help the connective tissues to regain a balanced state of fluidity and tone. This both supports the organs and tissues structurally and energetically and facilitates the passage of nutrients and wastes to and from the cells; this enables the cells to maintain a chemical and homeostatic balance most conducive to their healthy functioning. Thus somatic therapy can have far-reaching effects upon the general health and wellbeing of the person.

Repression

Although coming from a different philosophical position, Freud's work on repression nevertheless has direct relevance for the somatic therapist. As Badcock (1988: 7) describes, when we are first learning something, information related to that learning is accessible to the conscious mind; later on it becomes relatively unconscious. Both information and feelings related to the process and content of learning become unconscious. We see this to be true at a neurophysiological level. When we are learning new sensory-motor skills, for example, there is conscious cortical involvement. Once the skill has been mastered we no longer have to think about the complex coordinations necessary to carry out the task. Control is taken over by subcortical areas of the brain, and the actual mechanisms of the activity become unconscious to us. The emotional feelings associated with the process of learning or development also tend to retreat from consciousness, but continue to impress themselves on the special way we move, behave, and approach future learning and creative tasks. Juhan (1987: 272) describes the particular way an individual carries out specific gestures and movements as a 'sensory engram', a kind of template for a whole body signature that has been built up through past but forgotten learning experiences.

Psychoemotional experiences throughout the formative years of infancy and childhood are encoded in the sensory engrams, which thus contain material that has been forgotten or repressed during the course of development. This repressed material unconsciously influences the quality of our movement patterning, physiological functioning, and emotional behaviour. Birth is thought by some to be the most significant sensory engram, or organizing principle, upon which all later ones are built.

Our ability to form fulfilling relationships in later life is also profoundly affected by experiences during infancy. As the work of John Bowlby has shown, experiences of attachment and separation in our earliest relationships affect our ability to achieve intimacy and maturity in adult relationships (Bowlby, 1997-8). The work of Alan Schore has further developed attachment theory by showing how the brain itself is patterned in early life by the infant's experience of primary relationships (Schore, 1994); thus, what we might call 'relationship engrams' are also encoded into the developing brain of the infant. It is well known that, as adults, we tend to repeat experiences from early life, including destructive relationship experiences from childhood; neuroscience is now showing us that there is a neurological basis to this that, without effective therapy, can keep us bound to inevitable repetition. The neurological organization laid down in infancy will affect emotional behaviour and the potential to form fulfilling relationships in later life, as well as the physiological functioning of essential organ systems such as the digestive, immune and endocrine systems.

Emotional and relational patterning are also reflected in sensory-motor patterning, and information about this can often be accessed through bodywork and movement. In the practice of bodywork and somatic movement therapy, habitual patterning is brought back into consciousness to be processed at a cortical level. Through touch and movement, new sensory information can be experienced consciously and new engrams, or patterns of sensory-motor organization, are thus introduced. This opens up the potential for change as the client is offered the choice of a new and more efficient sensory-motor pathway over an old and less effective one. As a new pattern integrates, the centre of control then returns to the subcortical levels of the brain and in time the new way becomes another unconscious, but hopefully more healthful, 'habit'. Repressed emotional material may be brought back into consciousness, re-evaluated and released during this process, and more positive emotional and sensory experiences may become associated with the newly created engrams.

There is a natural process at work within the nervous system, whereby information becomes unconscious during the process of integration and development, but Freud noted that there is a selectivity as to *which* material is repressed. In his view, repression comes from the need of the ego to defend against instinctual forces that threaten to overwhelm it, in particular those of a sexual nature. His followers elaborate on this and postulate different drives and conflicts as the source of repression, but in general see repression as a defence against intolerable anxieties that come about through the conflict of opposing forces – such as the ego and the id or the reality and pleasure principles, love and aggression, or the individual and society. With this in mind somatic therapists, whilst having in their hands effective tools for accessing and potentially changing harmful unconscious patterning, must also take into account the anxiety and underlying conflicts from which defensive sensory-motor organization can be serving to protect the client. Bodywork that focuses only on releasing tension is not always successful as the energy held within the body may be needed for some important purpose that has to be understood and integrated before release can happen safely. This kind of bodywork can sometimes be counterproductive as it may open up defences too quickly, resulting in either a state that is too vulnerable or an increase of resistance in the client. It is here that the perspective of the psychologist and the psychotherapist trained to work with emotional conflict and trauma is invaluable.

Traumatic memories are laid down in a process called state-dependent learning (Van der Kolk and Van der Hart, 1989: 1530–40). When confronted with an emotionally overwhelming or potentially life-threatening situation, the person enters an altered state of consciousness. Whilst in this state memory is stored as somatic sensation or visual imagery (Van der Kolk, 1994: 253–65). At the same time as memory is being laid down, certain neuropeptides are released into the body (Van der Kolk and Van der Hart, 1991: 425–54). Traumatic memories can remain unconscious for years, even a whole lifetime. But memories and feelings associated with the traumatizing event can also be recalled by an experience that is in some way similar to the original event; this triggers the rerelease of the associated neuropeptides, and the re-entering of the altered state of consciousness. Care must be taken in all forms of therapy not to retraumatize clients by evoking such emotionally charged states before they are ready to enter safely and resolve them. Unconscious or unresolved trauma will inevitably affect our experience and functioning on many levels.

Bonnie Bainbridge Cohen also discusses the active selectivity of the perceptual process, with particular reference to the child's movement development. She observes that within the traditional model of sensory-perceptual-motor processing there are two additional phases. Firstly, there are 'preconceived expectations':

> Our perception of movement, i.e., our interpretation of movement, is dependent upon all of our previous experiences of movement, as it is for every other sense. We develop preconceived expectations based upon how we have perceived similar information in our past experiences. These expectations then precede new sensory input. (Cohen, 1993: 117)

Secondly, there is a process of 'pre-motor focusing'. This involves the ability to focus our sensory organs in order to select the information we will pick up. It is the motor aspect of perception:

> It is the motor ability to choose which aspects of incoming stimuli we will absorb or attend to . . . We can see this pre-motor focusing as motivation, desire, attention, and discriminating awareness . . . It is the *active* decision of what stimulation you will take in. However, this 'active decision' is usually unconscious, based upon previous experience. (Cohen, 1993: 117)

Although she does not elaborate upon the psychological dimension of such choices, Cohen's description does relate to Freud's concept of repression, and gives us a basis within neurological functioning for the mechanisms of selective repression. However, although we choose not to 'absorb or attend to' certain information, which might be either irrelevant or acutely threatening to the conscious ego, this information nevertheless impresses itself upon our neural pathways in a way that remains unconscious. Working with sensory-perceptual-motor processing may bring this unconscious information to light. Certain kinds of information that were once conscious may be selected out of conscious awareness through the process of active perception described by Cohen, and they can also be recalled again through somatic movement and bodywork practices. Psychological repression, dissociation, and the storing and release of trauma held in the body are all rooted in these underlying neurological processes.

Energetic pathways

Physical, mental, and emotional processes are interconnected in extraordinarily complex ways through the activities of the nervous, endocrine, immune, and neuropeptide systems of the bodymind. Appreciating this gives us a basis for understanding how somatic work can affect mind and emotion. However, there are further subtle ways in which these interactions occur, which lie beyond the realm of physical manipulations, neuromuscular repatterning, psychosomatic medicine, or the knowledge of orthodox Western medicine. For information about this we can turn to ancient systems of energy healing and spiritual development, such as acupuncture, Chinese and Tibetan traditional medicine, meditation, yoga, chi kung, or our own Western tradition of alchemy. These and other systems work with the relationship between the physical body and the subtle energy body, which organizes and influences the physical, emotional, mental, and spiritual levels of being. The presence of the subtle 'light body' can now be identified through methods such as Kirlian photography, and has been the subject of a number of scientific research studies. Some of these studies have been described in considerable detail by Richard Gerber in his book *Vibrational Medicine,* and in James Oschman's *Energy Medicine.*

We can no longer afford to ignore this aspect of existence when we talk about healing, just because it does not fit easily into our mainstream Western medical model. As homoeopath Gareth James writes:

> Although the efficacy of homoeopathy is now beyond dispute, a recent article in an American medical journal stated that homoeopathy had a long way to go before it can prove itself in terms of science. It is far more likely to be the case that science has a long way to go before it develops the technologies needed to recognise the science in homoeopathy. (James, 1995: 13)

In fact the use of light and vibrational energy is now being researched and proposed as the medicine of the future. Already orthodoxy is embracing the use of electrical energy in various therapies; electrotherapy has been used successfully to treat cancer and other diseases (Gerber, 1996), and laser light is now also being used in the treatment of some cancers. The medicine of the future promises to take us deeper into the realms of subtle energy, where already gifted healers are able to diagnose energetic imbalances before they manifest as serious physical disease, and to cure some conditions that prove untreatable by modern medicine.

Exploring the growing field of vibrational medicine, Gerber offers a scientific theory for the validation of energy medicine and describes a number of scientific studies that seem to give proof to the claims that physical and mental illness can be diagnosed and healed by energy alone. Energy medicine is rooted in the theories of new physics:

> The Einsteinian viewpoint sees human beings from the higher dimensional perspective of fields within fields within fields. Matter itself, from the infinitesimal subatomic particle to the level of the physical and higher vibrational bodies, is now seen as dynamic energy contained within the constraints of fluctuating energy fields. (Gerber, 1996: 495)

Like many practising healers, Gerber believes that the subtle energy fields are causative of the denser physical body, and thus healing can be most effectively addressed through the patient's energy bodies:

> This theoretical perspective is based upon the understanding that the molecular arrangement of the physical body is actually a complex network of interwoven energy fields. The energetic network, which represents the physical/cellular framework, is organised and nourished by 'subtle' energetic systems which coordinate the life-force with the body. There is a hierarchy of subtle energetic systems that coordinate electrophysiologic and hormonal function as well as cellular structure within the physical body. It is primarily from these subtle levels that health and illness originate. These unique energy systems are powerfully affected by our emotions and level of spiritual balance as well as by nutritional and environmental factors. These subtle energies influence cellular patterns of growth in both positive and negative directions. (Gerber, 1996: 43)

Furthermore, this approach to medicine sees consciousness as being embedded in cellular existence, and at the root of health and disease:

> Vibrational medicine attempts to heal illness and transform human consciousness by working with the energetic patterns that guide the physical expression of life. We will eventually discover that *consciousness itself is a kind of energy that is integrally related to the cellular expression of the physical body.* As such, *consciousness participates in the continuous creation of either health or illness.* (Gerber, 1996: 44, italics original)

Despite much evidence, we still have a long way to go before energy medicine will be accepted by the majority of conventional medical practitioners. In the meantime, a film of psychic diagnostician and healer Carol Everett, made during research at Tokyo University, might be of interest to the more sceptical reader. In the film, excerpts of which can be seen on the Internet (www.everetthc.oaktree.co.uk), the healer is shown diagnosing and completely 'dissolving away' an ovarian tumour. The treatment took about 8 minutes. Film of the tumour in the woman's body disappearing, recorded by thermal imaging techniques, and of Everett's brain wave patterns during the healing process, are both shown. It is believed to be the first time that such a psychic healing process has been recorded in 'real time'.

John Pierrakos, formerly a student and colleague of Freud, developed the study of energy using techniques which enabled him to see the aura, or energy field around a person. Eventually he developed the capacity to see without technical aids, and evolved the practice of core energetics, which uses the appearance of the aura as an aid in diagnosing and treating psychopathology (Pierrakos, 1990). As Pierrakos describes, philosophical and scientific research into energy has been a concern of both Eastern and Western cultures for a long time. Eastern energy systems have been evolving for several millennia, and we are now quite familiar with some of them. But in the West too there is a long history of enquiry into the nature of energy in life and healing, beginning with the ancient Greeks more than 2,000 years ago, affirmed by the 'miracle cures' of Christ and his followers, and finding renewed momentum in the last decades of the twentieth century, as science begins to evolve methods by which what was once invisible and intangible can now be clearly observed (Pierrakos, 1990: 30-54).

The chakras

Following Reich, Pierrakos held that at the core of each person is a source of positive energy which, in good health, will flow out towards the world without obstruction; here it meets and interacts with the unitary field of energy that infuses all of life. Energy from this universal source will also flow freely into the core of the individual if not obstructed. Physiological and psychological health depend upon a natural and unimpeded rhythm of energy flowing into and out from the core. The *chakras,* vortices or wheels of energy lying along the front of the body in front of the spine, serve to channel these flows of energy into and out from the core. Seven main chakras are usually identified, although there are many more secondary and minor ones (Figure 2.1). Each chakra is associated with specific physiological, psychological, perceptual, and spiritual functions; the condition of the chakras reflects health or disturbance in those functions.

C. W. Leadbeater was instrumental in bringing the Eastern concept of the chakras to the West. His book, *The Chakras,* first published in 1927, is held

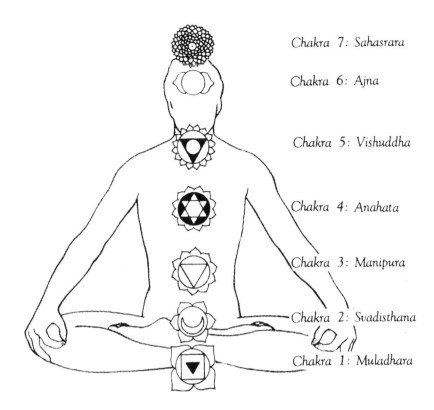

Chakra 7: Sahasrara

Chakra 6: Ajna

Chakra 5: Vishuddha

Chakra 4: Anahata

Chakra 3: Manipura

Chakra 2: Svadisthana

Chakra 1: Muladhara

Figure 2.1. The Seven Major Spinal Chakras. Reproduced with permission from Fritz Frederick Smith, *Inner Bridges*, p. 50.

by many as an authority on the subject (Leadbeater, 1927). The roots of the chakras are located at specific points along the spine and in the brain, and seem to be related to nerve plexes and endocrine glands lying close to them (Figure 2.2). It is believed that the chakras are intimately linked to the functions of the neuroendocrine system, and so to the regulation of the bodymind.

Although there is general agreement, subtly different systems of association between the chakras, emotions, and bodymind functions have also been evolved by various psychics and practitioners of energy medicine. (Some sources of information about the chakras and their association can be found in the following: Leadbeater, 1927; Smith, 1986; Brennan, 1988; Pierrakos, 1990; Myss, 1997); Carolyn Myss's approach should be of particular interest to the student of bodymind therapies. She relates the chakras to the body systems, organs, and glands, to associated emotional and mental issues, and to physical symptoms and disturbances. Her exploration of each chakra offers an inspiring and highly practical map for those seeking

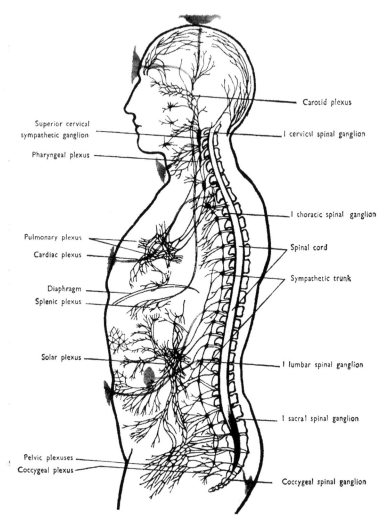

Figure 2.2. The Chakras and the Nervous System. Reproduced with permission from C. W. Leadbeater, *The Chakras,* p. 41.

to understand and participate more fully in their own psychological and spiritual growth, within the context of modern life.

Fritz Frederick Smith has been at the forefront of the exploration of the interface between modern physical medicine, and the ancient energy systems of the East. A chiropractic doctor and practitioner of traditional Chinese acupuncture, he developed a method of bodywork called zero balancing, which integrates the Eastern and Western models, and his findings are relevant to both the somatic therapist and the body psychotherapist. Smith noted correlations between the curves of the spinal column and the energy vortices, the chakras, of the yogic system (Figure 2.3). He observed that misalignment of the spinal structure and dysfunctioning of the chakras of the subtle body are related, and noticed that both affect the functions of related organs and body tissues, along with their associated psychological and perceptual processes. Therapy can intervene at any level to break destructive cycles and introduce a healthier relationship between physical structure, energetic flow, and psychophysiological function. Somatic therapies that address spinal and skeletal alignment can be of particular benefit in entering a cycle of destructive interaction between the physical and energetic bodies.

The energy body

Smith also describes how energy flows and circulates within and around the physical body but has its own anatomy and physiology, flows and currents; both bodies, the physical and the energetic, influence and are influenced by each other:

> In the human body, there is a great complexity of energy movement, currents, and vibrations. As in the ocean, body energy can exist freely, in layers, or in organised flows that maintain their integrity and have little tendency to mix. Energy can be blocked, flow freely, or vary in frequency of vibration; it can be in excess or deficient in quantity; and it can be of varying quality. (Smith, 1986: 25-6)

The energy of the body has an anatomy and physiology distinct from that of the physical body, yet formed and influenced by the physical structure. The physiology of the energy body is responsive to our thoughts, emotions, and imaginations, and as such it can be perceived and influenced from within, as well as being highly sensitive to external environmental and physical forces. Smith describes three main ways in which energy takes form in the body. First there is the background energy field. This is diffuse and unformed, influenced by forces from without and passing through it, and permeates the whole body in a general way. It also extends beyond the body as the *aura*, which can be felt and seen by some people. Every fluctuation in energy, thought, and emotion is registered here, and the quality of the energy field gives us a sense of the general feeling and vibration of the person; psychotherapeutic work engages with this level in particular.

Secondly, there are vertical energy flows that pass through the body in specific channels, and maintain our integrity both as an independent being and as an interdependent part of nature. The main vertical flow serves to connect us to the universe, to heaven and earth, conducting and transforming the energy that passes through us; this flow passes through the skull, spine, pelvis, and legs. Other vertical flows pass through the shoulders, transverse processes of the spine, pelvis, legs, and arms. These energy flows pass through the skeleton, being the densest of body tissues, and body therapies that focus on skeletal alignment will directly affect this level of energy. Craniosacral therapy and osteopathy, for example, focus on balancing

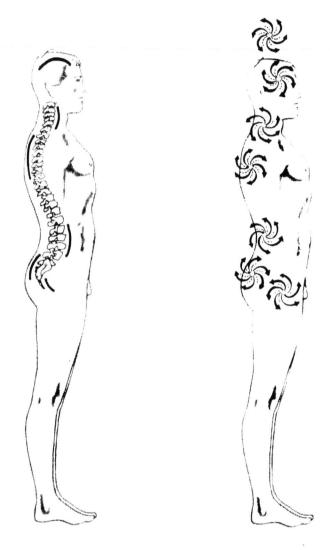

Figure 2.3. The vortices of chakral energy. Reproduced with permission from Fritz Frederick Smith, *Inner Bridges,* p. 51.

the central flow of energy through the bones, joints, membranes, and fluids of the cranium and spinal column; the craniosacral mechanism is an extremely subtle and influential process which registers and regulates functioning at all levels. The Alexander technique also focuses on the flows of energy through the vertical channels, as do yogic and meditative practices. Smith writes:

> The body is an armature with different densities of tissue. The denser tissues conduct the stronger energy currents, and the densest part of our structure is the skeletal system. Consider a skeleton. Even after a person has died, the skeleton is

holding an energy field. If it were not so, it would be dust. Energy is required to keep the molecules in the form of a skeleton, and the force fields of that individual are maintained within the bones. We can still gain insight into the individual who was once organised around that particular armature by feeling the tensions and torsions that remain in the skeleton. (Smith, 1986: 29)

The third form which energy takes, according to Smith's theory, consists of the internal flows – specific currents that circulate in identifiable pathways within the body. The deepest level flows through the bones and bone marrow. The middle level flows through the soft tissues of muscles, nerves, organs, glands, and blood. The superficial level of internal energy flows in a non-differentiated layer just beneath the skin, and serves to protect and insulate. It is our first energetic line of defence against harmful influences from outside, such as changes in temperature, vibration, wind, or humidity; if this energy is weak, harmful influences can penetrate to the deeper levels, causing imbalance and ill health. The condition of psychological boundaries is also related to this layer of energy; in exploring the skin and the layers of fat, connective tissue, and lymphatic vessels just beneath the skin, issues relating to psychological boundaries, holding, protection, and vulnerability often emerge. Thus this level of energy is also a concern of psychotherapeutic work.

This third aspect of energy flow has a closer connection to our emotional and mental life than do the vertical flows passing through the skeletal structure, and many healing systems, such as acupuncture and traditional Chinese medicine, have developed sophisticated models and methods to balance this energy system. Many somatic therapies will focus on this level, and it can also be influenced by psychoemotional factors and by psychotherapy.

The energy body and the psyche

Many therapies focus primarily on one level of energy, or the tissues that house a specific energy flow, but all levels interact and are mutually influencing. Attention to one level of experience, whether spiritual, psychological, physical, or energetic, can therefore affect many levels simultaneously, and an understanding of this can deepen and enhance therapeutic work. The homoeopathic view is that during the healing process symptoms do not simply disappear but that healing progresses from deep to superficial levels; the temporary re-emergence of old symptoms, or the appearance of new symptoms at a more superficial level, may indicate that the healing process is proceeding well:

> The physical is considered the most superficial aspect, the mind/emotion deeper, and the spiritual aspect the deepest. In the healing process, when a person first gets a glimpse of getting well, has hope rekindled, or regains a spark of life, it means that the deepest level has been stirred and improved. From here the healing will move up to the emotional/mental realm and in its final stages be manifest in the physical body. (Smith, 1986: 172-3)

The work of Barbara Brennan is also of great interest. Originally a research scientist at NASA, she later trained as a counsellor and body psychotherapist, studying bioenergetics with John Pierrakos. A natural ability to see energy, dormant since childhood, began to return as she counselled clients, and as she devoted herself to the exploration of this phenomenon, she developed an effective approach to spiritual healing. Her books provide perhaps the most comprehensive description available of the subtle energy bodies, and the practice of healing through them (Brennan, 1988, 1993).

Brennan describes at least seven subtle bodies, distinct layers of the aura, each one related to a specific chakra and the functions associated with that chakra. Healing may work through any or all of these levels, affecting all aspects of being from the physical body and its energetic systems, through emotional and mental functions, love issues, and spiritual development. She uses a combination of hands-on healing and bioenergetic psychotherapy, according to the needs of the client. Like her teacher and colleague Pierrakos, Brennan relates Reich's descriptions of character structure to energetic manifestations in the aura, and facilitates the creation of psychological as well as physical wellbeing by clearing and restructuring the aura and the chakras, using various healing techniques. Changes in the energy bodies can effect changes and healing at other levels; similarly, changes in our thoughts, emotions, actions, and lifestyle will also affect the appearance of the aura. Bioenergetic exercises are also sometimes used in her approach to help clear an energetic blockage, and support the free flow of energy throughout the physical and subtle bodies. Brennan writes:

> We stop our feelings by blocking our energy flow. This creates stagnated pools of energy in our systems which when held there long enough lead to disease in the physical body . . . The connection between therapy and healing becomes obvious when disease is seen in this way. The broad view of the healer encompasses the totality of the human being. In healing there is no separation between body and mind, emotions and spirit – all need to be in balance to create a healthy human being. (Brennan, 1988: 99)

The healing connection

Today there is growing awareness that the inseparability of body and mind offers enormous potential for healing and self-healing. Some therapies use both directions of the bodymind continuum, sometimes choosing to use physical means such as touch, massage, physical manipulations, or movement, and at other times, or simultaneously, using visual imagery, mental suggestion, or sensory awareness, to deepen and consciously direct the body process. Somatic practices such as the Feldenkrais method, Alexander technique, body-mind centering, and eutony all seek to integrate the effect of mind on body, and of body on mind, to cultivate a consciously aware bodymind, and more healthful patterns of functioning.

Clyde Ford has developed a system that he calls somato-synthesis. A chiropractic doctor who also trained in psychosynthesis therapy, Ford uses touch and gentle physical manipulations to access psychological material, which is then explored through methods adapted from psychosynthesis, such as guided imagery combined with related physical manoeuvres. He describes the healing journey as going from soma, to psyche, to centre or self, where a new integrating centre is experienced. Ford emphasizes the power of touch in accessing buried psychological material, and claims success with psychological problems that years of psychotherapy failed to address:

> As humans we were created, formed and birthed through the contact of skin. Touch is our first language. Before we could utter a word, hear a sound, see an image, smell a scent or taste a flavor, we could communicate through touch. In the womb, our barely formed body responded to the world through the only sensory system open to it, the sense of touch. (Ford, 1989: 11-14)

For the months after birth, touch continues to be the primary sense through which we learn about our world. We know that the earlier a system develops, the more important it is for our survival and future growth; so touch, the 'mother of the senses', informs our first and most essential learnings in the school of life. Later, hearing and vision will develop and come to dominate our ways of perceiving the world, but touch still continues to be the foundation for our interactions, as it was before and immediately after birth. The skin and nervous system develop from the same embryological layer; they are born of the same tissue, the same cells. Thus they function as if skin were the surface of the brain, or the brain no less than the innermost recess, the root system of the skin.

Therapeutic touch can create a special kind of connection between therapist and client:

> Any somatic therapist can attest to the often magical quality of sustained touch. It has an entrancing power not only for the client but also for the therapist. Touch promotes a state of engagement between therapist and client, a key factor in successful therapy whether somatic or psychological. What's amazing is that touch brings about this therapeutic rapport so easily. (Ford, 1989: 11-14)

Ford describes how this engagement between therapist and client induces an altered state of consciousness in both, and that this shared experience promotes a deep level of bonding, as the physical boundary between them dissolves (Ford, 1989: 128). It is during such states, when ordinary consciousness is suspended, that healing can occur. Smith also writes of the healing power of altered states of consciousness, which he terms the 'working state':

> The working state has a special significance in energy balancing therapies. This is one of the times that healing tends to occur. When a person is in an altered state of

awareness, he or she is removed from the ordinary mind set, which, among other things, contains a conceptualization of the imbalance. Any conception, vision, or neurological imprint of an imbalance tends to solidify the problem and give it form. If the mind set is altered *at the same time* we are providing the body/mind/spirit with the experience of being in a better state of balance, there is an energetic and experiential reprogramming of the imbalance or illness. A degree of healing has occurred. (Smith, 1986: 112)

Jacqui's story

As an example of a purely somatic approach, I would like to describe here a brief therapy that involved somatic work without any explicit psychological processing. It is an example of the use of bodywork and somatic movement therapy as reparative and healing, rather than as a means to access and open a dialogue with the unconscious. Depending on the needs of the client, this is sometimes appropriate. Although she did not have a great deal of previous experience with somatic therapy, this client had a particularly well-developed ability to sense her body, and to connect her thinking and feeling processes to bodily sensation and movement. This degree of integration enabled her to participate creatively in the healing process, facilitating very positive results; it also meant that the need for psychological work was not an obvious concern at that time.

Jacqui, a lively and intelligent 52-year-old woman, came to me for four sessions of somatic therapy over a period of two months, following surgery to her left ankle joint. She had received multiple fractures to the bones of both forelegs during a car accident 30 years ago, and had suffered pain and movement difficulties since this time. An arthritic condition had developed in her ankle joints, particularly severe on the left side; the talus and calcaneous (bones of the ankle joint and heel) had fused together, and eventually the tibia (shin bone) slipped off the talus. This led her into surgery, where the bones of the tibia and talus were cut and fused together with cross bolts. It was expected that she would lose all mobility in her ankle joint as a result of the operation.

She came to see me 3 months after the operation, and 2 weeks after the plaster had been taken off, walking on crutches and with great difficulty. She hoped to receive some help with restoring some mobility to the area. The injury also affected her postural and walking patterns, and she experienced pain when she put weight onto the heel of the injured foot, so she hoped for some help in adapting her posture and movement to the limitations the accident and surgery had imposed on her.

During our first session, her ankle and foot were red, swollen, and looked so sensitive and raw that I knew only the lightest of touch would be possible at this time. The bones of the ankle were deeply protected by the build up of fluids, so that they were inaccessible to my touch; my feeling was that there was too much pain and trauma at that level to allow direct contact. I made light contact and waited to see which body systems came up to 'meet' my touch. The first level was the interstitial fluid, and I simply followed and supported the subtle flows of movement I felt beneath my hands through this medium. In this way we were able, together, to feel and encourage a considerable amount of subtle movement in her foot and around the ankle joint; we agreed that supporting whatever potential for movement she had, at different tissue levels, was what was required. Through years of pain, the retraumatization of surgery, and nearly two months of immobilization in plaster, her ankle and foot had 'forgotten' that they could move at all, and it was necessary to reflect the tissues' potential back to them.

After this I was able to contact the bones of the foot and support some very subtle movement there and in the synovial fluid of the joints; the bones of the ankle were still too sensitive to be touched directly. We then focused on the flows of blood and lymph from the foot back to the heart, to aid in the drainage of the area. She was able to sense these flows as I gave feedback through my hands with a quality of touch that reflected their weightedness, rhythm, and direction of flow, again supporting the natural movement of her body fluids. This enabled her to experience the injured area in the context of her whole self, connected to the parts of her that were healthy and strong. I showed her some gentle movements that she could practise herself to aid this flow. Following this work Jacqui was able to find more movement in her foot, and even a very subtle movement in the ankle joint itself, as the energy was now moving through the fluids of the fused area. Work on the right side, which was showing signs of following the same pattern of deterioration, focused mainly on releasing compression in the joints of the ankle, and finding an open, balanced alignment of the bones. Learning a new walking pattern entailed taking time to release weight through the injured foot in such a way that the mobility she had found there could support her to distribute the weight through the whole foot with much less pain.

The next time we met her walking was much easier, and the ankle healing well, according to her doctor. She told me, half jokingly, about how she was taking care of her appearance: 'If I'm going to be a cripple, at least I will be a gorgeous one!' Her spirit was strong; she had clearly accepted that she would never walk normally again, and was determined not to become too despondent about it. This time there was less swelling around the ankle, and it was possible to contact the bones more readily. I felt a lot of movement between the bones of her feet and through the different fluids, and again supported this through gentle touch and tissue manipulations. The ankle was hot, whilst the calf area felt empty. Supporting the blood flow and working with the muscles of the lower leg helped to balance the energy between the foot, ankle, and leg. I showed her how the muscles of the calf move the bones of the foot, and how she could practise exercises for these muscles, despite the limited ankle joint mobility, which would help to rehabilitate the slightly atrophied muscles. Again some work to release and balance the joints of the right ankle was needed; she was given some gentle exercises to practise at home, which would help to align both ankle joints.

The mobility of her left foot continued to improve, and the swelling started to decrease. The ankle began to feel more substantial, bloodful, and some massage was used during our third session to help the circulation in the area. Once most of the swelling had gone down, and the ankle felt less raw and sensitive, it was possible to contact the many different tissue levels. I felt a confused, chaotic energy in the tissues, which is not surprising after a severe physical trauma such as the surgery she had recently undergone. I used a quality of touch and focus of attention that gives a feeling of 'holding' the tissues at the cellular level. The focus was on encouraging calmness and the flow of energy through the tissues, rather than holding it into the tissues as had been happening. At each level I was 'reminding' the cells and tissues of their natural function and potential. She reported that this felt 'wonderful', and when we returned to the exercises we had previously explored, she found more movement than she had thought possible.

Before our next and final session, Jacqui had taken a holiday, and had the chance to spend a lot of time walking barefoot on the beach – a wonderful exercise for the feet, as well as the spirit! When she appeared for the session she was walking so well that her limp could hardly be noticed, and she was no longer using any aids. We were both amazed that so much improvement had been possible in such a short space of time, and I shared in her joy. We spent the final session refining some of the work we had done so far, including releasing some of the torquing in the injured bone tissues and periosteum (connective tissue sheaths around the bones). She decided to stop therapy at this point, feeling that she had achieved what she came for and did not need to go further at this time.

Not every healing process is as immediately successful as this, and it is clear that Jacqui's own self-healing powers, her positive spirit, and her commitment to the process played an important part. Her responses to the work were generally not of an emotional nature, apart from her obvious joy at regaining her mobility, and a great interest and curiosity, so I did not feel it necessary or appropriate in this situation to address psychological material directly. Had she expressed emotional feelings arising from the work, or discussed other areas of difficulty in her life, then I would take this as an indication that another level of process needed to be addressed, perhaps exploring the meaning of her injuries within a psychological context; but as this was not the case, I respected the invitation to process through the body and allow her own inner resources, which seemed to be strong and healthy, to make the necessary connections and integrations.

CHAPTER 3
Embodying consciousness

Dialogue between the conscious and unconscious

In the practice of somatic therapy we consciously explore specific movement, energetic, and postural patterns by directing our awareness to particular tissues in the body, and touching or moving the body with the intention to effect change in those tissues. This may open us to feelings, images, memories, and sensations that we were not conscious of before. Past experiences that we have been unable to integrate, or that have been forgotten or repressed, are stored in the body tissues and fluids as bound energy; they are also stored in the unconscious psyche as images. Somatic work touches upon and awakens the unconscious store of memories, feelings, images, and knowledge held in the body, as the body softens and opens, allowing the life force beneath our habitual patterns of movement and behaviour to be contacted.

Somatic therapy engages the conscious mind in developing awareness of specific movement expressions, and directing or repatterning those expressions with conscious intent. The conscious mind penetrates unconscious and unexpressed areas of the body, awakening awareness in the body and integrating body and mind into a coherent whole. The dialogue between the conscious and unconscious mind is central to this work. However, if we only relate to the body with conscious intent, this may lead to an overly self-conscious or controlled way of being; in this we are expressing ourselves primarily through the nervous system, which can lead to disturbances. Consciously directed movement needs to be balanced by surrender to unconscious process, to the flow of the fluids within the body, and the free and spontaneous expression of the inner feeling self. The relationship between will and surrender is the issue here.

As a balance to the focus on conscious awareness and direction of movement patterning, which is central to many somatic practices, the practice of dance movement therapy (UK), or dance therapy (US), invites the unconscious to speak through the language of expressive movement. Dance movement therapy bridges the fields of somatic movement therapy and body psychotherapy, in its attention to the subtle expressions of the inner psyche through creative body movement. It seeks to integrate body, emotions, mind, and spirit in the dance of dialogue between the conscious and the unconscious. Expressive dance movement enables the psychological and spiritual dimensions of our experience to be embodied, made visible, and witnessed clearly by another. In my own practice and teaching, I use the discipline of authentic movement, a development within the field of dance movement therapy, to deepen, explore, and integrate the unconscious meaning of the feelings, sensations, images, and movement experiences evoked by focused somatic work.

The form of authentic movement offers a vehicle through which personal meaning can be integrated into consciousness. Where psychology and psychotherapeutic practice have developed complex integrations of different philosophical views, psychological techniques, and theories evolving from decades of clinical practice and intellectual endeavour, authentic movement offers a simple but powerful form within which the depths of the inner psychic world can speak directly through the body. It offers a holding space, a *feminine* container, and a practice of embodied awareness that goes beyond therapy, towards spiritual practice and embodied collective consciousness.

Dance movement therapy

Dance movement therapy developed in the USA during the 1940s, as pioneering dancers such as Marian Chace, Mary Whitehouse, and Liljan Espenak began to apply their skills in teaching dance in the community to working with patients in psychiatric settings. Originally it was practised as group therapy, adjunctive to treatment by a team of professionals under the supervision of a psychiatrist, and it was found to be very effective (Siegel, 1994: 72). The early pioneers began to research into psychological theories that would help to orientate, and also validate, their intuitive ways of working, and various theoretical approaches evolved (Lewis, 1986). Siegel describes an approach to psychoanalytic dance therapy, or dance-therapeutic psychoanalysis, which was greatly influenced by Freudian theories (Siegel, 1984). Espenak was more directly influenced by Adlerian theory, and Mary Whitehouse was the first of the dance movement therapists to be influenced by Jung in her approach. The system of movement analysis originated by Rudolf Laban, and further developed by Irmgard Bartenieff, was and still is a major underpinning of dance movement therapy theory and practice (Laban, 1974).

Dance movement therapy is based on the experience and perception that body posture and movement intimately reflect emotional and psychological processes. The creative use of dance movement allows the expression and integration of forgotten or repressed, preverbal, or inexpressible feelings and memories. As the client moves, the therapist witnesses her movement and then reflects back to her what has been expressed; she may use movement to empathize with or mirror back her client's movement, or she may use words, imagery, music or other methods. Unconscious material can gradually be reintegrated into consciousness, and a fuller sense of self can be developed. Thus the healing of personal history may occur, enabling a healthier developmental process to evolve. Joan Chodorow, a dance movement therapist influenced by Mary Whitehouse's approach, writes of this process:

> When therapist and patient can see and be seen by each other, the process re-insti-
> tutes the mirroring that is so fundamental to the parent-infant relationship.
> Expressive movement is the most direct way to reach back to our early experi-
> ences. By attending to the world of bodily felt sensations, the mover re-creates a
> situation that is in many ways similar to that of an infant who swims in a sensory-
> motor world. The presence of the therapist enables re-enactment and re-integra-
> tion of the earliest pre-verbal relationship. Over time, the quality of the therapeutic
> relationship may be internalised by the mover; it is as if a compassionate inner
> witness is constellated. In the end it is our ability to mirror empathically the
> expressive reactions of our patients which is fundamental to the success of dance
> therapy (Chodorow, 1994: 34).

Chodorow describes how dance movement therapy can take one of two basic directions, and it is important that the therapist understands which of these is appropriate to a particular client at a specific time. There is, however, a constant flow back and forth between the two directions in most cases. Movement can activate both conscious and unconscious processes: it can help to strengthen the ego-position by clarifying body boundaries and spatial orientation, creating a strong bodymind container through specific muscular activities; movement can also open us to the inner world of the unconscious psyche, a process of giving over to the unconscious, and allowing it to speak through our movement, to *move* us:

> The first approach emphasizes conscious, everyday reality, especially regarding
> time and space limitations, and it works to strengthen ego boundaries. The
> psychotic person usually derives great benefit from such work. Here, the dance
> therapist attempts to evoke specific movement responses which will help the
> person cope more effectively with the external world. For example, use of struc-
> tured rhythms, working within clearly organised spatial patterns, intentional use
> of weight, etc., will help the person develop a more realistic body image and
> strengthen his or her conscious viewpoint.
>   The second approach concentrates on using movement as a means of opening
> to the unconscious and will most likely involve some dissolution of ego bound-
> aries. Here, the movement may be based on more internally generated rhythms,
> spatial patterns may be more diffuse, and the person's eyes may be closed or have
> an inward focus. Awareness of and attending to aspects of inner reality become a
> central focus. As the brain receives an ongoing but diminished flow of sensory
> input, it may begin to create its own internal experience through increasingly

vivid imagery and, at times, body image distortion. Such navigation through the nonrational world of the unconscious can facilitate profoundly important insights and new levels of integration for people who have already developed a strong ego position. (Chodorow, 1977/1999a: 238)

The distinction between these two approaches is critical when working with a psychotic client, or one whose ego boundaries are not strong. To take the second approach with such a client may lead to the client being overwhelmed by unconscious content. To approach the unconscious with safety, ego boundaries must be strong enough to contain the emergence of disturbing or disorientating material from the unconscious. But, as Chodorow describes, dance movement therapy which takes the first approach can be helpful to such clients; movement experiences that clarify spatial, temporal, and body boundaries help to cultivate the sense of an embodied self, and can provide safety, structure, and an opportunity to strengthen ego boundaries.

Personal and transpersonal dimensions

Exploration of these two approaches has opened dance movement therapy into the area of transpersonal experience and growth, reconnecting us to the roots of dance in ancient healing rituals. Since the earliest times, dance has provided a vehicle for individual and collective healing. Ancient cultures practised dance to unite the community in a common feeling and purpose, to facilitate healing, to evoke the gods of fertility or hunting, and to induce altered states of consciousness that enabled the individual and the collective to experience connection with the spiritual source of life. Lewis writes:

We are not just intellects or even feeling intellects, we are embodied creatures. Every cell of our bodies relates and connects to each other. We are also filled with UR - the life force that interconnects everything. Thus if we are to be healed, our whole being, along with our relationship to the Source, must be engaged in the process. (Lewis, 1994: 41)

She describes how, since the beginning of time, dance has provided a vehicle for this unifying of body, mind, and soul with the eternal spirit. Dance has always been used to facilitate and celebrate rites of passage, to help relieve suffering and bring healing to body and soul, and to bring about 'the numinous connection to the spiritual'.

Chodorow also writes of this function of dance, and the need today to connect to its potential for transpersonal as well as personal healing: 'From the dawn of human history, dance has been a sacred language - a way of realizing our connection to the cosmos. Wherever we humans have withdrawn from a direct experience of our relationship to the universe, there too has the power of dance diminished.' We have now entered an age where the need to connect to transpersonal values and the inner reality of the collective is urgent; our survival depends on it, as Chodorow describes. To do this we must learn to embrace the opposites, whether they be within each individual, between people, or amongst the races and nations of the world She proposes that: 'To develop most fully the potential of that sacred dialogue which serves to unite the opposites, dance/movement must reclaim its original power. It may then take its place as our most powerful tool in facilitating the transcendent function' (Chodorow, 1977/1999a: 250).

The psychology of Jung strongly influenced the work of Mary Whitehouse, who developed the practice of authentic movement as an embodied form of Jung's process of active imagination. Whitehouse was the first dance movement therapist to differentiate movement originating in the conscious from that originating in the unconscious. She spoke about movement that is intentional and ego-directed, movement that is unintentional and has its source in the unconscious, and movement that comes from the Self. The difference between intentional and unintentional movement she described as the sense of 'I am moving', and 'I am being moved'; movement from the Self embodies both experiences (Whitehouse, 1958/1999a: 43).

Joan Chodorow has evolved an integrated theory of Jungian-based dance movement therapy (Chodorow, 1991). She discusses 'the mysterious interface that mediates between body and psyche':

> Jung calls this the psychoid level. He describes it as a transformative function in the depths of the unconscious that mediates between the realms of body and psyche, instinct and image. It seems obvious that the emotions are the stuff of that interface. An emotion, by definition, is at once somatic and psychic. The somatic aspect is made up of bodily innervations and expressive physical action. The psychic aspect is made up of images and ideas. In psychopathology, the two realms tend to split. By contrast, a naturally felt emotion involves a dialectical relationship – a union of body and psyche. (Chodorow, 1991: 3)

She goes on to say that working with the imagination – whether verbally through free association, or creatively through artwork, movement, or writing – takes us right to the emotional core of our complexes. Dance movement therapy may use all of these methods, with dance movement as the central focus, in order to reintegrate the somatic and psychic realms, and open a creative dialogue between conscious and unconscious processes. The ability not only to access and release, but also to contain and express symbolically our deepest emotions, inner conflicts, and also our innate qualities and wisdom, enables us to develop and grow. Dance movement therapy is concerned with the expression and transformation of emotions and feeling states which emerge from the unconscious, expressed as posture, gesture, and movement, into conscious awareness.

Janet Adler, another of Whitehouse's foremost followers, further differentiated movement from the unconscious, which has its source in personal history, and that which has a transpersonal or collective source

(Adler, 1987/1999: 149). As an example of a movement process that moved between personal, transpersonal and collective impulses, I would like to include here a personal movement story that evolved during an authentic movement retreat led by Adler:

> We are in Tuscany again. We sit for the first time in the circle, the surface of the wooden floor gleaming in the sun like a wide and empty pool of light. I am suddenly acutely aware of having no idea what will unfold this week; the unknown seems to sit in the centre of the space like a large and tangible presence. For a moment it all feels too much. Janet reminds us that some of us may work at the personal level, some at the transpersonal or collective level; she adds that we might also do nothing at all. I feel relieved. I need permission for nothing at all to happen.
>
> So I am surprised when in the first movement session I come quickly into something which feels like a universal and timeless experience. Following the subtle movements of breath, I am led to a posture with head and shoulders hanging. I am a prisoner of war. My hands are tied together in front of me and I am being dragged by a chain or rope across a barren wilderness landscape. It is dark - late evening or night - and very cold; but we, for I know there are many others with me, tied together by the long chains that bind us, have to keep on walking. We are beaten back onto our feet each time we drop exhausted to the ground. It feels like an endless, slow march. We have no choice but to keep going. The image of the prisoner returns several times during the week.
>
> We are in Italy, and so nearby a terrible war is going on. Just over the hills and water the people of Bosnia are driven to consciousness by the fighting and killing, in stark contrast to the protected place we enjoy here, where consciousness can grow through gentler means. The same sun shines on both sides of the water. Military planes fly overhead now and then, to remind us that the war is going on, and I hope that they are carrying aid, not bombs. My movement is a prayer.
>
> Each session is taking me deeper, as personal and collective images come together. I am a mother grieving the death of her son, kneeling in the centre of a circle of women, together making slow, strong, swaying movement and song, a mourning ritual. It is good to feel part of a collective of women grieving together, to feel the power and grief rise up through our bodies and begin to transform into a powerful but contained rage. My fists are clenched as my body circles and sways slowly between earth and sky. Here is a grief that could grow into rage that would cry out against the wars and violence. In my movement there is also personal loss. I have never had, and have longed so much for the opportunity to be supported through my own grieving with such rituals. I have longed *so* much for this. I am grateful for this moment, and grateful for the exquisite witnessing of it by my partner.
>
> A few sessions later, a small movement coming from my heart connects me to a deep feeling of loss and abandonment and utter aloneness. I choose to surrender to the feeling. I am a child abandoned by her mother, longing for the only one who could give comfort, the one who cannot be replaced by another. My movement takes me to that place where there is no comfort to be found. Then with a slow gesture of my hand and arm I find myself saying goodbye to the dear friend who died many years ago. Now I am really accepting that he has gone, letting him go, accepting it, feeling the aloneness, accepting it, feeling it, being with it. A sense of

surrender, close to resignation, but not quite. As I drop my arm I am giving up all hope, false hope, falling into stillness. But in that moment the stirring of new movement comes with the need to take a deep breath, and life goes on. I move to the wall to feel support, and the image of the prisoner returns. This time, out of the loss and suffering the deep will to go on is awakening, and the prisoner is transforming into a pilgrim. Somehow this way was chosen, for some sacred purpose.

Later, I am making sinewy, twisting movements across the floor, muscles tensed, complex convoluted shapes. It is a slow, slow birth. No pain and angst this time, just the knowledge in my cells of the movement pathways I took as I twisted and pushed and clawed my way out. Then I lie very still. I have been born and am lying on my back, my body arched slightly so that my heart is opened wide. I feel vulnerable and so very alone. The other movers seem to have retreated to the other side of the circle. They feel very distant. No-one comes to me, and I can't move, so I lie very still, barely breathing. I feel empty, and am aware of a choice to surrender into a bliss-like vacancy, or to remember that I was not welcomed at birth. I go numb.

I am carrying tears that lie so deep they aren't yet ready to be shed, and need a soft embrace to let go into. Instead there is violence in the circle. One witness sees a mother lion about to kill her cubs. I need a smaller circle to contain my grief and my small emerging self.

At the end of the retreat I am given this more intimate container, and complete my movement process. Out comes a sigh, a breath, soft at first, then a cry, then a roar, an urgent cry that says not 'I am afraid', but 'I AM'. My essential call to being. Then I am able to find my ground, to push up against the floor, against the wall, on my feet again. I find my shawl which I had used before as protection, and make a whip out of it, striding around the space whipping against the air and the walls of the room. Now I am the soldier who beats and bullies the prisoners as they march. This too.

The practice and discipline of authentic movement

The form of active imagination in movement, or authentic movement, was developed by Mary Whitehouse, and further evolved by Adler, Chodorow and others, as a container for the exploration and integration of the many levels of movement process. Adler's evolution of this work she names the *discipline* of authentic movement; her approach, which has evolved over nearly 30 years of practice and exploration of essential questions about the form, focuses upon the *direct experience* of both mover and witness. It is differentiated by Adler from *active imagination in movement,* which addresses more specifically the psychological process of the mover, in its embracing of the experience of both mover and witness in the presence of each other, and the relationship between them (see Geissinger, 1998, in which Adler describes her development of the discipline of authentic movement and the influences that contributed to it). Adler introduced certain concepts and structures such as the *ground form, long circle, witness circle,* and *collective body* into the discipline and language of authentic movement.

The ground form of authentic movement practice involves a mover and a witness. The witness creates and holds a safe space, the witness circle, into which the mover enters and begins to move, usually with eyes closed, following her own internal impulses. Both mover and witness attend to their own experiences as the mover's process unfolds.

By working with her eyes closed, or the vision inwardly focused, the mover is enabled to give full attention to her inner sensory and imaginal processes, with minimal distraction from outside. External influences, such as sounds or contact with other movers, may acquire meaning significant to her unfolding inner story when visual information and the perspective of objective reality are not present; unexpected disturbances often provide important impulses for new experience and awareness, or a catalyst for the discovery of insight. We live in a visually oriented culture, and our dominant visual sense is closely connected to our ego position and our *hold* on the world – many people use their vision, more than is physiologically necessary, to literally hold themselves in balance, to the detriment of the other somatically based senses. Letting go of this holding to our habitual orientation allows for other experiences, as we surrender ego to the unknown hidden worlds within.

Approaching the unconscious through attending to the body, we gain access to a great range and depth of sensory and emotional experience. We begin by listening inwardly to the flow of sensations, images, feelings, sounds, memories, and movement impulses which emerge into awareness: 'The unconscious manifests itself through an ongoing stream of body sensation and mental imagery. Its relatively formless products may include inner throbbings, pulsings, tinglings, pressures, surges, waves of differentiated and un-differentiated energies, inner voices, sounds, words, fantasies, feelings, moods, memories and impulses' (Chodorow, 1977/1999: 242).

The mover then begins to give form to these inner sensations and impulses. Mary Whitehouse (1963/1999: 52) described authentic movement as 'following the inner sensation, allowing the impulse to take the form of physical action . . .' During this phase of the process the mover attends fully to the movement itself; images may arise or not in conjunction with the movement. Sometimes an image may provide the impulse to move, and she follows her internal imaging process, giving expression to this in movement. The movement session usually ends when the witness gives a signal, such as the ringing of a bell, after a mutually agreed period of time. The time frame provided by the witness is a boundary that helps to create safety for the mover, who can enter her process for a circumscribed period knowing that she will be recalled by her witness; thus she can release the ego-function of time-keeping for a while, and more readily enter the timeless world of the unconscious.

After each movement session it is important to anchor the experience in consciousness; this can be done by recalling the experience to the witness, or by recording it through artwork or writing. In authentic movement practice the witness then offers her personal responses to the mover; her presence and witnessing help to bring unconscious material into conscious awareness, and help to prevent the experience from slipping back into unconsciousness again. The integration of unconscious material into conscious awareness is the ultimate goal, so that we may grow into an ever deepening and embracing sense of being.

During an authentic movement session we enter into our unfolding inner process, interacting with, responding to, and embodying in movement our inner figures. Ego reactions to the content emerging from the unconscious can be more readily understood and integrated when fully embodied in movement. Chodorow writes:

> Jung describes the ego as a complex datum which is constituted primarily of a general awareness of the body. (CW #18, para 18.) . . .
>
> Although the impulse to move may spring from a source in the unconscious, the body, which allows the impulse to manifest itself, remains firmly rooted in the fact of its own existence. The actual act of moving creates proprioceptive and kinesthetic feedback which serves to confront the unconscious with the body ego's reality. As the unconscious impulse and the body ego encounter each other's different realities, an intense and fully mutual education is likely to occur. (Chodorow, 1977/1999a: 246)

In the final stage of active imagination, Jung emphasized the importance of putting into practice the understanding and insight gained from the work. When a genuine inner change has taken place, integration will occur without the great effort and resistance encountered when we try, through will power alone, to make changes in our life, or act upon the ethical considerations that have arisen through the work. As Chodorow affirms, the actual physical and energetic embodiment of new levels of consciousness and integration, which occurs in the dance movement process itself, greatly facilitates the expression and integration of new energies and insights into everyday life.

The witness

Essential to the authentic movement process is the presence of the witness (The term 'witness' was first introduced into authentic movement language by Janet Adler. She credits psychologist John Weir as first introducing her to the use of this term. See Geissinger, 1998: 7). The witness creates the safe container within which the mover can surrender to her unconscious process; her presence helps the mover to return to ordinary reality at the end of the movement session, and to bring the fruits of her journey of descent back into consciousness. The witness sits at the edge of the space whilst the mover, usually with her eyes closed, enters the empty space and attends to the stirrings of her inner sensory and imaginal world. The witness does not generally intervene, unless she feels the mover's safety is at risk; her presence is non-intrusive, non-judgemental, and compassionate towards both the mover and herself. Whitehouse realized that it was the depths to which she had travelled in her own analysis that enabled her clients to work in depth. The witness embodies her own process of encounter with the unconscious and the depth of experience she has accessed, and this facilitates the in-depth movement work of the other.

To enter into the unconscious through an exploration of the body, whether through dance movement or bodywork, can be difficult and for some quite frightening, especially at the beginning, or when traumatic material is surfacing. The body interior can feel like a dark and threatening world in which it is easy to lose one's way. Resistance to the encounter may express in an inability to work with the eyes closed, a tendency to dissociate from body sensation or from feelings when moving, or to lose touch with the sensory and imaginal process and become lost in thoughts and disembodied day-dreaming.

Resistance is respected in this practice, but an important function of the witness is to support the mover, in her own time, to be able to enter her inner world in a way that is safe and creative. The encounter is made easier in the presence of another who provides structure and containment, and is willing to enter into the unconscious world together with the mover, and to meet the mover there. The witness's containing presence gradually detoxifies the mover's unbearable anxiety and fear, rage and grief, so that she is enabled more and more to contain her negative feelings herself. Non-judgemental, empathic, and compassionate witnessing by another is crucial to the process of fully integrating depth material into relationships and everyday life.

Over a period of time, the experience of being witnessed by another, with empathy, compassion, and clarity, enables the mover to internalize the presence of the external witness. She begins to develop her own internal witness, free of the concepts, judgements, and self-criticisms that so often cloud our clear perception of ourselves. Adler has explored in depth, and finely articulated, the important function of the witness. She writes:

> The ground of the discipline of Authentic Movement is the relationship between a mover and a witness. The heart of the practice is about the longing, as well as the fear, to see ourselves clearly. We repeatedly discover that such an experience of clarity is deeply and inextricably related to the gift of being seen clearly by another and, just as importantly, related to the gift of seeing another clearly. (Adler, 1994/1999: 6)

I look upon the art of witnessing as a form of meditation; indeed Adler has beautifully articulated the relationship between the discipline of authentic movement and mystical practice (Adler, 1991/1999: 9–10). The witness pays attention to the feelings, images, sensations, memories, and movement impulses that arise in her, evoked by the presence of the person moving. She owns these as her own experience, rather than projecting them onto the mover; she does not attempt to interpret or analyse the mover's experience in terms of her own judgements and fantasies, but owns these for what they are – her own direct experience, evoked by the presence and activity of the mover. In a similar way, in meditation practice the internal witness notices the impulses that arise as thoughts, feelings, images, sensations, and so on; but rather than interpret or judge or project them onto others, the meditator seeks to experience them directly, without attachment or aversion, thus allowing them to transform. In such a way, the witness enters into the mover's experience, whilst simultaneously maintaining awareness of her own; in this special moment of relatedness, both can see and be seen, and both may experience healing and transformation of consciousness. Adler writes:

> The witness practices the art of seeing. Seeing clearly is not about knowing what the mover needs or must do. The witness does not 'look at' the mover, but instead, as she internalizes the mover, she attends to her own experience of judgement, interpretation, and projection, in response to the mover as catalyst. As she acknowledges ownership of her experiences, the density of her personal history empties, enabling the witness at times to feel that she can see the mover clearly, and more importantly, that she can see herself clearly. Sometimes . . . it is grace . . . the witness embodies a clear presence. (Adler, 1994/1999: 6)

After moving and witnessing, both people speak of their own experiences; the mover speaks first, and the witness responds by sharing some of her own experience, choosing what it is appropriate to say, and what must be contained for the moment. In this way she provides the container which holds the mover's unconscious process, as well as her internal witness. The mover may feel clearly seen and accepted by the other, and her own experience can be enriched and deepened by sensitive and compassionate witnessing. She sees and accepts herself more fully, and can begin to own back that which she has projected onto the witness. Gradually, the mover is enabled to consciously integrate her unconscious material and her own internal witness. Through the presence of the external witness she learns to 'internalise the reflective function of the witness, i.e. to yield to the unconscious stream of bodily felt sensations and images, while at the same time bringing the experience into conscious awareness' (Chodorow, 1991: 113).

The art of witnessing has a wide range of applications, in both professional and personal relationships. In my own teaching and practice I use it in a number of ways. At times I use the form of moving and witnessing as a practice in itself, as described; or I may use it to explore, deepen, and integrate material arising from somatic work. When working with touch at the cellular level, I also focus on the art of witnessing the body through touch, applying the principles of non-judgemental and compassionate witnessing, and owning what I experience as I touch another; this gives the client space to accept or reject my perceptions, and thus helps her to connect to her own reality more clearly, as well as allowing her to feel met exactly where she is. I also endeavour to use the principles of clear witnessing in responding to a client's or student's verbal sharing, or artwork, and encourage group members to respond to each other in this way. This can have a powerful effect on the bonding process of a group, as each member is given space to express herself, in her own way, and is supported and accepted in this. The practice of witnessing can be viewed as an embracing attitude, a *meta-skill* (Mindell) underlying all technique and practice, which both guides and contains the work.

Although authentic movement as a discipline is not psychotherapy, it most certainly can effect therapeutic changes at the psychological level. A number of dance movement therapists and psychotherapists use it within a therapeutic practice, but Adler makes it clear that to do so one must also have appropriate therapy training. For some, it may then be used as a psychotherapeutic method, but it is not defined within or limited by such categorization; many use it as a resource for creative work, a tool for mindful living, or a contemplative discipline to support their spiritual growth. However, there are many parallels between the psychotherapeutic process and the discipline of authentic movement.

In her paper 'Who is the witness?' Adler (1987: 6-7) discusses the relationship between psychoanalysis and authentic movement. In both instances the client/mover does not see the analyst/witness, and surrenders to the process of free association, through words in the first instance and movement in the second. As both approaches evoke regression, long-term work is usually required, and the witness, like the analyst, may take on a nurturing, empathic, protective, and parental function. The verbal sharing after moving enables the psychodynamic and transference/counter-transference issues to be clarified and integrated. This form is particularly suited to the in-depth exploration of experiences related to preverbal life, the unconscious memories of which are held in the body. Through movement we *re-member* our past as it is revealed through the body, piece by piece, gesture by gesture, in order to cultivate a sense of integration, wholeness, and authentic selfhood.

Dance movement therapist and authentic movement teacher, Tina Stromsted, in an article entitled 'Re-inhabiting the female body', discusses the ways in which a woman may dissociate from her body as a result of traumatic and abusive experiences in early life; she describes how the practice of authentic movement can provide a safe space in which to reclaim the sensation, expressiveness, and power of the body that has been lost (Stromsted, 1994-5: 18-27). Her description is of course applicable to anyone who has lost touch with the full feeling and expressiveness of the bodymind and authentic self, because of hurt, violation, deprivation, or abandonment, which can cause numbing of feeling, and dissociation from the body. The importance of being witnessed in our moments of deep encounter with ourselves, our moments of transformation as we return home to the body and reclaim our full aliveness and expressiveness, is understood and honoured in this practice. Without the meeting that occurs in this personal relationship, depth and transpersonal experiences may not be fully integrated into everyday life.

The collective body

Sometimes in group movement processes, magical things occur that show us without doubt that we are in some mysterious way all connected to each other, and to the world in which we live – that our personal stories, unfolding through movement and sound, interact and evolve in ways that support each person's developing consciousness and healing, whilst also embodying a greater story in which we all play a special part. The interweaving of personal stories in a spontaneous and synchronistic embodiment creates a larger story, when each mover honestly and courageously expresses her own direct and embodied experience of the moment.

As movers in a group learn to witness each other and themselves, the power of the witness circles grows; it becomes strong enough to contain the energy of transpersonal and collective processes, as well as material from the personal unconscious. Consciousness of the collective body is the next evolutionary step that emerges, as each member of the group develops her conscious internal witness. Membership of a collective body becomes a possibility as personal stories are embodied and witnessed by the group.

Adler talks about the great longing that exists within each of us to belong. During the last century, the quest to individuate has been dominant; we have quite rightly sought to liberate ourselves from the constraints and limitations on personal freedom, choice, and consciousness, which group ideology, mass psychology, and religious dogma have imposed upon us. We have sought to develop personal consciousness, but a tragic result of this has been loss of the sense of belonging, loss of the embodied experience of belonging to a tribalbody, and to the earthbody itself. Adler writes:

> Over emphasis on individual development encouraged outside of a sacred circle has contributed significantly to the creation of unbearable rage, isolation, and despair. In response, the desire to return to one's unquestioned place in the circle can be awakened. But we can easily romanticize possible membership in the collective without fully understanding the shadow aspects of belonging, why the circle has become absent . . . Accepting one's place in the circle can threaten (the) process of the development of the self. If membership is unconscious, the loss of individual freedom results. (Adler, 1994/1999: 4)

Unconscious membership can thwart the process of individuation, and limit our choices and our capacity to take responsibility for our actions in the world. But when individual ego development and individualism is not in right relationship to the whole, conscious membership in the collective can also be threatened. Jung claimed that the way to participate responsibly as a conscious member of the collective is through rediscovery of soul. Our evolutionary task now is 'to bring the gifts of individuation into conscious membership in the whole, to find a way to be uniquely ourselves inside a sacred conscious circle' (Adler, 1994/1999: 4).

Adler states that this change in consciousness must be an embodied change:

> It is in our bodies where the phenomenon of life energy, a physical reality, is directly experienced. One by one, knowing (and knowing implies consciousness), knowing in our bodies that we belong, creates a collective body in which life energy is shared. I imagine the collective body as the energetic consciousness of the earthbody, which includes all living beings. It is the body-felt connectedness among people, profoundly related to the source of our humanity.
>
> Becoming conscious of our part in the whole through direct experience of membership allows exploration of the relationship between the personal body and the collective body. When our individual bodies have been wounded because of our suffering, we often are opened toward embodied personal consciousness. Our earthbody is wounded. Can we, because of personal consciousness, become opened toward consciousness of the collective body? Can we create a sacred conscious circle that evolves organically from the knowing body of each member, from the direct experience of each member? (Adler, 1994/1999: 4-5)

The discipline of authentic movement offers a form that can contain and support this evolution of embodied collective consciousness. Here, within the presence of the witness circle, the multilayered expressions of conscious and unconscious, personal, transpersonal, and collective experience are embodied, made visible, seen, heard, felt, and acknowledged. We come to feel and know ourselves as both individual members of the group, and as unique expressions of the collective body.

I would like to finish with a story of the collective body. This story is the creation of Janet Adler, in response to witnessing a *long circle* of authentic movement. (A 'long circle' is the name given to an authentic movement form developed by Adler where each group member can move or witness, according to her own wish, need or impulse. Members go in and out of the movement space as they choose, with a minimum number always maintaining the witness circle. These circles continue for extended periods of time, allowing a depth of work to emerge.) Each mover's process is witnessed and responded to as her personal story, but the witness may also experience the creation of a collective story, in which each individual member plays a part. This long circle took place during a five-day authentic movement retreat in Italy, where 25 women from different countries gathered together to study and practise the form with Adler; I was privileged to be a member of this group. Adler has named this story 'The call':

> Each time a voice called out, a particular archetypal aspect of the human psyche was acknowledged, accepted. In this story I saw how new energy repeatedly, cyclically

accrues from life, how it is gathered, contained, dispersed back into the collective through one body, then another, then another. I saw an embodiment of my experience of our present state on this planet .....

I see a senior woman standing on the edge of the circle, facing out, her arms folded in front of her: a gatekeeper on the edge of the earth. At her feet, I see a woman wrapped in a blanket: a baby, new. I see innocence.

A woman walks to the centre of the circle, her arms slowly lifting, calling.

I see a woman pounding, yelling, pulling her hair: destruction, despair, hatred, pain. I see suffering.

A woman suddenly stands, reaching her arms straight out to her side, calling.

I see three movers on the other side of the circle laughing, playing, tumbling: joy, beauty, love. I see freedom.

A woman begins turning, calling, a long steady call.

I see a woman standing, holding her hands in front of her as if she holds a thick tube reaching from the floor to the ceiling. She moves very little but tension visibly builds in her body, her focus steady and strong: energy accruing in one body. She releases the tension, pounding her heel into the floor: a body as vessel shattering, birthing new agony, which is sent into the earth through her heel. I see transformation.

A woman lies flat on the floor, calling into the earth.

Women clap and sing in rhythm with the pounding heel, and come to their feet, one by one, stomping and chanting: new energy is dispersed, flowing into many bodies.

I see one woman, crouched at the feet of the dancers, hiding her face: the one not ready.

A woman suddenly moves backward to the wall, screaming: fear of the unknown manifest as the new energy escalates.

Another woman, acknowledging fear, meets the screaming woman until the terror evaporates: fear of the unknown shared and thus contained. These two women – who is leading, who is following? – slowly re-enter the circle. Now a third woman walks with them. They walk so slowly.

The second woman continues, out the other side of the circle, arriving at the open window, calling out into the hills: a call to the gods for help.

A woman calls out from the other open window on the other side of the room: in response, in support, calling the gods for help.

I see a woman lying near the edge of the circle, silent, unmoving: the one who does not know what to do.

A woman sits on the floor with her legs open, breathing harder and harder: labor before a birth.

A woman wraps her legs from behind around the birthing woman. She pushes her pelvis forward, into the back of the birthing woman. Now she reaches up, out of her efforts and calls, a call for new life.

A woman is weaving shapes in the air with intense focus, directly in front of the woman who sits with her legs open: the cosmic mid-wife.

I see a woman moving around the entire outside of the circle, stepping into long deep strides, droning: the cosmic shaman, containing it all.

Again and again, I see a woman sitting on the floor with her legs open, breathing harder and harder: labor before a birth. Will new life occur? This birth is not about an individual who will save our earth. This is the birth of the collective body.

Now I see a woman sitting in a corner, raging: anger, frustration, violence, hopelessness.

A woman crawls towards her, waiting, listening at her feet. I see compassion.

The clock tells me to lift the bell and let it ring. It is time to rest. It is not time for the birth. How is readiness to be determined? For now, like children, we are in the process of remembering something we once knew long ago, and simultaneously, we are glimpsing our potential for discovering something completely new, something we have never before experienced. In the meantime, we are loving the best we can. (Adler, 1994/1999: 11-12)

PART II

Somatic psychology in practice – movement origins and the emergence of the sense of self

CHAPTER 4

Development of the sense of self

Personally and historically we have danced along a continuum between the experience of a unified bodymind, and of a split between body, mind, soul, and spirit that leaves us feeling less than whole, fragmented, ungrounded, anxious about our existence. There have been many movements during the twentieth century that have sought to heal this split; the fields of both psychology and somatology have developed numerous theories and methodologies to this end, each approaching the marriage of mind and matter, body and spirit from its own perspective. We are still in the process of moving towards this marriage. The separation has been long and deep, and reintegration is not a simple matter.

The humanistic and transpersonal psychology movements developed to support the growing variety of psychotherapies involved in the movement towards a more holistic view of the human being. Although body-oriented psychotherapy has been evolving since the time of Reich, it is only in recent years that body psychotherapy associations have been founded in Europe and the US, and efforts to establish body psychotherapy as a distinct discipline within the broader field of psychotherapy have just begun. Similarly, it is only recently that an international association for somatic movement education and therapy has been founded, with the growing need to establish somatics as a profession in its own right. Thus the movement towards integrating body-oriented therapies as professionally valid therapeutic approaches has been slower than the inclusion of transpersonal therapy; nevertheless, somatic therapy and body psychotherapy have grown into a field of immense depth, richness, variety, strength, and opportunity.

In this chapter we will explore some of the research that gives evidence for the central importance of the body in psychological development, and the need for its inclusion in holistic psychotherapeutic work. Ken Wilber's model of 'spectrum psychology' offers a container within which to explore the many theories of development and diverse approaches to therapy. Readers may be familiar with Wilber's work, as many integrative and transpersonal therapists use it today, but I mention it here as it will be referred to later. He offers a holistic mapping of the development of human consciousness through the natural life cycle, and indicates which therapeutic approaches may be most effectively used to address specific phases of growth (Wilber, 1979, 1980). His more recent work has developed and expanded the early model to include social and cultural dimensions of experience, but his original concept forms the basis of later developments and is relevant to our purpose here (Wilber, 2000).

As in the evolution of nature, growth and development in the human psyche is an evolution of ever more complex wholes. The development from amoeba to human is reflected in the development of each fertilized cell, into infant and adult. The force that drives evolution also propels the development of psyche and soma of each individual.

> We might say, psychological growth or development in humans is simply a micro-cosmic reflection of universal growth on the whole, and has the same goal: the unfolding of ever higher-order unities and integrations. And this is one of the major reasons that the psyche is, indeed, stratified. Very like the geological formation of the earth, psychological development proceeds, stratum by stratum, level by level, stage by stage, with each successive level superimposed upon its predecessor in such a way that it includes but transcends it. (Wilber, 1980: 2)

Wilber envisions the natural development of consciousness as a cycle with an outward and an inward arc, beginning with the 'ground unconscious' ascribed to foetal life. Within the ground unconscious all of the deep structures of body, mind, soul and spirit are embedded as potentials waiting to emerge as development proceeds, as if through a process of remembrance (Wilber, 1980: 83).

During infancy and childhood, development evolves through prepersonal, preverbal and ego/persona stages, to the mature ego of the adult. The cycle then moves through transverbal and transpersonal stages, potentially culminating in the ultimate realization of universal consciousness as the cycle dips into the mystical realm, below the horizon from which the individual ground unconscious originally emerged. This map includes spiritual as well as psychological development.

Wilber's model presents a potential healthy development, but in reality growth is rarely, if ever, as well ordered and sequential as the model seems to suggest. The perspective of a spirallic path, rather than a single cycle of progress, might be helpful to us as we struggle to integrate our personal traumas and deviations from this natural potential. We may well be fairly mature and able at times to access transverbal and transpersonal experiences, but we still have areas of 'unfinished childhood business' to resolve. Or life crises may plunge us into regressive processes for a period of time. In practice we may be dealing with issues related to several stages of Wilber's life cycle at any one time. As Jung observed, existential and spiritual crises occurring during the process of individuation usually involve infantile and even womb-like regressions. However, certain developmental processes generally predominate at specific phases of the life cycle; as Wilber shows, each requires a particular kind of therapeutic or spiritual practice appropriate to the developmental stage.

Wilber writes: 'Many structures on the Outward Arc that are "pre-" appear on the Inward Arc as "trans-". That is . . . pre-personal gives way to personal which gives way to trans-personal; pre-egoic moves to egoic which moves to trans-egoic . . . – and so on' (Wilber, 1980: 49). These distinctions are important in clinical practice, where transstructures are sometimes reduced to prestructures. The experiences of each are similar in certain ways, but not identical, and confusion between them can be damaging in practice. Reduction of a genuine transpersonal experience to a developmental pathology related to early childhood prevents the integration of an important experience; it can inhibit further growth and spiritual awakening, and may induce pathology. Similarly, mistaking prestructures for transstructures can be dangerous; someone engaging in spiritual practice, or accessing transpersonal experiences, from an unintegrated ego state may regress to an infantile state. Therapy that can address earlier levels of development may then be needed, to help avoid disintegration and psychosis. Wilber's model also gives a perspective from which to view the similarities and important differences between psychotic and genuine mystical experiences; the integration of the mature ego, and development of what he calls the 'centauric' level of development, the integrated bodymind, are integral to the safe immersion in unboundaried, mystical states of consciousness.

The relationship between prestructures and transstructures is important in bodywork and movement practice where preverbal and preegoic processes are often accessed, and can also open us to experiences of a transpersonal nature. Wilber's model offers a framework by which we can understand the evocation of transpersonal or spiritual experiences through somatic work, where the axis between prestructures and transstructures of consciousness may be opened. Unlike Freud and many of his followers, who viewed the body as related to unconscious drives and forces needing to be controlled by the conscious ego-mind, some transpersonal and many body-oriented therapists now recognize that consciously embodied process can lead to deeply spiritual and healing experiences.

We create our sense of identity by drawing successive boundaries between what we experience as self and not self; each boundary takes us further from the state of 'unity consciousness' where we are identified with the universal (Wilber, 1979: Chapter 1). At the first main stage of differentiation, the skin is the primary boundary separating self from not self, and we identify with our total organism but not the external environment. This boundary is necessary to the development of an individual sense of self.

Differentiation of ego-mind from body then occurs, with its inherent risk of splitting, and in our mentally oriented culture many of us come to identify the ego-mind as 'self', and see body as 'other'.

At the next boundary we come to reject 'unacceptable' aspects of the ego as not self, hence splitting ourselves into persona and shadow. This is a common process, at least in part culturally dependent, which can occur during the upward arc in Wilber's cyclical model. It leaves us reaching maturity with a very restricted sense of who we are, and large areas of our experience rejected as not belonging to us. To proceed through the inward arc to a more complete development, these split-off aspects of experience must be reintegrated, as we seek to realize the state of 'unity consciousness' and the ultimate fulfilment of our psychospiritual evolution. Effective therapy will use therapeutic or spiritual approaches appropriate to the levels at which these boundaries have been drawn.

Wilber's model offers a reference point from which we can look at the appropriateness of different therapeutic approaches, including somatic practices, body psychotherapy, or transpersonal therapy, in treating issues related to specific developmental processes. It also enables us to review the broad spectrum of psychology without judging one approach to be superior to another; instead we can see that each has its place and its value in treating specific developmental issues, each therapy representing a part of the greater whole. We see that there are many ways to heal the splits we experience within ourselves, depending on where the boundaries between self and not-self have been drawn.

Perception, self, and other

The life cycle that Wilber outlines begins with the infant and its fundamental task of developing a coherent sense of self through which it can interact with the world in a meaningful way. Our experience of self as adults is largely based upon the ways we navigated the formative years of infancy and childhood, and our relationships with those who were closest to us, as well as on our innate personalities. The subject of research from many different perspectives, developmental psychology has yielded a great deal of information and numerous theories about child development and the nature of the processes of integration and splitting that constitute our psychological health or lack of it. Daniel Stern's findings are of special interest and relevance to my own work as a body-oriented therapist and I will use his ideas to contextualize some of the somatic work explored in later chapters. He places sensory-motor processing through the body, and relationship through bodily experiences, at the centre of his theory of the development of the sense of self. Stern's research takes into account both analytic theory developed from clinical practice, and developmental theory derived from observation of infants and mothers. In the past these two areas of research have often yielded different information which has not always appeared compatible. Stern's work integrates both approaches in a fundamental reworking of developmental theory. At the heart of his ideas lies the importance of the infant's sense of self as it develops in relationship to others. The importance today of the sense of self as a clinical issue has been noted by Frosh:

> The classic Freudian patients were hysterics and obsessional neurotics – people with relatively clearly differentiate symptoms who could be understood to be suffering from too much repression . . . These classical neurotic patients, whose pathology was held to derive from Oedipal conflicts, were the bases upon which psychoanalytic theory was formulated and have dominated cultural images of analysis from the start, as well as dictating the therapeutic techniques employed. But over the post-Freudian period there has been a gradual shift in the nature of the typical analysand, from someone needing to liberate her/himself from unconscious conflicts, to someone desperately seeking for a secure core of self. (Frosh, 1987: 248)

Stern proposes that it is the *sense* of self and of other which is crucial to development; the emphasis on sense brings the question out of the realm of theoretical concepts and back to direct and felt experience, back fundamentally to the body, its sensations and perceptions. He describes four main senses of self: the sense of an emergent self, the sense of a core self, the sense of a subjective self, and the sense of a verbal self (Stern, 1985).

The sense of an emergent self

The sense of an emergent self develops during the first two months of life. Stern notes that from the very beginning parents instinctively treat their infants as if they were not only physiological systems needing care and regulation, but also social beings with feelings, sensibilities, and an emerging sense of self. Piaget and other theorists tend to view the sense of self as the *product* of integrating and organizing disparate experiences, but Stern is interested in the *process* of organization – the infant's actual experience of making the leaps and creating connections between previously unrelated events and pieces of sensory-motor information. He asks whether an infant can experience not only the already formed sense of organization, but the 'coming-into-being of organization' :

> In order for the infant to have any formed sense of self, there must ultimately be some organization that is sensed as a reference point. The first such organization concerns the body: its coherence, its action, its inner feeling states, and the memory of all these. That is the experiential organization with which the sense of a core self is concerned. Immediately prior to that, however, the reference organization for a sense of self is still forming; in other words it is emerging. (Stern, 1985: 45-6)

Various processes are available to the infant to make such organizations possible. One is 'amodal perception'. Stern describes research that shows that the ability to transfer sensory information received through one sensory channel to another is innate and present from birth. The representations the infant experiences are 'shapes, intensities, and temporal patterns', a 'global perception' rather than specific sights, sounds, and objects. We know that learning proceeds as synaptic connections are made between brain cells, and that there are complex connections between all areas of the brain; this would facilitate amodal perception. But Stern suggests that information transcends sensory channels and exists in a supra-modal form which is encoded 'into a still mysterious amodal *representation,* which can then be recognised in any of the sensory modes' (Stern, 1985: 51). This idea is reminiscent of Rupert Sheldrake's theory of 'morphic resonance' (Sheldrake, 1988), and also Candace Pert's research into the function of neuropeptides as the physiological substrata for emotion and mind. As discussed earlier, she sees mind as information moving through the networks of brain cells and receptor sites throughout the body. These ideas also closely relate to Mindell's theory of the 'dreambody', where processes are followed as they flow through various perceptual channels (see Chapter 9).

The infant also perceives affect, and what Stern calls 'vitality affects', qualities such as "surging", "fading away", "fleeting", "explosive", "crescendo", "decrescendo", "bursting", "drawn out", and so on' (Stern, 1985: 54). These experiences are of great importance in the forming of a sense of self. Stern claims that all domains of experience have equal importance in the infant's development: Piaget's self-generated actions and sensations, Freud's subjective experience of pleasure and nonpleasure, discrete categories of affect, infant states of consciousness, and perceptions and cognitions are all embraced as primary within Stern's theory.

The infant is gradually ordering the various elements of direct experience into patterned constellations that help develop the sense of self and other. All learning and creative action are rooted in this realm of emergent sense of self; it remains active as the other senses of self develop, and they are each the products of the organizing process experienced in the domain of emergence:

> This global subjective world of emerging organization is and remains the funda-
> mental domain of human subjectivity. It operates out of awareness as the experi-
> ential matrix from which thoughts and perceived forms and identifiable acts and
> verbalized feelings will later emerge. It also acts as the source for ongoing affective
> appraisals of events. Finally, it is the ultimate reservoir that can be dipped into for
> all creative experience. (Stern, 1985: 67)

The sense of a core self

Between the ages of about 2 months and 6 or 7 months the sense of a core self and core other develops. Infants now seem to engage in interpersonal relatedness as if there were a sense of being an integrated and coherent body, with some control over their actions, ownership of feelings, and a sense of others as being distinct individuals separate from them.

In contrast to psychoanalytic theory, which proposes that the infant gradually moves from a state of undifferentiation and fusion with the mother to a sense of separate self, Stern's observations suggest that the development of a sense of core self and core other is the infant's first developmental task, and that this occurs from about two to seven months. Only then can experiences of merger-like unity occur, and such experiences can and should be within the healthy individual's capacity throughout life.

This period is also the most exclusively social time of the infant's life. Prior to this, regulation of physiological impulses and needs forms the primary motivation for behaviour, and later on the infant develops an interest in the world of external objects. During the period of development of the core self, the infant is learning through the subtlest nuances of interaction with others, and the sense of core-relatedness between self and other develops. Patterns of relating are thus profoundly influenced by experiences during this time. Stern describes this as happening through 'representations of interactions that have been generalized' (RIGs). Social interactions, such as feeding at the breast, dressing, or playing a game, involve particular actions, sensations, and affects; many such interactions become generalized in a representation that is an average of all of these similar but slightly different experiences. The infant learns through this about the invariants of self and other which form the basis of developing the sense of a core self.

There are four primary experiences necessary for the development of the sense of a core self. Stern summarizes them as follows:

> (1) 'self-agency', in the sense of authorship of one's own actions and nonauthorship of the actions of others: having volition, having control over self-generated action (your arm moves when you want it to), and expecting consequences of one's actions (when you shut your eyes it gets dark); (2) 'self-coherence', having a sense of being a nonfragmented, physical whole with boundaries and a locus of integrated action, both while moving (behaving) and when still; (3) 'self-affectivity', experiencing patterned inner qualities of feeling (affects) that belong with other experiences of self; and (4) 'self-history', having the sense of enduring, of a continuity with one's own past so that one 'goes on being' and can even change while remaining the same. The infant notes regularities in the flow of events. (Stern, 1985: 71)

These four capacities of the core self have been observed to develop during this critical period from two to seven months. However, to some extent they are also present during and before birth. Research has shown that infants 'remember' speech and tones played to them in the womb (Stern, 1985: 92). Birth itself has a distinct element of volitional activity in which the experience of self-agency must be strongly stimulated. In my own experience of working with birth and prebirth movement patterns, a clear sense of self-agency and coherence is usually experienced by students and clients. It seems that the memory of actual historical birth is triggered by recreating the sensations and movement patterns of the birthing process. This is also true of movement patterns in utero. It seems likely that, because of the integration of the various domains of experience into a 'global perception', referred to above, the repetition of infant movement patterns evokes specific sensations, affects, memories, and responses in the client. It seems likely to me that a sense of core self is experienced to some degree during and even before birth; on emerging into a totally different environment when born, the infant may, as it were, have to begin again, as she experiences herself anew in this unfamiliar world of earth, air, and other. We will return to these ideas later.

The development of the sense of core self is an active process; the infant forms her self through her own somatic activity. Body psychotherapist Stanley Keleman is also interested in the way in which we are continuously in the process of forming ourselves somatically:

> If you want to know yourself, slow down. Stop what you are doing. But if you want to grow, if you want to form yourself, you must actively express yourself.
>
> The choice between knowing and forming is a choice that many of us are making today, often without realizing that we are making it. We wish to know ourselves, so we accept disciplines that ask us to curtail our activity. By slowing down and stopping, we can come to know ourselves by abstracting from our experience. But we also cease to form ourselves. To form ourselves, to grow, requires that we be expressive, that we try to shape our situations. To form demands that we accept the risk of the unknown. (Keleman, 1975: 124-5)

The sense of a subjective self

Between the ages of 7 and 9 months until about 15 months, the sense of a subjective self and intersubjective relatedness begins to develop. This is the time when infants begin to realize that they have minds, and that certain inner subjective experiences can be shared with another. Intersubjective relatedness develops out of the foundation of core-relatedness, which is 'the existential bedrock of interpersonal relations' (Stern, 1985: 125). Without the physical and sensory experience of an integrated sense of self, the sharing of subjective experience with another may be severely limited. But intersubjective relatedness does not replace core-relatedness; both coexist and affect the individual's experience of self and other throughout life.

This is the period of life that analytic theory describes as the time of emergence out of the merged state towards a more autonomous self. In Stern's view this is the time when both separation *and* experiences of union or 'being-with' in a new way can occur, because of the sharing of inner experience. Stern also proposes that intersubjective relatedness may be a primary psychological need, rather than an autonomous ego function.

The sharing of inner experience is achieved through 'affect attunements'. They go beyond simple mirroring acts that show infants that the other person knows what they actually did, but not necessarily what they felt. In an affect attunement, the other responds to the infant's actions with a response that conveys a similar feeling state, rhythm, and temporal pattern, but is performed through a different modality. For example, a vocal sound is responded to by a movement that echoes the infant's affective state; or the other's vocal intonations show an attunement to the infant's movement expression. Affect attunements are most often embedded within routine activities, and usually go unnoticed, but 'It is the embedded attunements that give much of the impression of the quality of the relationship' (Stern, 1985: 141). Furthermore:

> It is clear that interpersonal communion, as created by attunement, will play an important role in the infant's coming to recognize that internal feeling states are forms of human experience that are shareable with other humans. The converse is also true: feeling states that are never attuned to will be experienced only alone, isolated from the interpersonal context of shareable experience. What is at stake here is nothing less than the shape of and extent of the shareable inner universe. (Stern, 1985: 151)

Whilst categorical affects such as sadness, anger, or joy can be attuned to, attunement mainly occurs through vitality affects – the explosions, crescendos, surges, and fadings that concern *how* a behaviour is performed. This is an area of expression with which the dance movement therapist is particularly concerned, and dance can be a wonderful medium for working therapeutically with attunements in the domain of vitality affects. Rudolf Laban devised an extensive system of analysis of movement vitality affects, which is a cornerstone of many approaches to dance movement therapy.

The sense of a verbal self

During the second year of life the infant begins to develop language. This opens up enormous possibilities for new ways of exchanging and sharing meaning, of 'being with' another, and it enables the infant to begin to construct a narrative of her or his own life. Clearly language can greatly enrich interpersonal life in many ways, but it also begins the process of splitting life as lived from life as represented:

> [Language] makes some parts of our experience less shareable with ourselves and with others. It drives a wedge between two simultaneous forms of interpersonal experience: as it is lived and as it is verbally represented. Experience in the domains of emergent, core, and intersubjective relatedness, which continue irrespective of language, can be embraced only very partially in the domain of verbal relatedness. And to the extent that events in the domain of verbal relatedness are held to be what has really happened, experiences in these domains suffer an alienation. Language, then, causes a split in the experience of the self. It also moves relatedness onto the impersonal, abstract level intrinsic to language and away from the personal, immediate level intrinsic to the other domains of relatedness. (Stern, 1985: 162)

Language enables the development of the objectification of self; the 'categorical, conceptual, objective' self as distinct from the earlier 'existential, experiential, subjective' self now develops. This of course has value, but in distancing themselves from direct experience and the felt senses, infants can also lose touch with healthy instinct and the core sense of self. Winnicott's elaboration of the 'true' and 'false' self relates to this; an infant who is not sufficiently held, physically and emotionally, or appropriately attuned to at the earlier stages, may develop an overintellectualized sense of self as protection from early failures.

Winnicott observed that when mothering was inadequate or too erratic for the infant to assimilate and adapt to, a process of mental functioning began to take over to compensate for the environmental failure: "Mental functioning" became a "thing in itself"; the individual in effect was "seduced" away into his mind, with intellectual activity becoming dissociated from psycho-somatic existence' (Hughes, 1989: 136).

This 'hypertrophy of the intellect' leads to the creation of a true and false self. The authentic core self is isolated from the world and from consciousness, and it is through the false mental self that the individual relates. The false self is cut off from the experience of authentic psychosomatic process, from the felt-sense of bodily sensation, and from genuine feeling, which are attributes of the true self. When this happens, the wedge is firmly driven in, the boundary drawn between body and mind.

Language creates the possibility of sharing and 'being-with' in new ways, and the issues of union, separation, autonomy, intimacy, and so on, are encountered again at a new level in the domain of verbal relatedness. Language also has the capacity to transform or recreate experiences which have occurred at other levels of relatedness, so that two versions of life emerge - life as the original non-verbal, global experience, and life as the verbal account of that experience. This has implications for verbal psychotherapy, where the verbal account is the primary version available. Sometimes the verbal account beautifully captures the essence of the experience, but at other times the two do not fit well. Language can fracture preverbal experiences, which are perceived amodally and globally, by selecting out just one aspect and isolating it from the ongoing flow of experience. Some experiences at the level of the emergent, core, or intersubjective self cannot easily be put into language, and they 'continue underground, nonverbalized, to lead an unnamed (and, to that extent only, unknown) but nonetheless very real existence' (Stern, 1985: 175).

This results in the phenomenon of *double-signalling,* whereby two messages, usually a verbal one and a non-verbal one, are given out simultaneously. Normally we are held accountable for the verbal message, but can deny the non-verbal. Non-verbal messages are often unconsciously intended, and it is these that body-oriented therapists might attend to as they seek to understand their clients' unconscious process. In denying the non-verbal message to others, we can also deny it to ourselves; thus it becomes relegated to the unconscious. Stern has reformulated Winnicott's 'true' and 'false' self as a 'social', 'private' and 'disavowed' self. Awareness and processing of these double messages or 'secondary signals' (Mindell), expressions of the private or disavowed self, is central to many forms of therapy.

To summarize:

> Infants' initial interpersonal knowledge is mainly unshareable, amodal, instance-specific, and attuned to nonverbal behaviours in which no one channel of communication has privileged status with regard to accountability or ownership. Language forces a space between interpersonal experience as lived and as represented. And it is exactly across this space that the connections and associations that constitute neurotic behaviour may form. But also with language, infants for the first time can share their personal experience of the world with others, including 'being with' others in intimacy, isolation, loneliness, fear, awe, and love.
> (Stern, 1985: 182)

The senses of self in therapy

Each sense of self continues throughout life, but there is a 'sensitive period' when each first begins to develop. During these periods the infant is particularly vulnerable to the development of tendencies which could lead to disturbance within that particular domain of relatedness. Stern's proposal differs from analytic theory, which proposes a sequence of developmental tasks that must be addressed by the infant at age-specific times, such as attachment, separation, and autonomy; pathology in the area of a specific developmental task is related to chronological stages of development.

Unlike Mahler and the object relations theorists, who believe that the infant begins life in something like a merged state of symbiotic unity with the maternal universe, and gradually separates out and individuates, Stern proposes that infants begin life with an emergent sense of self in relation to others and are constantly and simultaneously negotiating issues such as intimacy, dependence, autonomy, trust, and relatedness throughout their development. This is also true for the adult, and pathology can have its roots of origin at any time in a person's life. In Stern's approach, the key questions would be 'in which domain of self is the client most compromised and wounded?' or 'what sense of the self carries the affect?' (Stern, 1985: 263).

In this view, from the very beginning of life the infant is dealing with reality, not fantasy as in Klein's theory, in the form of the subtle day-to-day interactions with caregivers. It is these interactions that are formative of the senses of self and of pathological developments, rather than intrapsychic conflict, in the earliest stages of development:

. . . Infants from the beginning mainly experience reality. Their subjective experiences suffer no distortion by virtue of wishes or defenses . . . Further, I assume here that the capacity for defensive – that is, psychodynamic – distortions of reality is a later capacity, requiring more cognitive processes than are initially available. The views presented here suggest that the usual genetic sequence should be reversed and that reality experience precedes fantasy distortions in development. This position leaves the infant unapproachable by psychodynamic considerations for an initial period, resulting in a non-psychodynamic beginning of life in the sense that the infant's experience is not the product of reality altering conflict resolution. (Stern, 1985: 255)

From all of this we can see that if the sense of a core self cannot fully form, the later senses of self do not have a secure foundation upon which to develop. It is therefore essential in clinical practice that any disruptions in the development of the core self are addressed. Stern suggests that failures at the level of the core self are unapproachable by usual psychodynamic procedures. However, bodywork, somatic movement therapy, dance movement therapy, and body psychotherapy may access this domain of experience more directly, and can be significant in the healing of wounds at the level of core relatedness. To further integrate direct, preverbal experiences into the realm of the sense of verbal self, these experiences must also be brought into consciousness through language and cognitive processing.

Stern shows that an empathic approach to therapy will primarily touch issues at the level of intersubjective relatedness, whereas an interpretative approach will first address material in the domain of verbal relatedness. He does not mention body-oriented approaches to therapy, but clearly they very directly touch upon the senses of emergent and core self. These distinctions are also present in Assagioli's model of 'body, feelings, and mind'; he describes an individual as identifying primarily with one or another of these aspects of the personality, and this information could be important in assessing the therapeutic methods to be used. We might conclude from Stern's work that a primary identification with one aspect of the whole self, and dissociation from another, could result from failure in the development of one or more of the senses of self, probably during the 'sensitive periods'. But disruptions to the sense of core self can occur at any time:

The sense of core self, as a composite of the four self-invariants (agency, coherence, affectivity, and continuity), is always in flux. It is being built up, maintained, eroded, rebuilt, and dissolved, and all these things go on simultaneously. The sense of self at any moment, then, is the network of the many forming and dissolving dynamic processes. It is the experience of equilibrium . . .

The sense of a core self, since it is a dynamic equilibrium, is always in potential jeopardy. And indeed, it is a common life event to experience and/or fear major perturbations in the sense of a core self. (Stern, 1985: 199)

Trauma or disruption to any of the senses of self can happen at any age; the sense of core self can also be disturbed within any of the four self-invariants mentioned above. Often we find traumatic experiences of a similar nature recurring throughout life (repeated accidents which result in head injuries, for example, or a series of relationships with physically violent partners). Whilst major traumas do, of course, occur in adult life, they frequently reflect in some aspect, or in the person's pattern of response, an earlier experience of disruption to the sense of self that is again being injured by the current event. A vulnerability is established in that area, which creates a propensity towards further disruption of that sense of self in later life; trauma can occur through a weakened ability to deal with stressful or threatening events that are in some way similar or related to a previous overwhelming situation. Without the inner resource of healthy instinct intact, which depends upon connectedness to the senses of authentic selfhood, we are left vulnerable to retraumatization (Levine, 1997: Chapter 1).

Sara's story

Sara had suffered from St Vitus' Dance as a child, following a major separation in her life. The disturbing effects of this period of illness still interfered with her full functioning in life, and her experience of many months immobilized in a hospital bed had clearly been traumatic. A disease that affects the body in such a way that children totally lose control of their movement functions is associated with disruption of the sense of a core self, primarily in the area of self-agency. The other self-invariants would also be significantly affected.

This client was born breach, which means she missed the fully embodied experience of the natural birthing movement, the first and most important full expression of self-agency and coherence with which the infant engages. (There are other preparatory experiences of self-agency and coherence in utero.) Her birth experience and her later illness can both be seen as disturbances of the sense of core self, in the area of agency primarily. Other events, accidents, and punishments in childhood, where her self-agency was interrupted or disturbed in some way, suggest a recurring pattern of traumatic experiences within the domain of the sense of core self. Most significantly, when she was ten weeks old her mother returned to work, leaving her in the care of various relatives; the loss of her mother for large parts of the day during this sensitive period, just when her sense of core self and core other was beginning to develop, must have had a considerable impact on her.

Sara's illness was like the 'final blow', which she experienced as a punishment for being too alive, too active, too spirited and uncontrollable. After she recovered she became cautious and obedient, not taking physical risks, avoiding trouble and unwanted attention. She described an image of merging into the wallpaper, not breathing, playing 'dead', so that she would not attract attention and would not be hurt. Her illness had engendered a belief that if she expressed herself physically and creatively, such as in dance, which she loved to do, something terrible would happen to her; and of course it always did, as confirmation of her belief system. So she forbade herself to desire anything or to challenge herself in new areas of achievement, to the point where she no longer knew what she truly wanted in life. As an adult in mid-life, she was tormented by an inability to know what she longed for, or to reach for and achieve desired goals, and felt that life was passing her by.

It was clear that movement carried strong affect for her, and was a powerful way into her core process. In one exploration, her two hands dialogued in movement. Following unconscious impulses, her hands told a story of an inability to move, then recovery as one hand helped the other to find movement impulses again, and finally a sense of integration as the two hands came together at the end in a gesture of unity; this brought her awareness to her heart and the feelings held there. The movement process evoked deep feeling and held special significance for her.

A little movement or bodywork produced powerful effects, and at times Sara needed to take breaks from it to integrate changes into her life. On one occasion she returned to therapy after an absence of several months seeming stronger, more embodied and coherent, less prone to dissociate into rambling trains of thought. During this period she made a decision to apply for a new job, which seemed a positive move, a first step towards taking her closer to where she wanted to be in life. She came to a session after being offered the job, having succeeded in not giving away her power by compromising her own needs, and talked of feeling changes in herself. She felt more present and alive, and had a more realistic sense of herself and her situation, which was not the depressing feeling of resignation that she had expected but something more grounded and workable. I felt her to be empowering herself in making positive choices which would better meet her own needs, and I experienced her presence as clear and strong.

She wondered whether it was true that inner work and internal changes could really have created these changes in her sense of herself, and in her ability to deal with the external realities of her life. She described some sessions that had felt particularly significant, and relevant to the changes now taking place within her. Each had involved some powerful movement experience. During one session she had worked on a dream. In the dream she had been excluded from membership of a meeting that she dearly longed to be part of because she had arrived late. The situation accurately reflected how she felt about her life – the feeling that she was unable to participate fully, and her longing to do so. As she physically embodied the different characters of the dream, she was able to enact different choices of action and relationship; in particular, she felt the quiet power and assertiveness of the doorkeeper, who represented the guardian of her inner sacred space, and was able to embody and identify with the energy and the purpose of this important and protective figure. After this session she showed a new quality of presence, and more energy; there was a clarity about her, as if stronger boundaries and a clearer sense of self were beginning to form. The simple process of physically embodying her inner figures, and fully identifying with and expressing these unowned psychological energies through movement and enactment, had created a powerful transformation at an energetic level. She could experience herself as being in command.

Another session that she felt had been a catalyst for the changes she was now experiencing also involved embodied process. She had begun by talking about an internal conflict between wanting everything to be achieved immediately on the one hand, and giving up, wanting nothing at all, or not knowing what she wanted and so not even trying, on the other. This inner conflict kept her stuck in a situation that felt familiar and safe, but did not satisfy her. She was inhibiting her desire for something because she was sure she would never get it. She had no memory of ever trying to get something she wanted and not succeeding; it seemed that she had given up expecting her needs to be met at a very early age, and so had also given up trying. Such beliefs and choices, which we make unconsciously early on in life, are somatized into the developing neuromuscular system, and embodied in the movement patterns that are emerging at that time. For Sara, the difficulty in seeking what she longed for was embedded in the actions of pushing through her arms to support herself, and reaching out with her arms towards another.

We decided to explore this conflict experientially, as talking about it was taking her into mental abstractions. I suggested she find something in the room that attracted her, and she chose a cushion which had a design of a tree and a red moon on the cover. It represented the qualities of 'warmth, solidity, strength, security, and beauty', which she acknowledged were the things she longed for. At this stage Sara was not able to make a direct connection to her longing for the absent mother, but it seemed clear that the cushion represented the qualities of the mothering of which she had not had enough as an infant. The cushion was placed on the floor between us, and she was invited to explore reaching out towards it, connecting to her longing for the qualities represented by the image on the cushion. She explored several ways of doing this. The first time she reached out and quickly grabbed it; this felt awkward and an unnecessary effort. Then she tried sidling up to it, and tentatively laid her head on the cushion; this way of approaching it made her feel vulnerable and very small, like a young child, but it also felt good to rest her head on it. The third time she approached it face on, but became very tearful as she thought of reaching out towards it. Later she said that she had needed it to come to her, as if she was too young to be able to reach out on her own behalf. Sensing this, and in order to avoid the risk of retraumatizing her by repeating old frustrations, I gently passed the cushion to her as she connected for the first time to her great longing for the warmth, strength, and security that it symbolized; she held it and cried deeply. Afterwards she held and looked at the cushion, saying that she felt grateful, and that she needed these qualities within herself. She became eager after this session to look for ways to nurture this connection and to begin to internalize the qualities that the image of the tree and the red moon evoked for her.

Several sessions later, and having been accepted for her new job, Sara expressed some concern that she might put in too much effort and get very tired again – a pattern of hers was to put a great deal into her job so that everyone would like her, no one could fault her work, and thus she would avoid all conflict with other staff members. This pattern was burning her energy out, and she was concerned not to repeat it. We had talked about this issue before; this time we explored it in movement. I invited her to push against my arm to see how much effort she needed to use. I felt her using a great deal of energy, but using it to hold her arm quite rigidly so that there was little contact with my arm and very little strength flowing out towards me. In fact she realized she was not pushing at all, but felt as if she was following my movements; this, she acknowledged, kept it 'safe' between us. She talked of not being allowed to express her exuberant energy as a child, and how she would be punished for it. She developed a way of being always alert and sensitive to what was going on around her, so that she would know if there was any threat or danger; however, her alert, sensitive approach to life left her unable to act, and thus unprotected, vulnerable, and unable to motivate herself. An imbalance between sensory and motor functions had been established in her nervous system, and to alter this she first needed to experience a new relationship between her receptivity and the active initiation of movement.

We then played with different ways of pushing, until she found a softer but more powerful way that connected her whole body in the action. Our movement then turned into a playful 'dance', and Sara recognized that power also had a positive side, and could be fun. In previous sessions she had experienced a great deal of fear of her own power, but this way of playing with it made it feel safe and helpful to her. Again she mentioned her image/feeling of 'merging into the wallpaper', and I suggested she try out her new-found power by pushing against the wall. She experimented with 'merging into it', but found that in reality this was impossible – she could now feel that the wall was too solid. As she pushed against the resistant surface of the wall, she was consolidating her boundaries, her sense of coherence, and self-agency. Afterwards she commented that she felt more substantial, and was clearly energized by the movement.

These are some examples of Sara's work; each was a small event in the ongoing course of therapy, but because of the importance of embodied experience for this client, they had quite significant effects on her feelings about herself, her energetic presence, and her ability to make choices and begin to take control of her life. She was consciously and experientially discovering her physical integrity and ability to act, and as her sense of core self was strengthened by this, her desire for life, and the belief that she *could* reach out for and get what she desired, were beginning to emerge.

Early origins of the developing senses of self

Despite the comprehensiveness of their perspectives, there is an important area of development that neither Stern nor Wilber fully addresses – the experiences of birth and prebirth, and their effects on the development of the senses of self.

Perinatal experiences

Otto Rank was one follower of Freud who diverged widely from classical analytic theory by claiming that birth trauma was the origin of all neuroses, not the Oedipus complex. He noted, as Freud himself had done, that all anxiety attacks were accompanied by physiological processes similar to those present at birth. In his view, separation at birth, in weaning, through symbolic castration, and all other separations from a loved one were the primary cause of anxiety, and were patterned on the birth-separation experience. This took two forms: the fear of life and the fear of death:

> The life fear is the anxiety which occurs when the individual becomes aware of creative capacities within himself the assertion of which would bring about the threat of separation from existing relationships; it is 'the fear of having to live life as an isolated individual'. The death fear, on the other hand, is the fear of losing one's individuality, of being swallowed up in the whole. All his life each human being is pushed forward by the need to be an individual and express himself more fully and drawn back by the fear that by doing so he will cut himself off from the rest of society. There are two possible solutions to this dilemma, that of the 'normal' person who wholeheartedly accepts the standards of his society as his own and that of the creative individual who is prepared to stand alone and create his own standards. The neurotic can accept neither of these solutions. (Brown, 1961: 53)

The similarity to the birth dilemma can be seen here, as the infant struggles with the existential choice between loss of relationship to the all-embracing uterine world and emergence as a separate individual, or engulfment in an increasingly uncomfortable and limiting universe. Whilst Rank's methods were not altogether successful, his ideas have nevertheless been influential, and are precursors of approaches such as primal therapy, rebirthing, and the holotropic therapy of Stanislav and Christina Grof. Analyst Nandor Fodor also put forward the view that birth trauma is influential on all aspects of behaviour; and Phyllis Greenacre, through her scientific research into foetal and infant responses, believed that: 'Constitution, prenatal experience, birth, and the situation immediately after birth together play some part in predisposing the individual to anxiety' (Brown, 1961: 54-5).

Apart from a few bold pioneers, this area has not received very much attention in the field of analytic or developmental psychology. One who has done extensive research into perinatal experiences with adult patients is the Czechoslovakian psychiatrist and Freudian analyst, Stanislav Grof, but the radical nature of his approach and findings has excluded his work from greater recognition within conventional circles.

Grof's exploration began with LSD research; finding that his experiences with this drug did not fit into the accepted paradigm, he turned to studies of anthropology and shamanism. This led him to develop natural methods that could induce states similar to those experienced under the influence of hallucinogenic drugs, and to propose a new paradigm that viewed altered states of consciousness not as signs of insanity but as naturally occurring phenomena essential to the healing process. His approach, holotropic therapy, uses a combination of breathing exercises, specific massage techniques, and music, to bring the patient into deeply altered states of consciousness. As a result of these methods, patients may vividly relive perinatal and birth experiences.

From observations of thousands of such sessions, Grof developed the model of the basic perinatal matrices, which he discovered to underlie the birth process. By reliving traumatic birth experiences, patients can release energy that has been blocking development, and also frequently report blissful and transpersonal experiences as they resolve trauma associated with perinatal processes. Grof believes that pathology arises from incomplete processes, and his work claims to take patients through trauma to resolution, usually accompanied by the re-experiencing of powerful affects as deep memories and energy in the body are awakened and released.

COEX systems

I have found Grof's model useful in contextualizing students' and clients' experiences when working with perinatal processes. (This will be explored in Chapter 6.) His concept of 'COEX systems', or 'systems of condensed experience' is also useful: 'A COEX system is a dynamic constellation of memories (and associated fantasy material) from different periods of the individual's life, with the common denominator of a strong emotional charge of the same quality, intense physical sensations of the same kind, or the fact that they share some other important elements' (Grof, 1985: 97).

He observed that many such incidents originating from different periods of the client's life might emerge simultaneously. They are experienced in many modalities, and can also be evoked through any perceptual channel; a smell, an image, a body sensation, a movement, a particular sound, or an atmosphere, can all evoke a complete COEX system that is experienced through the different senses. Grof found that most COEX systems are connected to some aspect of the birth process, and that perinatal material has specific relationship to experiences in the transpersonal domain: 'It is not uncommon for a dynamic constellation to comprise material from several biographical periods, from biological birth, and from certain areas of the transpersonal realm, such as memories of a past incarnation, animal identification, and mythological sequences' (Grof, 1985: 97).

Grof also noted that physical trauma appears to have a far more profound effect upon individual pathology than has been acknowledged by those schools of psychology and psychotherapy whose focus is primarily upon psychological trauma. In particular, an accident, illness, or other event that threatens the physical survival of the individual has, Grof claims, a greater impact than emotional trauma. Peter Levine, working for over 25 years to understand and develop natural methods of healing trauma, confirms that traumatization is a physiological process; to aid recovery from trauma he has developed a method called *somatic experiencing* (Levine, 1997: 119–20, 152, 196, 205).

Traumatizing events frequently reflect aspects of the birth process, where physical survival is also acutely threatened. These would be classed as traumas affecting the sense of core self, and hence are primary and fundamental to the development of the other senses of self. According to Grof:

> Experiential work makes it obvious that traumas involving vital threat leave permanent traces in the system and contribute significantly to the development of emotional and psychosomatic disorders, such as depressions, anxiety states and phobias, sadomasochistic tendencies, sexual problems, migraine headaches, or asthma. (Grof, 1985: 98)

Grof's work introduces an important dimension into the field of psychology; however, I am not entirely in agreement with the view that the birth experience is the primary cause of patterns of experiencing and behaviour, and that neuroses develop as a result of birth trauma. In my own view, the birth experience may be partly causal, but more significantly, it is the first clear reflection of the individual's tendency to perceive, to organize experience, and to act in particular ways. On many occasions of working in groups with birthing processes, I see how individuals appear to 'recreate' their original experience, no matter what the supporters do or do not do to facilitate a supportive rebirth experience. Each experiences different aspects of the process as significant, and each perceives it in her own individual way, even though the conditions for each are as near as possible the same.

I believe it is the same with our original birth; although external events and conditions undoubtedly profoundly influence the birth drama, the birthing child brings to it her own energy, agency, patterns of response, and a tendency to perceive and experience in certain ways. From a Buddhist point of view we would call these the 'karmic tendencies' which we bring along with us even at conception. We are not a 'blank slate', even in the embryonic stages, but an individual consciousness with history and the potential for a particular path of development and personality formation. It is the meeting of both worlds of self and other that determine the specific developments, but our tendencies are innate.

A developing sense of self in utero?

To find possible evidence in the developmental literature for this point of view, we must go to the fascinating work of Alessandra Piontelli. A medical doctor and child psychotherapist, Piontelli has extended research into the development of the sense of self to a study of life in the womb. Using ultrasound scanning, she has observed the movement behaviour of a group of foetuses in the womb, and followed their development through birth, infancy, and childhood. Whilst noting that her research is in early stages, and offers no concrete scientific evidence as yet, and also noting the ethical considerations of observing infants in utero, her research nevertheless points towards some interesting conclusions.

It is only in recent years, with the advent of ultrasound scanning, that it has been possible to accurately observe movement in utero. Discussing such research studies, Piontelli writes: 'We can now state almost with total certainty that foetal motility is endogenously generated and not a mere response to external stimulation' (Piontelli, 1992: 28).

Observations have shown that the foetus makes strong whole body movements, as well as slow movements using only parts of the body. Purposeful movements, such as bringing the thumb into the mouth, have been observed to occur frequently, and in early stages of development. These observations suggest that the self-invariants of agency and coherence (Stern) might already be experienced in utero. The repertoire of movement that can be accurately observed is quite impressive. Visible movements first appear around 7 to 8 weeks, involving slow flexion and extension of the spine. From 10 weeks many movements can be seen, such as stretching, yawning, tongue movements, and hand-to-face contacts. The repertoire develops rapidly from this time; by 12 weeks the hand comes to the mouth, sucking and swallowing can be seen, and there are fine finger movements. By 15 weeks the foetus possesses an almost complete repertoire of human movement capabilities. Piontelli affirms that:

> No neonatal pattern can be considered to originate at birth, as the fetus has already the full repertoire of movements which will be found in the neonate. The only difference lies in the quality of movement, most probably because of the increased influence of gravity after birth. Besides movement, no other function is seen to originate at birth either. (Piontelli, 1992: 30)

With so much learning and forming of neural connections taking place before birth, it is reasonable to propose that some, at least embryonic, sense of self might be experienced in utero. Experiential explorations of prebirth movement patterns frequently evoke memories, feelings, and images of intrauterine life, as well as of animal species, related to those stages of evolutionary development – amoebae, star-fish, fish, and other water-dwelling creatures; the evocation of memory, feeling, and imagery associated with uterine life suggests the existence of some form of consciousness during this phase of development. It is also clear that foetal movement plays a vital role in normal neuromuscular and behavioural development, and inadequate movement development in utero can result in problems in these areas. Premature infants, and infants of mothers immobilized during pregnancy, may have received inadequate stimulation, and may suffer developmental problems as a result.

As well as the development of the typical movement repertoire of the human foetus, individual quality, style, and movement behaviours can also be clearly discerned. Through observing the child in utero, through the birth process, infancy, and into childhood, Piontelli noticed that specific uterine movement behaviours continued almost without interruption after birth. Particularly traumatic birth experiences did affect behaviour, but did not fundamentally change the basic behavioural tendencies observed in the womb, and in some cases could be thought to have resulted from them. In order to explore the extent to which individual variations might be due to influences from the maternal environment, she made special studies of both monozygotic (uniovular) twins and dizygotic (binovular) twins. She observed clear differences in temperament and behaviour emerging from early on in gestation, and continuing into childhood. Distinctive patterns of relationship were also observed, expressed in various behaviours such as mutual stroking, punching and kicking, seeking contact or withdrawing:

> With twins it was possible to note clear individual temperamental differences between the two members of the couple from the early stages. In this respect twins seemed to behave like ordinary siblings, each with their own distinct temperamental endowment. Individual differences found their expression in various somatic manifestations, such as the choice of preferential postures, the repetition of certain activities and patterns, the higher or lesser frequency of bodily movements and their quality, and so on . . .
>
> Each couple, in fact, from the early stages seemed to have its particular mode of relating, which continued throughout pregnancy and could still be noted in postnatal life. Therefore from the very early stages one could observe the emergence of both individual and couple patterns which continued to be seen in later life. (Piontelli, 1992: 112)

This fascinating evidence suggests that a sense of self is already emerging during foetal life. The quality of consciousness, intersubjective relatedness, and affect cannot so easily be assessed, but experiential work with adults into these early stages of development definitely suggests that consciousness, emotional feeling, and some rudimentary sense of relatedness to other may be present in utero. Interestingly, Montagu reminds us that infants do not reach the level of maturity of other mammalian neonates until about 9 months of age, when they are able to crawl on all fours. He suggests that gestation continues outside of the womb for a further nine months after birth, early birth of the human infant being necessitated by the rapidly expanding size of the head in relation to the dimensions of the birth canal (Montagu, 1971: 53–4). Thus gestation is a more-or-less continuous process from conception until about 9 months of age, briefly punctuated and stimulated by the monumental event of birth.

The area of development that the work of Grof and Piontelli opens up clearly expands the domain of the emergent sense of self and prepersonal structures to include the period before birth. This area also touches upon the realm of consciousness which both precedes and completes Wilber's cycle – the realm that lies before the prepersonal and beyond the transpersonal domains of consciousness, which Wilber refers to as 'unity consciousness'. At this level there are no boundaries; preconception would relate to this realm, as well as fully enlightened states of consciousness at the absolute completion of the cycle. For elucidation of this dimension of consciousness we must look to the mystical texts. In this developmental scheme, the primary step in the process of individuation out of the unboundaried state of consciousness could be said to occur at conception, and at conception the process of embodiment and of the development of a sense of self begins.

We will now turn to an exploration of the process of infant development from the perspective of the body and the process of sensory-motor learning, beginning with the life and consciousness of the fertilized cell, the embryo, and the foetus in the womb.

CHAPTER 5

Touch, boundaries, and bonding

Somatic learning

The foetus, infant, and young child learn somatically. They learn through direct embodied experience about themselves, and the world in which they live and move. First learning is through the perceptions of touch and movement, and the nervous system matures through the continuous interaction of motor expression and sensory feedback. (For a discussion of movement as a perception see Cohen, 1993: 114-18.) But even before the nervous system begins to develop, the cells of the growing embryo are touched in various ways, they respond with movement, and experience new contact as a result. The interactive processes of action, perception, and response have their basis in the earliest experiences of cellular activity in the womb.

As the nervous system develops, a process called myelination takes place, during which nerves are covered in a fatty insulating sheath; as a nerve is myelinated, conductivity is greatly increased so that the nerve can function with a dramatic increase in speed, accuracy, and efficiency. The sequence of myelination throughout the nervous system shows us which functions develop first, and from this we can understand which functions are primary for survival and growth. So it is interesting to note that the motor nerves myelinate before the sensory nerves; first I move, then I receive sensory information about that movement. Thus I learn about myself and my world. It is also noteworthy to the somatic therapist that the first of the specialized cranial nerves to myelinate are the vestibular nerves; they help to organize movement and postural responses, and register changes in relation to gravity, speed, and direction of movement.

There is a natural process of development, a sequence of perceptual and movement potentials, which we all pass through on our journey of learning to walk, talk, and interact with our world in a multitude of ways; through embodying this process of development, we gain a sense of mastery over our own body and the physical world around us, and are thus more fully able to

95

express our individual potentials, and relate to others in a coherent and meaningful way.

When particular phases of the sequence are not fully embodied, a weakness or gap in the developmental process is created, which means our progress to the next stage will feel less supported, less secure, and the challenge of learning new skills less wholeheartedly met. If the foundations of early sensory-motor skills are not established in a strong and clear way, our potential at other levels of development – social, psychological, intellectual, spiritual – may be compromised. Stress, weakness, or imbalance is established in the bodymind, which can create vulnerability towards various symptoms of physical and psychological disturbance, or ill health.

A specific sensory-motor patterning marks each phase of development. The primitive reflexes appear first, and as they are integrated and the necessary nerves myelinated, the basic neurological patterns, or *developmental movement patterns* can emerge. They are more complex but specific movement coordinations that appear in a more-or-less universal sequence of development, and are basic patterns inherent within the nervous system. Gradually, and through much effort and perseverance, the infant gains the neuromuscular coordination and strength to master these patterns in a controlled and voluntary way, so that she can move independently and act with willed intent. There are four basic neurological coordinations traditionally identified in the developmental process; these are *spinal, homologous, homolateral,* and *contralateral* patterns of locomotion (see Figure 5.1). They were described by Temple Fay, out of whose research the Doman-Delacato method of treatment developed (Wolf, 1968). Bonnie Bainbridge Cohen has expanded this description with the addition of several patterns which commence in utero and underlie those that develop after birth; these are *cellular breathing, navel radiation, mouthing,* and *prespinal* patterns (see Appendix 1).

The failure to embody movement potentials fully

Many movement, postural, perceptual, and also psychological problems can have their roots in this early developmental process. If specific movement patterns have been inhibited for some reason, or not fully embodied and expressed during the natural process of development, we might find places of weakness, low tone, or excessive tension in the body, or a lack of integration between the parts. A particular movement quality and mind state might dominate, whereas others are inaccessible, leaving the individual with less choice in terms of movement and perceptual awareness. Embodying and clarifying the early movement patterns can help to open up more choices, and gives support for subsequent development; corresponding effects on states of mind can also be experienced.

This happens, Cohen believes, because the early movement patterns are controlled most naturally and efficiently by hindbrain and midbrain centres.

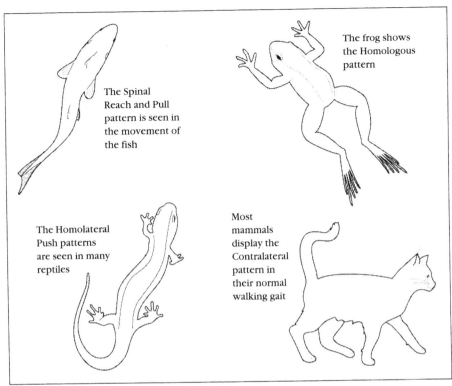

The frog shows the Homologous pattern

The Spinal Reach and Pull pattern is seen in the movement of the fish

The Homolateral Push patterns are seen in many reptiles

Most mammals display the Contralateral pattern in their normal walking gait

Figure 5.1. From Linda Hartley, *Wisdom of the Body Moving,* pp. 53, 74, 76, 80.

If there is dysfunction at this level, or if patterns have not been fully integrated so that they can be performed automatically, then higher cortical areas take over the coordination of the movement. This is done at a more conscious level, and means that less cellular potential is available for the development of the social, intellectual, and creative skills which are the proper functions of the higher brain centres. The practice of developmental movement therapy, where the full embodiment and expression of the basic patterns is supported, affects sensory-motor functioning by strengthening lower brain centres. A 'by-product' of this focus on early movement learning and sensory-motor integration is often improvement in other levels of functioning, such as perceptual, emotional, social, and cognitive skills. (Case studies of work with children with early learning difficulties have been documented in Mills and Cohen, 1979.) Cohen writes of the process of embodying movement potential: 'All natural phenomena fall into patterns. The nervous system is designed to function by patterns. The nervous system has the potential for innumerable patterns, but the patterns are not accessible to us until they are actually stimulated into existence, until we actually do them. Patterns will fall on a continuum between efficiency and inefficiency' (Cohen, 1993: 99).

We may be inhibited from fully embodying and expressing a movement pattern for a variety of reasons – constitutional, physical, emotional, and environmental factors all play a part. For example, an infant may not feel herself securely held, and thus cannot internalize a sense of being grounded, rooted in the earth, and in her own instinctual body; an underlying sense of non-specific anxiety and fear may result from this. Feelings of being unsafe in the world, of not being loved, or of being alone and having always to 'hold oneself up' and 'do it alone', could also accompany this state. The fundamental experience of feeling connected to, and supported by, the earth is the basis for later movement patterns, and these may be compromised as a result of an early holding failure.

Or a child may reach out in play, in curiosity to touch something, or for love; if its gestures are constantly rejected with spoken or unspoken messages such as 'no', 'don't touch', 'you can't have it', 'I won't hold you', or with physical gestures of rejection or punishment, the child may learn not to reach out for what she wants. A way of relating to the world is established, which involves a need, such as – 'I need to play/be loved/be given attention'; a belief system, for example – 'I can't get/don't deserve to get what I want'; a feeling – 'I hurt/I'm angry/I feel rejected/I feel worthless'; and a way of behaving as a consequence of such a sequence, which may be saying 'I won't try that again'. Thus the child, and later the adult, learns to repress her desires, not to reach out for love, companionship, or to achieve her heart's desire and goals in life. Such responses are embedded in the nervous system when the child first learns that reaching out is dangerous or futile, and an inhibited perceptual-motor pattern is established.

When we explore the movement patterns that involve reaching out, these feelings and memories may reemerge. But as we embody the movement patterns more fully, we are given a chance to consciously change the neurological programming that underlies the cycles of needs, belief systems, feelings, and behaviour, established as a result of childhood conditioning or trauma. This can have benefits at many levels. Keleman refers to one research study into movement development:

> In a well-known study, two researchers showed that when a child's creeping and crawling are interfered with, he has trouble with his speech functions and often ends up as a stutterer. Their study was a revelation insofar as it demonstrated that when certain locomotor patterns are not connected up and developed, certain socializing patterns do not fully emerge. The same researchers then found that encouraging the stutterer to creep and crawl once again served to call up the immature motor patterns in order that he might develop them. As he did so, his speech and his other socializing activities improved. (Keleman, 1975: 120)

Cellular touch and holding

The physical body is the ground and container through which children embody themselves, and through which they learn. If the child is unable to embody herself fully, if her body is not a safe and supportive container for her growing self, she will not be able to learn and develop her full potential as an instinctual, loving, trusting and creative being. For Winnicott, the mother is the environment within which the infant learns, and the infant's relationship with her mother's body is crucial in determining how she will relate to life, to other people, to her work. He described the 'facilitating environment' as providing the right balance of boundary for security, and space within which the child can explore and take risks:

> . . . According to Winnicott's theory, it is not possible to talk about self-control or internal boundaries until there is an integrated self which makes sense of the terms 'inner reality' and 'shared reality'. The fundamental boundary is, therefore, the limiting membrane between the 'me' and the 'not-me' which corresponds to the skin of the body; the fundamental space is the place within this boundary where growth takes place along 'natural' lines according to the maturational processes, and where the self and the inner psychic reality begin to be. Until integration is achieved, the father supplies the circle around the mother and infant that protects them, and society is arranged so that this can happen. (Davis and Wallbridge, 1983: 146)

Feminist theorists question such clear-cut definitions of the roles of mother and father in relation to the child and society, and they raise some important criticisms of object relations theory in general, with regard to social and political issues (Frosh, 1987: 179–92). However, Winnicott's ideas about boundary are of great significance to the somatic therapist and body psychotherapist. The creation of internal psychological boundaries depends on the infant's experience of the primary boundary, the skin, the membrane that separates 'me' from 'not-me'. It is through touch that the infant receives the feedback which defines this essential boundary; the quality of touch and holding determines the ability to differentiate clearly between what is self and what is other, the distinction between 'total organism' and 'environment' in Wilber's schema. It influences the integrity and intactness of the core self, and excessive failure from the environment to provide appropriate and adequate touch stimulation results in damaging psychological and physical consequences. In his seminal book, *Touching,* Montagu (1971) cites numerous examples of research studies that affirm this. A number of studies have also documented the occurrence of 'deprivation dwarfism' and even death in institutionalized infants, due to lack of physical touch and holding (Gardner, 1972).

Before even the skin of the growing embryo has begun to form, the membranes of the cells give a rudimentary sense of boundary. From the earliest moments after conception the new life growing in the womb is defined by the skin of the cellular membranes, and the embryonic experience of boundary, and of self and other, has already begun to develop.

Individual life begins as the one-cell, the ovum that, on fertilization, commences its own unique process of development, related to but quite distinct from the other cells of the mother's body. During the first days, growth is by cellular reproduction and cells at this stage are all of basically the same nature, undifferentiated from one another. The cells embody an innate awareness and intelligence, a responsiveness to their own needs and the activities of surrounding cells. As Pierrakos writes: 'Consciousness invests every specific unit, from the smallest subatomic particle yet to be discovered up to the totality of being, the macrocosm. Each unit has a special function, a plan for fulfilling its potential, inherent in its fact of being' (Pierrakos, 1990: 16).

Cellular breathing

The body's basic life processes are all carried out within the membraneous boundaries of the cells, made possible by the process of internal respiration that enables the cell to absorb oxygen and nutrients from the surrounding fluids, and release wastes. The cell is the basic unit of organic and sentient life, and the first movement of new life is the pulse of internal respiration as the fertilized cell expands and contracts, fills and empties. *Cellular breathing* is the first of the developmental movement patterns, the first movement made by the new life forming in the womb.

The cell has a life force; it is the basic unit of organic life, and within its DNA structure it carries the intelligence of the organism. The cell can perceive movement, vibration, and chemical changes within its environment, and when in a healthy condition it will respond actively and appropriately, and to the benefit of the whole organism, to the information it receives. The cells dialogue with each other at this microscopic level to maintain a dynamic balance within the internal milieu of the body. Mind, as Pert suggests, might be thought of as the 'immaterial substrata', the flow of information, which communicates between and unites all of the cells. We experience mind in the movement within and between cells.

It is the intelligent life processes of the cell that constitute somatic existence. Through touch, through imagery, or perhaps through simply meditating upon the presence of the cells, we can become aware or help another to come to an awareness of cellular presence. In this approach we seek to access the *mind,* the innate intelligence and awareness of the cells of the body. This cannot be done through our normal mental functions; it requires a shift in consciousness, in our fundamental way of perceiving and being. A visualized image of the cells might help us to make this shift, but ultimately the cells are experienced directly, kinesthetically, and beyond the threshold of normal consciousness. Cohen calls the process of kinesthetically experiencing the body tissues and cells 'somatization'; it is the sense of experiencing cell, experiencing body from within, rather than the dualistic stance of observing the body and its structures as if from outside.

This way of focusing attention brings us to an experience of being present that is similar to that met with in some forms of meditation practice. Allowing our mind to settle into this kind of awareness might also reveal insights, as the cells appear to be the physical 'carriers' of memory, knowledge, and what we often refer to as intuitive knowing. Intuitive insight, in my understanding, is the result of a complex receiving and processing of information through many channels, which occurs beyond the threshold of conscious awareness; access to cellular wisdom is an important basis for this subliminal process. When we awaken cellular awareness and perceive *through* the cells and the integrated bodymind, we gain access to levels of information which might not be accessible through our external senses in normal states of consciousness.

Experiencing the process of cellular breathing can be healing in itself; simply focusing on allowing each cell of the body to breathe and be fully present helps us to connect to our inner healing resources, and is the basis of finding balance within the bodymind. We might also discover much about ourselves, our problems, and what we need to receive, let go of, or integrate in order to move towards health and wholeness. Through focusing awareness in the body in this way we also experience moments of integration of body and mind, as we allow our thinking mind to settle and be grounded and present in the body.

Touch and holding

When working at this level I might begin by touching the client with my focus on the skin, the body's primary boundary, and then deepen the focus to imagine I am simultaneously touching and gently holding the membrane or skin of each cell that lies beneath and between my hands. When the cells feel themselves to be touched, met, and held in this way, they come to experience their own presence within the body; frequently there is a sense of expansion as the cells breathe more fully, of release as they let go of holding and come into relationship with gravity, or various movements, flows, pulses, and vibrations as the subtle cellular activities are sensed. We make contact with an open and receptive mind, not judging or intending any specific results but simply being present to what we sense under our hands and to the person as a whole. This contact can be felt to be deeply nurturing; through our hands we are witnessing the other at a very deep and subtle level, and such non-judgemental witnessing can create a safe and trusting environment within which healing can take place (Hartley, 1995: Chapter 1).

This way of touching may be a preliminary to bodywork involving intentional touch and repatterning techniques – a non-invasive and receptive way of making contact and accessing information from the body; it may provide a space for relaxation and recuperation; it might also be used within the context of psychological process when addressing preverbal issues. Cellular holding relates firstly to the holding of the embryo and foetus in the womb, and later to the holding of the infant; I may use this approach with a client who has experienced trauma or inadequate holding in these early stages. Process at this level of development cannot usually be accessed without attention to the body, and cellular process is a basis for this. Cellular activity is of course the basis of all life processes, not only in the early stages of development, and contact at this level may be effectively used as a support for clients dealing with issues rooted in later periods of development. Touch and holding facilitate the experiencing of safety and flexible boundaries, no matter where we are in the life cycle, and this can be especially beneficial to people going through crises and change.

Cellular holding and bonding

A positive experience of holding in the womb is a foundation for bonding at the cellular level, which underlies bonding at other levels of relatedness. First there is a sense of bonding to the experience of self, as cells become aware of their own presence through the feedback of touch; then bonding to earth and mother's body as the cells relate through touch, movement, and the sensations of gravity to the physical world around them. According to Lowen:

> The ground is always interpreted as a symbol for the mother. Ground equals earth equals mother is a basic concept of bio-energetic analysis. The way a person stands tells us much about his early relationship to his mother. The insecurity of that relationship becomes transferred to an insecurity in standing and becomes the basic insecurity of life. (In Boadella, 1976: 186)

Issues of trust or mistrust in the universe's ability to hold, support, and nourish one are constellated during the womb experience, in response to the quality of holding and nourishment experienced there. This may be either reinforced or countered by experiences after birth. Some psychologists believe that autistic and psychotic conditions are expressions of acute fear and anxiety, which have their origins in inadequate holding or traumatic experiences in utero. Kurtz and Prestera write:

> The mother who, for whatever reasons, experienced negative emotions toward her unborn child, even as it grew within her, might very well have cut off some of the life energy she had available for this purpose [of nourishing the child]. Sometimes poor physical health or emotional distress unrelated directly to the child can result in decreased amounts of energy input to the growing fetus. We carry this inheritance within us as a quantum of life energy . . .
>   Our relation to our cosmic mother closely parallels that to our physical mother. In that first connection is the seed of all later expectations and fulfilments. If, in the uterus and early extrauterine environment, we were poorly nourished, we will find it emotionally difficult to receive any energies. Somewhere within us the experience of not receiving full warmth and love is imprinted. We will be untrusting, unable to open ourselves to the available nourishment around us. (Kurtz and Prestera, 1976: 72–3)

Early trauma and holding failures

Janov has described three levels of development, and three kinds of trauma associated with them, which he relates to different kinds of psychotherapy and also to different areas of the brain. Trauma at any stage of development creates a split in the sense of self, and disruption to the functions that are developing at that time (see Rowan, 1988: 18).

According to Janov, 'third-line traumas' relate to the verbal period of childhood (Stern's sense of a verbal self), and issues surrounding the Oedipal drama; this is the area with which classical psychoanalysis is primarily concerned. Third-line traumas are registered in the cerebral cortex, and language and meaning have great importance here.

'Second-line traumas' relate to more primitive preverbal stages, when emotions are differentiated and intensely experienced, and the one-to-one mother-child relationship is of primary importance (Stern's sense of a subjective self). The object-relations school addresses this level. It relates to the limbic system of the brain, which incorporates parts of the old forebrain and the midbrain. Intense emotional affects, primitive behavioural patterns, and the drugs which influence these, are connected to this area.

'First-line traumas' are even more primitive, and connected to the earliest stages of development where survival issues are of paramount importance. At this stage emotions are not yet differentiated out of the psycho-physiological ground of being (Stern's sense of an emergent and core self). The hindbrain, or reptilian brain, is involved here, and trauma in utero, around birth, and in the first few months of life. Clearly therapy at this level must be able to affect psycho-physiological functioning, and such trauma cannot be accessed through words alone, as the experience is preverbal.

Discussing Janov's theory, Rowan summarizes how first-line traumas are the most primitive:

> . . . going back to the time before any differentiation of the emotions took place, and where survival is the main issue. This involves the reptilian brain or R-complex – the most basic and oldest part of the brain, which we share with most of the animal realm. There is hardly even much sense of two-ness here – just deep fundamental feelings of positive or negative. (Rowan, 1988: 18)

Rowan also emphasizes his own belief, different from Janov's, and with which I agree, that experience is not reducible to brain function alone, and that there is a conscious experiencing of the *meaning* of physical and traumatic events in the womb. There is now much evidence to support this view, based on the work of therapists and researchers such as Verney, Chamberlain, Grof, and Swartley (Rowan, 1988: 15). Consciousness is embodied in the cell before the development of the brain and nervous system is complete; though it is not reducible to cellular function either, consciousness of early experiences can sometimes be accessed through focusing on cellular presence.

Specific trauma suffered in the womb, such as attempted abortions, conflict within the mother or between parents over the pregnancy, a previous miscarriage or death of an older sibling, can create woundings which are very hard to understand and heal because their source is shrouded in mystery and often goes undetected. Swartley has also defined seven basic categories of womb trauma, occurring between conception and the end of the first hour after birth, which have a basis in the natural physiological processes. They are: conception trauma, fallopian tube trauma, implantation trauma, embryological trauma, uterine trauma, birth trauma, and bonding trauma (Rowan, 1988: 15. Reference to a 1977 interview with Swartley published in *Self and Society,* volume 5, no. 6.) Bodywork can give a space for the healing of these wounds which are held cellularly in the body, and it may also open up memories of the roots of trauma so that the issues can be addressed more consciously.

Experiencing cellular presence

In exploring cellular presence and the subtle movement of cellular breathing, or internal respiration, students sometimes report images of amoebae, or sensations of floating in water. The experience is frequently felt to be deeply restful and recuperative, and also empowering, as awareness is brought into the body tissues in a more fully embodied way. Some vestigial memory of early life in the watery world of the womb, or of evolutionary origins in the oceans of the world, seems to be held in the cells themselves and reawakened when we touch to this level of consciousness.

It is possible to differentiate between the cellular membrane and the fluid content of the cell. The condition of, or our relation to, the cellular membranes reflects issues related to psychological boundaries, to containment, taking in, letting go, and being in relationship at the most fundamental level. The quality of the cellular fluid can give information about the vitality and general state of health of the person. Cellular boundaries may be too pervious, allowing passage through their fine walls without enough choice or discrimination. Or they may be too rigid, too unyielding and unresponsive to internal and external requirements. Cellular immunology is concerned with the subtle decision-making processes which take place at the boundary of each cell of the body, and the breakdown of this process can lead to physiological and psychological imbalance and disease.

A client was experiencing a lot of physical pain and tension, and felt this to have its source at the cellular level. When we focused our awareness at this level, she described the cells of her body as being isolated, out of communication with each other, each one doing its own work but as if oblivious to the presence of the others at the membranes. This gave a feeling of lack of connection and integration. We focused on the passage of fluid through the cellular membranes, into the intracellular spaces, and back out into the interstitial fluid, the internal 'ocean' in which the cells live. Experiencing the free and unboundaried flow of movement within the interstitial fluid, which flows through every body part, enabled her to regain a sense of integration that was more fluid and responsive than her former state.

Later on in this session her attention was drawn to difficulties with her digestive process; as we explored this through awareness and dialogue with the organs of digestion, a difficulty with knowing what to accept into her body and what to reject emerged. The mouth is, like the cellular boundaries, a place of choice, of acceptance or rejection, and the first organ to actively express this choice. Through exploring early mouthing movements, she discovered that it was hard for her actively to say 'no' at this basic level, causing her to ingest what was unwanted and then be unable to digest it properly. She was able to relate this pattern to her early relationship within her family, which we had explored in earlier sessions, and to a wounding she had suffered through 'ingesting' at a very early stage of development a conflict between her parents regarding the pregnancy. She felt that negative attitudes towards herself as a woman, in a female body, had origins in this early parental conflict.

In this process, discovery of a lack of ability to respond clearly at the cellular membranes led to the unfolding of a process related to a general difficulty in accepting or rejecting, in choosing and acting upon what was wanted and good for her, and what was not. In such a way, we frequently see that issues manifesting at the cellular level are reflected at many other levels too. Through bringing awareness to this life-long problem, she was able to begin to make conscious choices about what to accept, and what was bad for her and should be rejected; this included the acceptance or rejection of others' judgements and attitudes towards her.

One student described the cellular fluid as a place where she felt 'very clear and awake'. She expressed finding it difficult to go into this experience alone, feeling a lack of initiation or motivation for awareness, but when witnessed by another felt 'very present and very aware'. This speaks of the need for witnessing at this earliest and most basic level of human experience. The foetus is held or not by the *quality* of its mother's attention, her witnessing of its presence, though still unseen, expressed through the mother's own cellular presence. This student's response suggests that the experience of being witnessed, perhaps even at the earliest stages of life in the womb, is important for the development of her conscious awareness, motivation, and the ability to initiate and express her creativity. The practice of *cellular holding* can be about 'remothering' at the earliest intrauterine stages of growth.

Another student described some of her experiences with the process of cellular breathing in the following way (it should be noted that most of the students whose accounts are included here do not speak English as their first language – I have lightly edited their texts but on the whole have kept to their original wording in order to preserve the quality of experience that their writing conveys):

> The fluid mind of cellular breathing seems to me to be on a very different level [of awareness] than that of daily experiences in Western-modern life . . . The first time I experienced cellular breathing I felt an incredible activity, mainly when I was touching another person. There was a lively sssss-sound, concrete and transparent at the same time . . . After practising cellular breathing a lot, the rhythm of the breathing and the feeling of the time of the fluid/osmosis became dominant and the almost nervous activity (ssss-sound) gradually disappeared. Studying the different body systems, cellular breathing became like a bowl to contain this diversity. In bodywork and movement improvisation cellular breathing is almost always my starting point and also my point of reference whenever I feel lost or absent or too nervous. Cellular breathing is very helpful to balance activity and awareness . . .
> I'm now able to connect very easily to the quality and the rhythm of cellular breathing . . . I would say that I'm reconnecting physical and spiritual in a conscious daily meditation on being.

This woman described the experience of connecting to cellular presence as being for her 'the physical base for spirituality'. She also uses this as a support in her work with others, and described how she used it to help herself stay present in her body in a difficult situation. She was working with a client for whom touch was threatening. In one session, a focus on cellular breathing helped the client to bring awareness into her body for the first time during their work together. However, the feeling of being alive in her body was connected with forbidden sexual desire, and the client reacted strongly after a few moments. The student commented: 'To stay present, and not to make breaks as she does all the time, I took the cells as a point of reference, to help me stay strong. The main work was to be present, to create presence within and without, to support me in my work.'

This woman's experience relates to what was discovered by Marion Milner, a colleague of Winnicott, who applied what she had learnt from the mother-child relationship to that between analyst and patient. She recognized the importance of the analyst's fully embodied physical presence for the client whose own psychophysical boundaries had not been well defined during infancy. Some of her insights developed from a documented case with a severely disturbed patient, 'Susan':

> Above all what Milner needed to accomplish in herself in order to 'hold' Susan had a 'deeply physical aspect'. As time went on, she came to believe that the words she said were 'often less important' than her 'body-mind state of being.' A state of '"concentration of the body" . . . a kind of deliberate filling out of one's body with one's consciousness.' (Hughes, 1989: 155)

This passage reflects upon the importance of the body, the therapist's as well as the client's, in the therapeutic process. This 'body-mind state of being', a sense of embodied presence, is a characteristic of the bodymind integration of the total organism that Wilber describes as centauric consciousness. Such integration and perception is one of the central aims of somatic therapy, where one not only becomes aware *of* the body but also perceives and communicates *through* the body; in this way the therapist can 'hold' and 'understand' the client at a non-verbal level. Jourard has called such perception 'somatic perception' (Jourard, 1994).

The student's comments at the beginning of the transcript, above, also suggest that we are evoking altered states of consciousness when we engage in this kind of bodywork. Today we are beginning to recognize again what ancient cultures have always known – that altered states of consciousness are vital for individual and collective health, and are fundamental to spiritual experience. We can access a ground of awareness, unlike ordinary consciousness, when we connect to our physiological source and ground of being in the cells of our body. As these women describe, connection to self at this level gives a sense of fullness, presence, awareness, and clarity; it is an experience of being that is akin to experiences encountered in meditation practice. This seems to support the theories of Wilber and Grof that we can move fluidly along the axis between prepersonal and transpersonal realms of experience, and may encounter transpersonal and spiritual experiences when engaged with somatic work and perinatal processes.

Differentiation and integration

Psychologically it is necessary to differentiate aspects and functions of the psyche in order to reintegrate them into a more fully and efficiently functioning whole. Psychotherapy concerns itself with this process, which also has a basis in movement development. The second basic neurological pattern to emerge in utero is called *navel radiation* (Cohen), and it facilitates the differentiation of the limbs of the body, and their integration through the navel centre into a whole body pattern.

Navel radiation pattern

As the cells of the growing embryo begin to differentiate into specialized functions and structures, the different tissue layers, limbs, and organs begin to evolve until, by the eighth week, a tiny but fully formed foetus has developed. The foetus is attached by the umbilical cord to its supply of nourishment, and the navel functions as a centre of movement organization during the next phases of growth. Movements of the limbs frequently initiate at this centre and may involve one limb or all limbs simultaneously. This pattern can also be seen in the newborn (Hartley, 1995: Chapter 2). Although many of the movements do not appear to be intentional, in the sense of having a specific goal or focus, they are nevertheless functional and extremely important to normal development; the nervous system is fed by the constant supply of sensory information received from the foetus's movements, and contact to the skin as it moves. This sensory nourishment is essential for the development of the brain and nervous system. In fact infants whose movement in utero has been seriously restricted are sometimes unable to develop fully, and neurological dysfunction can result. Thus the foetus's movement-play is as vital to the development of brain and nervous system as is the play of infants later on. She is beginning to learn about the body-self, and about body boundaries and unboundedness as she turns, rolls, floats, punches and kicks, strokes, sucks, and explores, through a myriad of movements, her own physical being and the sensations of water, womb, mother's bodily activities and sounds, and the pull of gravity, which are her world. As mentioned in the discussion of Piontelli's work, foetal movement has been well researched and documented.

Cohen observed that organization of limb movement around the navel centre forms a basic pattern, a matrix, for these explorations; some foetal movements relate to the primitive reflexes necessary for the development of basic locomotion and survival skills, and others appear to be unique and idiosyncratic expressions of the foetus's developing personality (see Piontelli's work). During this sensory-motor play, the body parts experience themselves and their relation to the centre of the body, through the sensory and proprioceptive feedback generated by the movements themselves. Thus the bodymind is coming to 'know itself', to develop a rudimentary self awareness. I would suggest that this stage relates to an underlying and primitive formation of the sense of emergent self, in Stern's terminology, based primarily in sensory-motor experience, but influenced by factors such as the mother's health and emotional states, other environmental factors, and the foetus's unique way of experiencing and relating to these.

In this movement pattern, the limbs are first differentiated, each one experienced in relation to its own movement and to the body centre; then each is integrated into a whole body pattern, where each limb can know and dialogue, through movement and touch, with each other limb and body part, and with the surrounding fluid-filled womb. This process provides an underlying basis for the potential experience of psychological wholeness and integration; as Stern describes, self-coherence is one of the four primary experiences necessary for the development of a sense of core self, and its physical basis evolves during intrauterine life.

The integration of this pattern can be supported through hands-on work. Focusing on cellular breathing and communication between the cells of each limb, from extremity to the navel, is one way to bring awareness to the connection of limb to centre. Gentle and rhythmic compression and extension of the limb into and out of the centre, stimulated through another's touch or by self-generated movement, also facilitates proprioceptive feedback and integration. Movement improvisation evolving out of the subtle sense of cellular breathing through each limb can be a profound and enjoyable way to reexperience and support this early movement process.

Students and clients often report experiencing new and unfamiliar movements, and altered states of consciousness, as with cellular breathing. They may also describe these experiences as old, remembered, familiar. One student described her experiences during movement explorations of the navel radiation pattern, in this way:

> I stayed on the floor – wonderful harmonious movements, like a fish. It touched me deeply, so that tears came to my eyes. (The lost paradise? The longing for security – *Geborgenheit.*) Immediately, when I lost the concentration, it didn't feel harmonious any more. Light and shadow behind my eyes were like light and shadow at or after my birth. It was difficult to open my eyes and approach another person to exchange afterwards. You are in a completely different world.
>
> The second time, 3 months later, it was easy. The movements with the breath felt very harmonious, those influenced by my will unharmonious. I loved moving on the floor – I normally don't like floor work – and I even loved the 'pushing' which was not my favourite before.
>
> I think I'm very used to doing things with my will, and at that time trusting my inner self to do the 'right' thing was very new to me. I remember this feeling of complete harmony of movement, light, and that it was so *effortless*. It was like a stream going on and on. I was in an inner world without losing the outer world. I felt very safe in myself. And I had found a source, MY source of movement which I had the feeling I had lost somewhere during my dance education. The discovery of this inner source was one of the seeds from which I learnt more trust in myself, an inner strength, and that there is something that is caring for me, beyond my will.
>
> In general, from this work I feel more grounded . . . I feel more of a balance between my will and my intuition. I feel more of a balance in my body.

This woman's experience suggests a coming home to the self, to a place beyond the ego-will where a sense of trust in life can be nurtured. This might be a return to a phase of development prior to disruption of the sense of core self, her 'lost paradise', which can serve as a safe ground for the exploration of later disturbances, a place to return to; or the experience she describes may come as a result of some healing of early intrauterine disturbances which prevented her sense of core self from developing fully and securely. Another student also described some of her experiences with the navel radiation pattern:

> In the very first exploration it felt like entering a totally new state of mind, like being on a threshold, and it was very amazing and fascinating that this was a place with much space - not, as I would have expected a threshold to be, a place that is narrow and that exists mainly to pass through, but it had a very strong quality of being a space to stay, to be, to move.
>
> Being there also had a very powerful quality, a feeling of being carried by a deep innate pulse or rhythm.
>
> I enjoyed very much moving in the navel radiation pattern, and also receiving a light pressure being fed in from my body peripheries to the navel centre by a partner. Both experiences had a strong quality of nurturing something in me, and of making up for something very basic.

I taught navel radiation in every group that I worked with, because I felt it to
be so basic for my teaching and for moving.

At one point when I worked with it in a group they went/I led them really
deeply into it, and afterwards one of them gave feedback that it felt like being led
into a trance. This was a strong impulse for a reflection on my teaching, and I
found out that exploring altered states of mind, and training the flexibility and
ability in that, was a strong interest in my teaching that had been unconscious up
to that moment.

This student's questioning about leading her group members into a 'trance'
stimulated our own group into a discussion of this issue, which led us to
explore connections between this work and shamanic and mystical trance-
inducing practices. There seems to be an intrinsic connection between
bodywork and movement practices which evoke intrauterine experiences,
and the 'incubations' and 'death-rebirth' rituals which form an essential part
of the mystical initiatory practices of ancient and indigenous cultures (Eliade,
1972). The accounts of these students also suggest that this work holds the
potential for healing and transformatory experiences, which have enabled
them to develop new abilities, awareness, and spiritual qualities.

Bonding and defence

The two processes of bonding and defence are absolutely essential to our
survival in the world. They are the expressions of all our longings, needs,
desires, our fears, dislikes, and urges to power. In Buddhist psychology, all
thought and activity in the samsaric world is based upon attraction and
aversion, and until our minds are completely free of delusion, nothing we do
is free of these two motivations.

These two fundamental movements – towards what we love and desire,
and against or away from what we find distasteful or threatening – have a
physical basis in the primitive reflexes that are developing in utero, within the
matrix of the navel radiation pattern. They continue to emerge and integrate
after birth. Reflexes are specific movement responses elicited by specific
stimuli, such as touch or pressure to particular areas of the skin; tastes, smells,
sounds and visual stimuli; passively induced movements or changes in relation
to gravity (Cohen, 1993: 233–56). Initial responses are expressed as a simple
movement towards the stimulus, which is the basis of *bonding,* or a
movement away from the stimulus, which underlies *defence.* The primitive
reflexes facilitate these basic responses in a semi-automatic way.

They tend to work in modulating pairs that balance muscle tone and
activity throughout the body. Problems arise when one reflex dominates and
is not modulated by its counterpart. The unconventional approach taken in
body-mind centering practice is to facilitate the embodiment of *all* of the
reflexive patterns, bringing into expression those which have not been able
to fully develop. They can then function to modulate and counterbalance

those that might have temporarily dominated; this gives greater freedom and choice and allows the natural developmental process to continue to unfold. Bringing into awareness, embodying, and balancing the reflexes can also be of great benefit to the normally functioning adult; the process can bring greater spontaneity, integration, fluidity, and efficiency to movement, and also positively affect mind states.

Rooting reflex

One important reflex that develops in utero is the *rooting reflex*. When the skin around the mouth is stroked, the foetus and infant, unless tired, overstimulated, or otherwise absorbed, will usually move towards or away from the stimulus, depending on whether it is perceived at that moment as pleasurable and desirable, or not (Comparetti, 1980). In the example at the beginning of this section, I used this reflex to explore with my client the basic 'yes' and 'no', which is first expressed through the mouth by turning towards or away from the source of stimulation.

Such responses are the basis of our ability to move towards, open to, and make contact with another – the process of bonding; or to move away from, create distance, separate – to defend ourselves. The alternating rhythm of approach and withdrawal enables us to negotiate our relationships throughout life, and one of the first ways in which we experience this is through exploratory movements in the womb and in early feeding, via the mouth.

Mouthing pattern

Along with this develops the *mouthing pattern,* where rocking motions of the head and spine are initiated by the sucking actions of the mouth, as in feeding; this pattern underlies the birthing movements, and dominates during the early weeks of post-natal life. Psychoanalytic literature (the work of Melanie Klein in particular) has devoted much attention to the satisfactions and frustrations experienced by the infant during the 'oral phase' of development, around the all-important activities of nursing. The infant has been viewed by some theorists as primarily passive to environmental circumstances; however, the aspect of self-agency, necessary to the developing sense of core self, is an essential part of the infant's experience of nursing, and of the mouthing pattern. As an underlying initiation for birthing movements and later spinal locomotion patterns, it is involved in powerful acts of self-agency, and is well developed before birth and actual nursing begin.

Melanie Klein regarded loss of the mother, represented by the 'good breast', as the primary source of infant distress, and central to the development of neuroses. The infant is seen as proactive as well as reactive, and nature dominates over nurture in her view. Her model is based on bodily functions of oral incorporation and anal expulsion: 'Where Freud believed mind functioned like a machine, Klein saw it working like a digestive tract.' She created: 'Rich imagery associated with mind as body, as opposed to mind as machine' (Hughes, 1989: 50).

Klein's work is of relevance to the somatic therapist and body psychotherapist, as it addresses preverbal experiences concerned with physiological functioning and the person's relationship to nurturing and nourishment of the body. Such early experiences might be recalled through body-oriented therapy; disturbances associated with nursing frequently emerge when working with the mouth region, and movements initiated there. Whereas Freud viewed external objects as only physiologically significant to the young infant, Klein also saw them as psychologically important from birth onwards, and influential upon the earliest development of the psyche. Satisfaction or frustration at the breast were critical, as was the appearance and disappearance of the breast-mother. The breast was imbued with qualities such as love, frustration, fear, hatred, security, and comfort, which were introjected as the 'good' and 'bad' breast.

Moro reflex

Another reflex closely connected to the bonding and defending instincts is the *Moro* or *'startle' reflex*. A sudden shift of position, loud noise, or other surprise, will cause the infant to first open wide its arms and upper chest, drop back its head, and cry out. This is a shock reaction, but it also provides a widening of the upper body in preparation for embrace. The second phase involves flexing in and holding on. When there is a body or object to hold, the infant establishes a firmer contact through this two-phased movement. The defensive startle reaction resolves in a holding embrace when the pattern is completed. However, sometimes startle reactions cannot be completed in this way; the nervous system is left in a state of alert, in shock, and the whole body can be thrown out of alignment as the incomplete extension phase, or an unresolved flexion/embrace, crystallizes into a habitual postural pattern. This reflex demonstrates the need for a healthy balance between defence and bonding, withdrawal and approach, and for the resolution of high-stress situations with experiences of comfort and release.

The presence of an incomplete Moro reflex became apparent when working with one client. We had been exploring the issue of lack of support in her life and how this expressed in her body through postural and breathing patterns. As we followed the process of her breathing, she made a movement of reaching out and grasping with her hands, reflecting a grasping that happened at the beginning of the inhalation; she would then cut off the inhalation and quickly exhale. Noticing tension and restriction in the movement of her chest, I worked gently with the muscles and joints of her ribcage to create more openness there, then returned to her movement. I suggested she grasp for my hands, instead of the air, and she opened wider, reached out and pulled me into an embrace – an expression of a fuller Moro reflex. We rested for a long time like this; she said it felt good to pull me in and hold me, and she could now breath more fully and relax. I felt a clear message from her body to stay with her, and I was aware of experiencing a 'merged' state whilst she relaxed into the embrace. She connected to the sense that as a child, once the 'emergency' or 'practical necessity' was over, she could not expect to continue to be held by her mother; she began to let go of me, but tension remained in her hands and the grasping breath returned. Clearly her body was expressing the need for holding and bonding, not withdrawal, whilst her mind had learnt that she could not expect her mother to hold her once the emergency or practical necessities were over. The residue of this unresolved stress appeared to have become embodied in a posture of slight flexion in the upper body, as if still attempting a holding embrace, a stiffness in the neck, and a grasping breath, which expressed the frozen movement of reaching out for contact and security.

Patterns first embodied in the reaching, grasping, holding, and expelling activities of the mouth are frequently repeated in the way we reach, grasp, hold, and let go with the other senses, and with the hands and feet. In the following session with this client we sourced back to the mouth and jaw, where I noticed a holding pattern similar to that expressed through the grasping of her hands. She responded well to an exploration of the mouthing pattern, and her jaw released considerably; she felt an openness and freedom after this work, her head more easily balanced, and she was able to feel connected through to her feet as we developed the movements through the whole body. In the movements that she did at the end of this process, she was balancing flexion and extension, an integration of the two phases of the Moro throughout the musculature of the whole body, which is necessary to a supported posture. Her work continues, as the openness and internal support she experienced after these sessions allowed another level of process to emerge.

Movement and the senses

The mouthing pattern and rooting through the mouth underlie perception and movement initiation through the other senses, and can be a support for how we orientate ourselves through smell, hearing, and vision. This forms a base for how we relate, for what we choose to move towards, bond with, and what we choose to move away from or defend against. In a two-week seminar, the first part of a year-long training programme, a group of students explored the developmental process in depth. One woman described some of her experiences of this; she spoke of the work with mouthing and the sense perceptions:

> In many patterns the question of 'how do I get support for what I do?' was a big issue . . . With the mouthing, I learnt I could open my mouth much more than usual, and then going into grasping, I felt a lot of fun and joy as I reached for things.

An important experience was being on the level of a baby, just perceiving what's going on, without doing, or manipulating, or coming into activity. At the end of the two weeks we explored a long phase of perceiving through the senses. After this perceiving process, I came into contact with someone (in a movement improvisation). It was such a light way of making contact; it came out of noticing what is around me and just responding to my perceptions, without wanting to get anywhere. Out of this came a curiosity about the world and things and people – I had the feeling there is so much you can explore, and for me it was a new quality of being in the world. Not so much judging or deciding 'I want to do this or that', or 'I don't want to have anything to do with these people'. It was a feeling of opening up into the world. This curiosity came to a point when, after returning home, I placed an advertisement (in the paper) to find a partner. In this advert I used the words 'I want someone who is curious about the world and other people and himself'. These words came out of this experience. And I found the man, and I think in a way he is the right one, besides all the struggles!

I had a strong feeling that I want to be in relationship, and to have a place where I feel at home and have support for myself and my daughter. At the beginning (of the seminar) it was not consciously an issue, but at the end when we reflected on what was going on for us, and what were the important points, for me it was to look for people that I feel supported by, and not be with people with whom I'm not really in contact. So when we returned from Tuscany, I decided to leave the flat where I live with others because I don't feel comfortable and good about our relationship.

The cellular breathing and navel radiation work gave me the feeling – 'oh, it could be like this. I could feel like this – integrated, satisfied, completed!' Out of this came the feeling of stillness I look for. Then I could recognize what would bring this into my life. The course crystallized these needs, and also helped me feel the strength to handle it and bring it to actuality . . . It had to do with the atmosphere in our group – feeling what can be between people, how communication can be, and then to see what the lack was in my life.

Her last comment reflects on the quality of bonding which took place in this group, and was greatly facilitated by the work on early movement patterns, perceptual processes, touch, and holding. In exploring this process, students have a chance to relearn early responses established in the preverbal stages of development, and to make new choices about opening and defending, bonding and the making of boundaries, within a supportive community.

Sinead's story

Sinead was in therapy for a period of nearly three years. When she first came to see me she was in a state of exhaustion and extreme stress. Her father had recently died, and she experienced this as a 'double grief', as it brought back the memory of the death of her younger brother 16 years earlier. The stress within her family was overwhelming her; she felt that she was the one always called upon to support others, whilst there was no emotional support for herself. She also feared that she was 'carrying' the pain of other family members who were less able to cope than she was. She felt over-burdened by her family situation and history, and was unable to draw boundaries between her own feelings and those of her mother and an alcoholic sister. Her inner life was unfocused and chaotic, and she feared being unable to cope with the externals of life. She was also suffering from menopausal symptoms, and a stressed and over-vigilant way of being in the world.

The eldest of four, Sinead had been given the responsibility of looking after her younger siblings since early childhood, and as an adult had developed a tendency to feel overly responsible for others. She had chosen not to have children of her own as she felt she had spent all her childhood being responsible for other children, and did not want to do this any more. Her sister Angela, the second child, and brother Joe were both sickly children, needing a lot of attention; the family's way of coping was to get ill, but whenever Sinead was ill there was always someone else worse off than her, so she would be the one required to cope. She developed a defensive attitude to hide her vulnerability and a deep unmet need to be witnessed and understood. These family patterns had continued on into adulthood, and the emotional demands of her mother and sister had now become unbearable.

Much of our work focused on the issue of boundaries between herself and her mother, her sister, and a close female friend. A level of enmeshment and codependency had evolved from the cellular and energetic levels, to the psychological and spiritual. She indicated that she was seeking a birth of soul into a situation not burdened by her family history, and connection to a spirituality that would be more 'tangible, substantial, and nurturing' than her Catholic upbringing; she was seeking an immanent, embodied, more feminine connection to her spirit. Bodywork that helped her to come out of her anxious, vigilant mental processes, back into her body, formed part of this work. For example, allowing her head to be held, she could more easily let go and come back home to the body; coming into the organs and blood allowed her to feel more substance and nurturing. We also worked through movement, drawing (which was an important medium through which to access her unconscious process), and dreams, to explore the boundaries between her self and her mother and sister. Gradually, painfully, over the years she was able to separate from the women in her family and create space into which her inner self could emerge.

The issue that emerged as central to Sinead's process was the death of an older sister, Cathy. Cathy had died at only 7 months of age, and Sinead had been conceived 3 months later. She had only learnt about her sister's existence and death 7 years previously; such a family secret can create bewilderment in the psyche of a child who senses feelings around the subject but has no information to relate these feelings to. Knowledge and information give power and protect us; dark family secrets never mentioned create vulnerability and a fundamental disempowerment. The lack of knowledge about an issue that emerged as essential to Sinead's psychic life created a veil, a sense of deep enmeshment and enchantment, which she had been unable to penetrate. This veil-like quality still pervaded her relationship with both her mother and younger sister, for whom she had always had to take responsibility; she was still 'in the dark', enwombed in her mother's unconscious pain and unexpressed grief.

At a point in her therapy when Sinead was beginning to experience some space from her sister's demands, she was also working to let go of a man with whom she had been involved some years ago. It was an unhealthy relationship that she was glad to end, but she felt he was still part of her inner life and often appeared in her dreams. She felt his presence in her solar plexus, and after exploring these sensations an image of him as a small 'aborted' baby emerged. During the next session she drew another image, this time of another baby that she recognized as being connected to herself; she took this to mean that when she let go of taking care of his child, there was space for her own inner child to emerge. A dream that this man was leaving, and another that she was pregnant seemed to confirm this understanding.

The second drawing initiated a process of understanding for Sinead. She had drawn the image with sensory organs but no arms and legs – its ability to act in the world cut off, but very sensitive to everything coming in. A question mark hung over the baby's head, asking 'why?' A few sessions later she returned to this drawing. She had realized that her dead sister was present in her drawing; she was a 'gauze-like', ghost figure who 'wafted about' but did not speak, and had Sinead's own puzzled expression on her face. She felt she was partially identified with Cathy, and realized she had been conceived and born into her mother's grief over her first child's death. Now she sensed that Cathy's ghost was still within her, and needed to be let go of. She had even acquired two birth certificates, as if her sister were truly still with her, like an invisible twin. The question 'why?' from her drawing now made sense; she needed to find out from her mother exactly what had happened.

She knew that her father had never seen Cathy; he had been in England at the time, and her mother had been alone with the child in Ireland. After this session Sinead talked to her mother and was able to get more information. She discovered that although they married later, her parents had not been married when Cathy was conceived and born. Her father, his brother, and sister-in-law sent her mother to Ireland to have the illegitimate baby 'in secret'. She had no support, and hoped to have the baby adopted, but was unable to arrange for this; Cathy became ill and died in hospital at 7 months. Sinead and her mother were able to cry together after this story was finally told; for 50 years her mother had held in her grief, and Sinead had felt biologically connected to it, carrying and feeling responsible for her mother's pain.

Although this understanding and sharing of grief with her mother enabled some healing within their relationship to occur, Sinead needed to complete on many levels the work of freeing herself from her mother's pain and from responsibility for her sister's woundedness, which she felt she was carrying.

In the womb, she had quite literally ingested her mother's unshed feelings of grief, and probably guilt and anger too, through her very life-blood. At this earliest stage of life, even before she was born, Sinead had been exposed to and impelled to absorb so much; boundaries at the most fundamental cellular level had been invaded with toxic psychic energy, and this pattern had continued throughout her childhood and adulthood, not only with her mother, but with her sister and close female friend too.

Drawing and movement were important avenues for exploration of this early preverbal material. In earlier sessions, before this issue had become completely conscious, she would sometimes curl into a foetal position on the floor when moving, and if I touched her head during somatic work, her body process would lead her into the initiation of birthing movements. Clearly she was needing to address issues related to her womb and birth experience. For a period of time a negative transference manifested, mostly taking the form of anger at the therapeutic situation. She would complain about our seating arrangements, or the quality of the carpet on the floor, or the form of therapy itself which she feared was going to 'pathologize' her. Because her process had its roots in prenatal development, I imagine her anger signified that she experienced the womb as 'hostile', a negative or unsafe space which she had tried, unsuccessfully, to defend herself against. She also feared not being seen clearly, as her mother had not seen her because Cathy was always there in her mother's mind, like a shroud of grief. It was important that she could express her anger about the therapeutic space without the 'womb' disintegrating – the boundaries of the therapeutic container, and the therapist, being destroyed.

After further work, a ritual finally enabled her to let go of Cathy, and to begin to differentiate her own wounds from her sister's. She came to feel that her own deepest wound was that of not being witnessed – not being seen, heard, or understood by her mother. She realized that roles must have been reversed, even as a child, so that she was required to mother her own mother from the very beginning of life.

Sinead's work spiralled around these core issues, coming back to the early processes concerning Cathy and her mother, then moving out into her current relationships in the world many times. Somatic work, both before and after the sessions focusing on her dead sister, helped to deepen and integrate her understanding at a bodily and energetic level. She came into one session, quite early on in our work together, in distress at 'doing the feeling for her family', taking on the pain of her mother and younger sister. She cried and asked to be held; she was beginning to connect to the hurt and sadness she felt beneath her strong and 'coping' exterior. As she lay curled up on the floor, she allowed me to hold her, and talked about her infancy – how she was in the womb with her mother's grief, then born between her dead sister, Cathy, and her sick sister, Angela, so that there was no space for her, no positive holding.

As she connected to her inability to separate from others' pain, she felt she could not breathe fully. I gave her cellular touch, and suggested she focus on her navel, imagining the breath to be coming into her body through the umbilical, as it had done in the womb. She became more relaxed and we stayed with this for some time; I continued to give cellular touch, and a slight compression as she exhaled, as a way of supporting and witnessing her through her breathing. We worked non-verbally for most of the session; I was drawn to follow and reflect the flow of blood from her heart to and from her feet, then spent some time holding her organs, initiating a gentle rocking motion that allowed them to release tension and become more present and supportive. When she finally felt ready to emerge from this process, she said she had at last the sense of breathing for herself, her own breath; she had made up a kind of mantra that she chanted to herself as she breathed, affirming herself in this way. For her to begin to experience her core self consciously it was essential for her to feel in her cells that it was her own breath she was taking in, and not her mother's grief-laden breath.

On another occasion she had felt 'strangled' by the situation with her mother and younger sister, Angela, and had released some of her feelings by 'strangling' a cushion; this led to pushing against the cushion with her hands and head, which she felt was about trying to get out of the stuck and intolerable situation she felt trapped in. This was also a metaphor for birth, and we decided to recreate a womblike situation and see if a birthing process was called for. I began simply placing my hands on her curled-up body, giving cellular touch, and she discovered that she was not ready for the birth; it was necessary first to rest within the cellular holding, to experience a 'positive womb', before she was ready to emerge. Eventually she expressed feeling 'bigger', less embryonic; she found a clear and strong but gentle pushing action from her feet through her whole body, which carried her easily out of the enclosed space as if 'moving through water'. Having allowed the time to receive what she needed, it was an 'easy birth'.

Sinead's essential work was to differentiate herself and her own feelings and needs from others, particularly her mother's and sister's, and to create psychological boundaries that would enable her to protect herself from the toxicity that seemed to flow into her from her family's wounds. This pattern had been established in the womb, and reinforced throughout her childhood. She learnt to let go of the ways in which she had colluded in the destructive family patterns, and in doing so made space for her own inner self to emerge. She learned to say 'no' to the unreasonable demands of others, and 'yes' to her own needs, and found a central core of awareness from which she could disidentify from negative conditioning and distressing relational patterns. Coming into her body, being with her feelings and body sensations in a deep and attentive way, brought her to experience her core self and helped her to connect to an embodied spiritual practice.

During the last phase of our work she was looking at the question of intimacy; the possibility of renewing a relationship with a man from her past offered a ground within which to explore questions around relationship. Her relationship with her mother also became easier, and she felt more able to give appropriate support to her now elderly mother, without becoming enmeshed in the old patterns; her mother, too, seemed to respond positively to the changes Sinead had undergone. Coming into relationship from a more empowered and conscious place, after learning to separate, to say no, to create boundaries, would complete the cycle. A series of drawings showed a movement from a closed, victimized stance, to a protective gesture, to an image of reaching out towards a loving hand; the drawings seemed to offer a map of her journey and its potential fulfilment. Body symptoms also led us, appropriately, to explore holding patterns in her shoulders and upper chest, the relational area of the body connected to gestures of defence, of reaching out, and embracing. With great courage, and a deep commitment to the healing process, Sinead continues to develop her resources and her awareness from a place that is more grounded, empowered, and spacious.

CHAPTER 6

Embodying self: birth and the process of movement development

Embodying the sense of a core self

In the womb the adventure of embodying self through movement and sensation progresses, as the foetus prepares herself for birth. The movements initiated at the mouth are the foundation for active, intentional movements of the whole body, which will eventually birth the child and gradually enable her to embody her full movement potential. With the mastery of each developmental stage, another level of coherence and agency, a new level of expression of the will, has emerged.

Prespinal and spinal movement patterns

Evolving out of the mouthing pattern is the *prespinal pattern*. This involves sinuous movements of the whole spine, head to tail, which flow through the spinal cord or digestive tract (soft spine) rather than the bony spine. It is usually initiated by the mouth or other senses of the head, and underlies the *spinal* patterns of the vertebral column (hard spine). This pattern is present in utero, and during early postnatal life. It reflects fish-like motions, a reminder of our watery origins, and develops a fluid connection between all parts of the spine.

During an advanced training seminar on the brain and developmental movement patterns, students explored embodying the brainstem and spinal cord, and early movements related to this, including movements of the foetus in utero. They described it as 'a place of stillness and centredness', of 'coming home to myself', 'feeling myself in a clear way, without having to do or be anything in particular'. This suggests to me that the prespinal stage of development is closely related to the emergence of the sense of core self, and that this may be already well developed in utero. The prespinal pattern is also a support for birthing.

There are four spinal patterns that develop out of the prespinal pattern: a *spinal yield and push* pattern initiated first by the head, then by the tail of the spine; and a *spinal reach and pull* pattern, again initiated first by the head then by the tail. All of the movement experiences in utero are preparing the foetus for birth and life beyond the womb, and the spinal patterns are developing upon the foundations of all previous levels of organization; but it is not until the actual birthing process that the spinal patterns are fully embodied (Hartley, 1995: Chapter 3).

Birthing

For the infant, birth involves a pushing movement that initiates first with the crown of the head searching for and pressing into the cervical opening; the resulting compression levers through the spine to the tail, and there is a responsive push initiated by the tail of the spine against the contracting uterine walls; the feet are also involved. These rhythmical movements give powerful feedback to the spine, and greatly stimulate muscular and organic tone throughout the whole body. At the actual moment of birth, the head breaks through the cervical opening and the pushing action transforms into a reach forwards of the head, which pulls the body into its new environment beyond the confines of the womb. This powerful moment of transition brings the infant into a whole new world, from water and enclosed space, to earth and air.

Students and clients exploring the movements of birthing report a wide variety of experiences. Memories of their original birth are often graphically evoked, and under the right conditions, trauma and unresolved stress can be gradually worked through. In my training programmes students explore the birth process in small groups; three or four people form the 'womb', and replicate the cellular holding for one who curls up within this container. They gradually offer more pressure, simulating the increasing contact of the uterine walls as the foetus grows to fill the space, until the one inside feels a readiness and impetus to move. Together they work with the rhythmical contractions and release, the 'womb' being responsive to the movements within. The 'birth' comes when the whole body integrates in the powerful rhythmic contractions, and a deep source of will, strength, and intention is embodied. In this way, each one can feel how her own power, heart, and will are engaged in the birthing process.

Many different issues and feelings can be evoked: feeling at peace; feeling trapped and helpless with no way out, like a victim; feeling safe, held, and secure; feeling joy and power when the rhythms of the contractions of 'baby' and 'mother' synchronize and support each other; or feeling fear, struggle, anger, or frustration when they do not. The experience can be very empowering as she connects to her own active part, and her physical strength and power as active coparticipant in her own birth. Birth trauma can sometimes be resolved; when, in the rebirthing process, it is experienced as different from the original birth, a whole new basis for perception, choice, and bodymind experiencing is introduced, and new patterns of behaviour can be developed out of this. It would clearly take more than a single experience to resolve and integrate birth trauma, but if the student or client has been prepared by working through issues at other levels, the birthing process may be the catalyst for important change.

The basic perinatal matrix

In these explorations I use Grof's model of the basic perinatal matrix to contextualize experiences (Grof, 1985, 1988). This model explores the development of the will, the expressive function of the self, through the birthing process. My integration of developmental movement therapy with the basic perinatal matrices described by Grof seeks to integrate psychoemotional experiences evoked through the embodiment of the birth process.

Grof's model evolved out of his research with altered states of consciousness; his early research explored drug-induced states, but later other methods were developed using breathing techniques, bodywork, and music, to induce similar states of consciousness. In exploring deep states, sometimes occurring spontaneously during periods of transition and crisis, and sometimes induced in a therapeutic context, Grof identified four main phases of bodymind experience, which reflect stages in the birth process.

The first phase denotes the original state of preconscious unity of the foetus with the universe, her mother, where blissful harmony, oceanic feelings of at-one-ness, and trust, are potential experiences.

Second is the stage where contractions begin; the foetus begins to feel the constricting walls of her universe pressing in on her but does not yet feel the ability to respond effectively. Feelings of vulnerability, helplessness, pain, separation, victimization, or the acceptance of limitations may ensue.

During the third stage the foetus actively engages in the birthing process, potentially discovering her own will and power, either in cooperation or in conflict with the 'other', the rhythms of the contracting womb.

The fourth and final stage of birthing is the culmination of the process, as the newborn emerges and is reunited with the mother. This can be experienced, in Maslow's terms, as a 'peak experience', if all previous stages have been fully embodied, accepted, and fulfilled. There can also be an experience of catastrophic annihilation, as union with the old way of being and the holding environment of the womb is completely severed; adults going through this process may experience what has come to be called 'ego-death' at this point.

Perinatal experience and the developing will

Attachment, failure to complete, unwillingness to accept, or conflict at any stage of the process reflects difficulty with a particular stage of development of the will. As a result, personality patterns develop, which consist of specific needs, desires, attitudes, beliefs, and behavioural patterns.

If we are unable to fully integrate the first stage we may develop a pseudo-mystical desire for a world that is always in harmony, free from pain and conflict, an all-is-one perspective. If the will is caught at this stage, the experience is of not knowing one has a will; any use of the will would be unconscious, and thus possibly manipulative or controlling. Underlying issues connected with this stage relate to experiences of harmony and mystical union and a fundamental sense of trust or mistrust in the universe is established here. A range of problems from anxiety to psychosis may evolve from a negative experience of the womb.

Issues related to the second stage are associated with feelings of victimhood. They are constellated when the experience of confining limitations, separation from the original sense of at-one-ness, and loss of the security and harmony of the first stage are not accepted. Here we experience that there is a will, but we do not have it; we are stuck and there is no way out. A healthy resolution of this stage is the acceptance of limits and suffering, and recognition of the love that underlies our pain; issues connected with vulnerability and love underlie difficulties at this level.

During the third stage we find that we do have a will, and begin to use it to actively birth ourselves. We might experience our will working in co-operation with the 'other', which can evoke a joyful, life-affirming and powerful experience of self. In contrast, if we resist and find ourselves in conflict with the outside force, feelings of antagonism and rebelliousness may be constellated; our will is experienced as being in opposition to that of the other. Issues of power and self-assertion are connected with this stage.

If all stages have been fully embodied and accepted, the moment of release and reunion with the mother can be experienced as the joy of simply *being* will; this is a moment of individuation, of the experience of self in relation to other, which may have a transpersonal dimension. However, the experience of the fourth stage is momentary; attempts to hold on to it and prolong it beyond its natural course return us to the mystical longings of the first stage – a desire to return to the idyllic and blissful world of the eternal womb.

The core experience of the will, and the personality development associated with it, will be reflected in the way we experience subsequent stages of development, including the learning of new skills, the emergence of potential qualities, engagement in creative processes, and passage through major life transitions. All of these are like minor and major birth processes, occurring throughout the life cycle. Unless we bring awareness to, and complete or resolve stages where our will is stuck, the original pattern may be unconsciously repeated in these later passages.

The birth experience is not purely causal of later personality developments or neuroses. The child is not a passive participant in her own birth process, but an active cocreator; experiential study of the movement process of birthing affirms this belief. Each of us comes into life with an innate tendency to experience, respond, and exert our personal will in particular ways. The birth process is the first time our personal will is fully embodied and comes into relationship with the will of another; hence it is the first time that innate patterns crystallize and are experienced. Working with the birth process can resolve difficulties around our original birth experience at the energetic and physical level; it can also yield useful information about our basic orientation to life, our patterns of willing, and central issues of the personality which need to be integrated.

Embodying the birthing process

In integrating this psychological model with developmental movement therapy, the foetal movement patterns that prepare the baby for birthing are first embodied. We then simulate the womb experience for each person in turn, through the touch of several other participants. At the first stage we use a gentle touch with the focus on cellular holding, giving time for feelings of safety and trust to develop. Then pressure is gradually increased, to reflect stage two, until the pressure begins to stimulate a movement response. We then endeavour to recreate the movement and rhythm of the contractions, giving appropriate resistance but also yielding to the person's push; this reflects the third stage, where will and power are fully engaged in pushing movements through the whole body (the spinal yield and push patterns). At the moment of release the movement changes into a reach and pull into the new environment, reflecting stage four. Here we must be attentive to the needs and wishes of the 'birthing' person, being sensitive to the kind of contact and meeting they need as they 'emerge'. The quality of welcome into the world is of crucial importance, especially for our generation who were largely the victims of quite brutal postnatal treatment.

The four stages of the basic perinatal matrix relate to four stages that can be identified at every level of the developmental movement process. Each stage of movement development evolves out of the foundation of cellular breathing, which is a basis for *bonding*, or *grounding* at later levels; then there is an active *yielding*, a choice to surrender to the pull of gravity or another force acting upon the body; this is a preparation for the activity of *pushing* against the resistant force or supporting surface, which initiates movement through space; and finally, as the resistance is released, a movement of *reaching and pulling* into space takes us beyond our known boundaries to a new level. This process is repeated at each new stage of movement development, and also offers a movement-based model for the process of psychological development and creative growth throughout the life cycle.

One student, Inga, described her rebirthing process in this way:

After the birthing process I had the feeling I can do things easily. I don't have to fight so much. But it depends a lot on the people who are communicating with me, and I had the feeling that there must have been resistance from my mother (during my birth), which prevented us from coming together. It was very important to see that both mother and child have to work together in this process. Making this experience in my body - that I came out smoothly, and it was very easy – I didn't trust it, and said I have to do it again - it couldn't be like this. So I did try again, with much effort, and hurt my neck a little!

This woman had been working on herself through somatic therapy for a number of years; I imagine she had prepared herself well by working through many issues at different levels, and was now ready to experience a new and easier, more empowering and joyful birth. With supportive companions sensitive to her needs, strength, and rhythms, she was able to harmonize her pushing movements with those of her 'womb-mothers', and experience her own power and joy in the process. Her attempt to recapitulate what her mind told her it should be like, perhaps had been like at her original birth, resulted in a less fluid, more effortful and injurious experience. My choice would be to trust what her body knew in this situation.

When people complete this process, they often appear transformed – clear, present, alert, more fully embodied. A sense of coming into oneself is often experienced, similar to that described with the prespinal pattern, but more active and dynamic. Birthing constellates a sense of physical integration like no other activity we know, as every muscle, every nerve, every cell of the body must engage fully, and great learning takes place as a result of the prolonged tension of birth and the stimulus to the nervous system that this creates. From observing the effects of this work on adult students and clients, and having had the opportunity to observe newborn babies in this state of quiet but dynamic alertness and presence, it is my feeling that a clear sense of core self may be experienced at birth. However, the infant now has to learn to live in a totally new environment, and must go through a further phase of development of the emergent and core senses of self in relation to this very different world.

With clients in individual sessions I may work by giving sensory feedback to the spine, and with movement exercises that reflect the principles of the spinal patterns and birthing movement, when a sense of self and of core support is needed. Psychologically this can relate to inadequate holding, in its broadest (Winnicottian) sense, during the very early months of life. The spinal yield and push patterns evoke a mind of inner attention, a being present to one's inner core. The spinal reach and pull patterns evoke a mind of outer attention, of presence to world and other.

Sensory initiation of developmental transitions

The shift from domination of the spinal yield and push phase to the reach and pull phase also reflects a transition from the stage of the developing sense of emergent self, to the beginning of the development of the sense of core self, where relationship to others begins to evolve. This transition happens around two months of age, when several important sensory-motor skills are being mastered: visual coordination and acuity develop and the infant's visual sense begins to dominate; she can lift up her own head when lying prone (on her belly) and look at the world from a vertical (human) position for the first time; she can bring her hands together at the mid-line of the body, the significance of which is great – there is a sense of touching and knowing self as this happens, which brings a new level of self-awareness; and hand-eye coordination, which enables manipulation of the outer world, is developing. These events bring the infant to a new level of consciousness, a new level of sensory-motor functioning, and into the phase of development of the sense of core self. In therapeutic work, the spinal movement patterns, and other related sensory-motor reflexes and activities can be practised, in order to support the development and full embodiment of the senses of emergent and core self.

Relating: bonding and separating, boundaries and space

As Stern proposes, the many issues with which the infant, child, and adult are confronted in the process of developing relationship to self and other, are not processes to be dealt with once and for all at age-specific stages. Rather, we are continually engaged with the dissolving and recreating of the senses of self, moment to moment and throughout the life cycle. A similar spirallic patterning of developmental tasks can also be observed in the progress of the infant's mastery of sensory-motor skills. Certain principles recur at each stage of development, so that the infant is repeatedly confronted with the processes of merging, separating, dependency, autonomy, and so on, embodied within her developing movement capabilities.

The four basic neurological patterns

There are four basic neuromuscular coordinations that the infant embodies, in sequence. They are: *spinal* (fish-like movement – propelled by the spine); *homologous* (amphibian/frog-like movement – two upper limbs and two lower limbs move simultaneously); *homolateral* (reptilian movement – right arm and leg, and left arm and leg move simultaneously); *contralateral* (mammalian movement – upper limb moves simultaneously with lower limb of opposite side) (see Figure 5.1 in the previous chapter).

Bonnie Bainbridge Cohen observed that the way in which a movement was initiated, sequenced through the body, and completed, was also significant. She defined two patterns of initiation: a yield and push, which levers the body out of a supporting surface; and a reach and pull, which draws the body into space (see Appendix 1). Each of the four basic locomotion patterns is first mastered in relation to the earth; the infant yields her weight into the ground, or other supporting surface, and through this contact is able to push herself up out of, or along, the supporting surface, as in crawling. The yield and push patterns are associated with an inwardly focused attention, an absorption with body sensation, weight, gravity, movement, and the muscular effort required to lift the body up out of the ground. They concern the process of embodying a sense of emergent self. As each new pattern of organization begins to develop, the infant returns to the yield and push initiation, in order to gain stability at the new level. Once mastered, the push transforms into a reach into space, and the body is pulled along in the direction of the reach. Here the space and outer environment support the infant's outwardly focused attention. These phases mark a greater curiosity in and attention to external events, people, and objects, as the world is explored through the senses of touch, taste, smell, hearing, and vision; the sense of core self and core other is developing.

Bonding – yielding weight into gravity

As described earlier, a basis for bonding and establishing boundaries has already been experienced at the cellular level, and this will affect the infant's ability both to bond and to establish personal boundaries as she negotiates her relationships with others. Yielding is a physical expression of, and support for emotional and social bonding; bonding is first experienced in relation to the body of the mother, and the earth, as the infant yields her weight into her supporting surfaces. If the support is not felt to be secure and responsive to her needs, the infant cannot yield fully, and bonding will not be complete. Adequate physical touch and holding are essential to the bonding process, and to physical and psychological wellbeing; this begins in the womb at the cellular level, but continues in various forms throughout life. A pronounced and prolonged lack of touch and holding in early life are now recognized as causes of severe dysfunction and even death. Questioning the diagnosis of AIDS amongst babies in Romania, Molly Ratcliffe writes:

> Haunting photographs and TV footage showed infants and children wasting away, staring forlornly from inhospitable rooms, lacking even the basic necessities of survival; rocking themselves obsessively in corners and lying immobile in cots. Their symptoms were respiratory infections, failure to gain weight, recurrent fevers, mental retardation, stunted growth. On the surface it looked like an epidemic, a tragedy of epic proportions . . .
>
> But . . . the list of symptoms mimics with startling exactitude those observed, since the turn of the century, in babies reared in orphanages elsewhere . . . Evidence from a wealth of research indicates that what they actually suffered from was sensory deprivation, ie. not receiving enough physical contact. Sparse staffing was found to be the cause; infants were dying of loneliness and inadequate stimulation (Ratcliffe, 1995).

Understanding of the importance of mutual holding between parent and child has led Judith Kestenberg and her colleagues to develop therapeutic programmes for mothers who are experiencing difficulties in bonding with their infants. Concurrent with infant therapy, the mothers are trained to be aware of their own bodies, and to develop postural and movement patterns which enable them to hold, and thus bond with their babies more securely. Their work shows that:

> (1) Early failures in mutual holding lead to a distortion of the body image, to an insufficient development of trust and empathy, and to a difficulty in holding-oneself-up and becoming self-reliant; (2) movement training of mother and infant is a method of choice to prevent sequelae of holding failures; (3) insight gained from infant-therapy through movement retraining helps us understand adult patients whose body attitudes reveal their attempts to hold themselves up by putting strain on their neck, back, or shoulders; (4) the analysis of the defensive use of certain parts of the body for self-support reveals the underlying fear of falling, collapsing or falling apart (Kestenberg and Buelte, 1977).

Separating – pushing to support oneself

At each level of movement development, and building upon the experience of bonding with the mother or primary carer, the infant first yields her weight into the earth, creating relationship to a supportive ground from which she can move. This enables the impulse for pushing or levering out of the ground through the supporting limbs of the infant's body. In this way she masters rolling, crawling, and a multitude of manoeuvres that enable her to move around. As the infant separates from the mother-ground in this way, she gradually gains more independence and autonomy, in preparation for later reaching out in an intentional way towards contact and union with another.

The pushing activity gives proprioceptive feedback through the nervous system, stimulates body tone, and helps to establish the sense of a body-self boundary. The continuum of movement process from yield to push embodies the transition from preconscious bonding or merging experiences, to separation and individuation, and it is a continuum we are constantly moving back and forth along, balancing and rebalancing as our need for these experiences changes. However, what we learn from the movement process is that if the yielding and bonding are not fully embodied, the push will not be supported in an easy and natural way, and may be fraught with effort and insecurity.

Working with the continuum from yield to push can be helpful for clients who need to feel their boundaries more clearly, who feel unsupported or have difficulty in trusting self and other, or who feel insecure in their ability to stand up for themselves. In working with one student during a workshop, I was gently feeding in pressure through her hand, and asking her to explore pushing against this resistance, as a preparation for the push patterns. Her response was either to collapse and give in to the pressure, or to sharply and rigidly extend out her arm against my hand. She connected this to a life pattern which she described as 'all-or-none with no gradual in-between. In my desire to get there and be useful, I have great difficulty in living through the in-between time – the time of transition from conception of a hope, a dream, to its incarnation or birthing.' The push patterns are also about fully incarnating, embodying, discovering our own strength, the power to act in the world; when supported by the responsiveness of the yield, our pushing, asserting actions can bring us into clear relationship with whomever or whatever we are engaged. Without the continuum of yield to push, we may collapse, give in, stubbornly resist, or rigidly defend, which takes us out of right relationship.

In order to clarify and strengthen the yield and push patterns, the limbs need to integrate into the body centre, as in the navel radiation pattern, and specific alignment and bodywork techniques are sometimes used to facilitate this. Emotional issues relating to support, boundaries, self-assertion, and will are often associated with the yield and push patterns, and exploration of these movement patterns can support work in such areas.

Another student described her experiences during a training weekend that focused on the integration of the upper limbs into the spine through bodywork and the developmental movement patterns:

> . . . When allowing spontaneous movements I would move into a pattern of torsion whereby my left arm and shoulder would twist around to my back (as if having my hands tied behind my back); the feeling would be that my shoulder needed to twist more to be able to tap into something, but it never quite made it.
>
> . . . After the first day I had a strong dream regarding issues around male viola-tion of my boundaries, especially around my sexuality. The next day more work on my left shoulder: I became aware of the image of an empty warehouse with cobwebs in there. Over the lunch memories were coming back to me of a traumatic period several years ago in a relationship. I start 'seeing' how much of the sexual blame I took for things that weren't my fault. The term 'shouldering the blame' kept coming to me.
>
> During the afternoon, more work on the shoulder, and the torsion became very strong. I felt a great pressure in my heart and throat as if I had been hit so hard that I was winded and could hardly breathe. Many memories of male violation and fear came up.
>
> Even though there were many tears and feelings of pain, I was also aware that underneath all that I had been healed.
>
> After the work, I initially felt relief, an understanding of the source of the torsion, another insight into my own body and life experience, and a good feeling to experience the deep healing underneath.
>
> The long-term effects will be filtering through for a long time. However, there has been a major issue in the last six months about a particular man violating my space and not taking any notice of me saying NO! This recently came to a head and I confronted him in front of the group that we were both part of. I felt 'heard' by others in the group and also 'heard' by his unconscious violator; even though he

still pleaded his innocence, something in me felt 'listened to'. This situation made many connections for me as I travelled back to the source of this pattern. Afterwards I was aware that something energetically had been completed which had been there most of my life.

Relating – reaching out into the world

The continuum proceeds from yield to push, to reach to pull, and as some of the experiences described in this section show, the transitions from one to the other are all-important. Each phase supports the next, and if one phase is not fully embodied, later movements will not be so well supported. In working with the developmental process we are particularly concerned with how transitions are made, with how each new phase is learnt, paying attention to what will support the transitions. For the infant, the major stimulus to move from the inwardly directed attention of the yield and push patterns, to the externally focused reach and pull patterns, is sensory information received from the environment.

Once a certain degree of security on the ground and within one's own sense of body-self has been established, curiosity and desire draw the infant to explore the world around her. The senses perceive, and actively initiate movement towards or away from people and objects, and new movement skills are mastered in the process of exploration and play. It is a phase of constant new discoveries and learning. Through the practice of yielding and pushing the child has internalized the support of the ground, and is now supported by the space as she reaches out and enters into new realms beyond her own body boundaries. If the push patterns have not been well enough integrated, reaching out and moving beyond known boundaries may feel insecure, unsafe, or she may lose her sense of self as she reaches too far out from her inner ground. Movement is now strongly motivated by desire, curiosity, and playful interaction, once gravity has been mastered, the support of the ground internalized, and the sense of one's own body boundaries integrated.

During explorations of the developmental sequence, Anna described yielding as difficult for her to fully embody, but once there she experienced rest, recuperation, playfulness, satisfaction, contentment:

> The yielding underlies the motivation to reach . . . If I allow myself to really go into yielding, I find my own timing. From there my liveliness awakens, my creativity, curiosity. If I don't allow myself to arrive, I can't find my own timing.

For her, the push patterns gave feelings of security, playfulness, alertness, enjoyment, and the wish to make contact, when moving close to the floor. At higher levels she experienced more difficulty and feelings of helplessness were evoked. She observed: 'I feel a connection between this pattern and a kind of childlike obstinacy.' When attempting the reach and pull patterns she felt she lost her connection to the ground and could not reach into space fully; this created anxiety and caused her to tire quickly. She found that the support of the mouthing pattern helped her to reach out into space, but became aware of a tendency: 'It is difficult for me to go for something unreservedly, not to give up. Often I lose the motivation, the power.'

She described a process of finding ways to deal with an uncomfortable pattern of symptoms that she often finds herself suffering from:

> I have seemingly no energy, or very diffuse energy. I am tired and nervous at the same time. I don't know what I can, or want to do. I don't enjoy anything really. I can't find calmness in myself.
>
> When I am in this state of mind, hands-on work is helpful. At first it is necessary to feel the ground. The hands of a partner help me to arrive. My awareness goes to her touch, and so other things become unimportant. I can leave my intention to have to do something. I can allow myself to rest, to yield. But if the touch is unspecific, after a while my attention goes away, inside myself. If I am only passive it is often not satisfying to me. To get in touch with the connective tissue or with the blood in the muscles wakes me up. I can relax and feel awake at the same time. Random movements without direction come up, playful movement. I want to feel into the space. I become curious. Mouthing. Then I want the touch within the movement. Through the touch more pleasure in moving comes up, and the wish to push. To push against someone. And with the pushing I change level. With the pushing I feel more structured and clear. I can start to move into space. I feel clear and awake and ready to do something. I can feel my power. My energy goes either into powerful movement or I feel like a little child and want to play with others. Now I can feel a clear energy.
>
> I think in this presenting symptom I lose my connection to my body. To get in contact with the connective tissue is the best way for me to find the connection again. I need the feeling that all parts of my body are connected. And through the blood I come in contact with the energy, which wants to go out into space. I feel lively.
>
> One effect of this experience is that I know how to come out of this terrible nervous energy. I know places in my body, where I feel more comfortable. I have started to use the energy of the connective tissue in my daily life.

Anna's process, discovered during a bodywork session, very clearly encapsulates the whole developmental process of embodying, of reinhabiting the body fully. She begins by receiving cellular touch, and can yield into the ground as she is met at this level. Attention to the blood and connective tissues of the body help her to find the random, playful movements of the navel radiation pattern. Then mouthing becomes a support, and curiosity is awakened. The pleasure of touch and movement bring her into pushing, and she can move to a higher level, feeling clear, powerful and awake, ready to play and to act. Again the blood connects her to the energy she needs in order to reach out into space in a lively and related way.

In working to find a transition from one stage or process to the next, we need to begin where the person feels secure, and look to the kind of support needed to make the next step. Without the appropriate support we stay, in a certain way, stuck at one level of development, unable to move forward and fully embody the next stages. This limits our choices, both as children and as adults, for action and relationship. Anna's process, outlined above, describes the need for support at the very first phase of cellular touch and yielding, in order for her to move through her developmental process in an organic and unforced way. Being witnessed through touch at the cellular level is the support needed for her to fully embody herself through yielding and pushing, and from this to move out into playful interaction and relatedness.

Archetypal movement processes

Inga, mentioned earlier, also described her explorations of the homolateral yield-and-push patterns:

> We were moving to music, very earthy. I came into moving from one side to the other side. Suddenly I feel as if I'm a bear, a little brown bear, very compact, but very able to move, and with a lot of power and joy in playing. It was such a strong image, and I needed a long time to come out of it. I had the feeling it must be similar to (native American) Indian women or men dancing, and suddenly there is the connection with an animal. I had the feeling it was 'my animal' coming to me. This feeling gives me a lot of power.
>   Normally I'm cautious when people talk about Indian and shamanic things – it's something from another tradition, and we are Europeans. But from this experience I had the feeling that maybe it's similar to what they do.

In exploring the early movement patterns of crawling, creeping, and so on, people often connect to other forms of plant and animal life, to moving in different environments, such as water or mud or air, and to feeling powerful changes in movement quality and energy, as this woman did. Grof (1985: 92–137) also noted the occurrence of identification with other life forms during perinatal experiences, and describes this connection to the transpersonal dimension in detail in his writings. Inga associated her experience, evoked through exploring the early movement patterns, with the sacred traditions of the shaman. Again we see that, as we go beneath or beyond the control of the ego and the mental self, we access other dimensions of being which connect us to our transpersonal nature, the level of collective mind, Jung's archetypal realms, where we may open into the spiritual core of our being.

Daniel's story

To elucidate the therapeutic application of some of these ideas I would like to describe Daniel's developmental movement story. I began working with Daniel when he was 7 years old, and we met weekly during school term-time for nearly four-and-a-half years. He was diagnosed as severely autistic, and thought to have additional learning difficulties. He also had a beautiful spirit that could not fail to charm and delight all who knew him. Daniel smiled and laughed much of the time, unless perturbed by something, when he would frown and jump up and down, nervously picking at his fingers. Despite his autistic symptoms, a mischievous, fun-loving, and warm personality shone through his typically bizarre behaviour.

In working with Daniel as a dance movement therapist, I used the theory and process of developmental movement therapy to orientate my work. Movement was our primary medium; psychological and relational process was contained within the movement work itself. I had access to little information about his personal history or development, so I allowed Daniel himself to guide and teach me, moment by moment. Staying present to a child who has difficulty in being present in the moment seemed an essential ground from which to work. Witnessing his movement was my primary tool; 'sticking' to him, a principle developed in T'ai Chi Ch'uan partner work, enabled me to follow the quick and subtle changes in his bodymind expression, and to be present to the fleeting openings that might invite contact.

From a developmental movement perspective, Daniel was not well embodied; he seemed to have missed fully mastering many of the early stages of movement development. He moved almost constantly, hopping up and down from one foot to the other on his tiptoes, as if trying to escape his body altogether and fly away to some higher world. Whenever there was an opportunity, he would climb. He was frequently to be seen balanced precariously on the ledge of a blocked out window, only toes and fingertips hanging on, or sitting on a chair that he had placed on top of a table. All of his efforts seemed to be striving to get him as far away as possible from the earth, and from the feeling of weight and substance that was his physical body. It is common for 'normally' functioning adults and children to show similar tendencies in their movement and postural expression, but not to the same degree as an autistic child displays; I found children like Daniel to be great teachers because they embody in such a visible way certain bodymind expressions that we may all share to some extent. We are different not in process but only in the depth of the disturbance. They display their inner desires and fears with such a total lack of inhibition or censorship that the unconscious is made transparent through their movement. An inability to complete the normal socializing process allows such children to express a purity of being rarely seen in a child or adult with ego functions intact.

My first goal with Daniel was to establish contact and create a trusting relationship, with movement as our medium. As he did not possess verbal skills, movement and also music were natural choices of therapy for him, and he was happiest when moving, whether dancing, swimming, or horse riding. Of course, making contact is the most difficult and probably frightening thing for an autistic child to do. Daniel would turn his face towards me, but determinedly avert his eyes; at the same time he would make complex manipulations of his fingers, quite unrelated to his gaze. A child who is unable to coordinate eyes and hands cannot clearly relate to and master his physical environment; it is an essential task which usually develops between about 3 and 6 months of age, the time when the core sense of self is also developing. A child like Daniel could not integrate a sense of core self; his movement expression showed a fragmentation of experience that would inhibit this. Further psychological development would also be limited, as there was no basis for the emergence of the senses of subjective and verbal self.

With Daniel I found that eye contact and hand-eye coordination could not be achieved without first going to earlier levels of development to find support for this major step. It was through the senses of touch and movement – proprioception and kinesthesia – that I was first able to make contact with him. As he gradually became accustomed to my presence in the room with him, and to being witnessed by me, he would allow moments of physical contact. Initially this might be as small as touching fingertips as he ran around the room in circles, one of his favourite activities. In time his movement would quieten and he would permit more contact.

Alongside establishing contact, another primary goal for Daniel was to support him in coming into his body and down onto the earth, dropping down from his constant hopping, jumping, balancing, and running activities. Until this could happen, he could not really start to fully embody the successive stages of the developmental process, or come into conscious relationship with another. Through witnessing and following his movement over a period of time, I could discern relative 'resting' phases, very brief, transitory moments when another energy entered his activity. These became openings for making fuller contact, and once he had experienced this, and felt safe enough, he began to enjoy being held and rocked. This reflected a very early developmental stage where full body contact, holding, and rocking, such as in the womb and in early infancy, enabled him to begin to feel his physical body, its weight, substance, and boundaries. Through such experiences the sense of an emergent self could be nurtured.

I would use these opportunities to encourage in him a sense of boundaries and containment, through gentle compression through the limbs, for example; this was a precursor to his eventually being able to push against my hands or feet. Daniel tended to avoid pushing, and thus had not mastered the basic creeping and crawling locomotion patterns. He rarely came down to the floor, and once down, did not know how to move about there, or how to get up again; he would fling his body into the air in a kind of horizontal leap if he wanted to stand up again. So from the body contact, we began to explore yielding weight and pushing. I also used some of the primitive postural reflexes which help to integrate the movements of the spine, arms, and legs that are necessary for coordinating more complex movement patterns. Eventually he was able to push himself over to sit or crawl or come up to standing in a fluid and integrated way. This enabled him to use the space more three dimensionally, and gave him more control of his body.

Out of this, we were able to explore his relationship to space more clearly. This can only happen once the child has developed a sense of body boundaries through experiencing the sensations of contact, weight, compression, and pushing movements, which help to establish the sense of a core self. A child like Daniel initiates movement primarily by reaching into space, and has not embodied the process of yielding weight into gravity and initiating through pushing against a supportive surface like the ground. We easily feel lost in space when we have not developed this foundation for movement, and this seemed apparent in Daniel's constant turning, hopping, running activity – he seemed never to come fully to rest and actually be in one place, fully on the earth.

To facilitate the transition into a more conscious relationship to the external space, we played with righting reflexes and equilibrium responses. Often we would sit or stand together in such a way that I was partly or wholly supporting his weight. Through small shifts of weight, moving in time to the music, I would bring him to the edge of his balance. His tendency when about to lose balance would be to curl up and simply fall to the ground, with no attempt to stop the fall or protect himself; it was as if he experienced no fear and no pain, though this pattern could also develop from feeling so much fear that normal responses are paralysed. So my focus here was to train his nervous system to embody the natural protective responses to loss of balance, so that he could master his relationship to gravity and space more fully. We spent a lot of time playing in the tiny moment between balance and falling, allowing him to experience fully the moment of imbalance; by supporting his body to find the protective responses that would stop him from falling, or enable him to fall safely, he could stay present and conscious in those moments.

For Daniel this was important work; it was through these games that we made our first real contact. Previously I had felt rather like an object, another piece of the furniture that he would sit on, or climb on, or be held within, merging in an unconscious way. Now our relationship began to develop in a more differentiated way, and he would respond to my movements playfully, dialoguing through the subtleties of touch and movement. The unpredictable quality of my movements in the balancing games seemed to bring his attention into the present, and he discovered that it was enjoyable, not threatening, to actually be here. In fact he delighted in these games so much that he would always request them. One challenge in working with such a child is that every new step mastered may become a new habit; once safe in a new activity, the child may want to stay there and retreat from further exploration. So we try to keep moving forwards, exploring the next challenge as his own readiness allows.

Following the developmental process, Daniel's mastery of space and of his own weight enabled him to embody with greater clarity and coordination the more complex movement patterns. He was now able to initiate movement by reaching into space, without losing his orientation. He could move more easily from standing to lying, could sit, crawl, and stand again in an integrated way, and without using excess effort. He now stood with his feet more firmly on the ground, and some of the tension in his body had released as he allowed the support from the ground below to hold him. I must add that these changes were often subtle and partial; he still liked to jump and climb, and sometimes he would still avert his eyes and play with his fingers. But he had also experienced other possibilities. He learned to coordinate his eyes with his hand movements, and would do this when he was not too distracted or nervous. Much time spent bringing awareness to his own movements and discovering where his curiosity and interest lay enabled him to eventually coordinate his gaze with an object he held in his hand; work with the primitive reflexes and with sensory stimulation facilitated this important step. He could also make eye contact for relatively extended periods of time, usually after we had moved together and experienced some meaningful contact through our shared dance. Daniel was not able to *consciously* develop his own dance movements, but he did learn to follow some of my movements, and to be aware when I mirrored his.

The developmental movement therapy occurred within the context of dancing together, often with music, and the general patterns of Daniel's own idiosyncratic movement repertoire. My focus was to introduce activities, or offer support for new movement experiences whenever an opportunity arose within our movement interactions; interventions were dependent upon the developmental tasks he was needing and ready to embody. It was never my intention to force him into a specific movement experience, but to facilitate him to complete the very subtle movement initiations embedded in his own habitual rituals, but not yet fully embodied. It is work that takes time and patience, but it is rewarding work when the light of conscious awareness is ignited in the child.

The process we went through over the years was not as linear as this description might suggest; there was much going back and forwards to integrate earlier stages of development, even while new skills were emerging. It is important that the child has a secure base from which to learn something new and he will often return to earlier stages of development that feel comfortable when about to take a step into something new and unknown. Beginning from a place that feels secure and safe enables new learning to take place organically. With a little support and encouragement, Daniel was able to make each transition into an unfamiliar and often feared experience by himself. This is an important aspect of the work; the moment when a new pattern is first embodied is the moment of greatest learning, and when the child makes this step for himself he realizes that he has achieved this through his own efforts. As for every child in the natural course of development, Daniel was always conscious of such moments and would express joy and pride in them. The effects of this learning are to enhance self-awareness and self-esteem, and give the child the confidence in his own ability to learn and master future tasks.

When working with such a child, our expectations must always be within the child's realistic capability. It is most likely that some achievements will always be beyond Daniel's reach. When I finished my work with him he was still unable to talk, although he could make some meaningful sounds and seemed to understand a lot of what was said to him. He was thought to have a speech impediment, distinct from his autistic tendencies, but I sensed that he longed to speak and communicate with us fully. After one session where we had both thoroughly enjoyed moving and dancing together, I was sitting on the edge of the table resting and talking to Daniel about our dance. He came up to me and looked intently into my mouth as I spoke, pointing in an inquisitive way. I had the clearest feeling that he wanted to know how I was making the sounds that came out of my mouth; he wanted to know how to speak, but all he could do was gesture with his hands. I asked what he was trying to say to me. He came close and dropped a light kiss on my cheek, then skipped away as if both shy and happy. It was a touching moment for me, and I felt that he too was aware that a depth of communication had taken place between us during the session that was quite special for him; his gesture seemed to be an acknowledgement of this.

It is unlikely that Daniel will emerge from his autism completely, as some more fortunate children do, but I content myself with knowing that small gestures such as this, and the consciousness they embodied, marked important moments for him; another crucial step in his development had been made, as he acknowledged a relationship that had become important to him. I often feel that I may have learned and received more from Daniel than I could ever give to him. His presence in my life was a gift, for he had the power to connect me to my own heart and spirit.

PART III

Somatic psychology in practice – the language of the bodymind

CHAPTER 7

Inner landscape of the body

When we explore the interior of the body, beyond skin surfaces and the contours shaped by muscle and bone, we discover a landscape as rich and varied as that of the earth, and an 'ecosystem' at least as miraculous as the complex interactive processes that constitute the living system that is Gaia herself (Russell, 1988; Lovelock, 1991). A whole universe exists within the boundaries of our skin that mirrors in all its extraordinary microcosmic detail the workings of the greater universe of which we are each a part.

Approaching any body, a human body or the body of the earth, we first meet with those structures which contain and define, protect and defend the integrity of that unique and individual life form.

Containment, protection, and defence: the integrity of the whole

Before we even touch the skin of another being, we encounter the person's energy field. The subtle body is thought of as an energetic matrix for the physical body, and extends beyond it into the space around us. Like the earth, the human body has a protective energetic 'skin', an invisible but palpable membrane that contains our subtle energy body. The earth's protective membrane, the ozone layer, ensures that harmful levels of ultraviolet radiation from the sun do not penetrate our atmosphere. But as we know, the pollution that we are manufacturing threatens to damage significantly and even destroy this first layer of defence. So too with the human body and its energy field; healer Lily Cornford (unpublished training notes) describes how certain drugs can damage the protective membrane of the aura, or subtle body, as can trauma and severe emotional stress. Disintegration of this 'skin' has profound and widespread effects on the person's mental and physical health. Cornford claims that schizophrenic states are associated with damage to this layer – an unboundaried state where the person is vulnerable to influences from both within and without, and the sense of integrity of the core self is lost.

Richard Moss claims that the acute openness and sensitivity of the schizophrenic can be experienced positively when the person is in a group of people sharing in an expanded and higher state of consciousness, such as occurs in the seminars he leads (Moss, 1986: 137-9). In such a situation where the collective energy becomes coherent, there is no need for the individual to defend against loss of boundaries, and the schizophrenic can feel comfortable and supported in this milieu. He also noted that smoking causes a person's aura to become more closed, more dense and boundaried, and suggests that people who are normally very sensitive and open to collective energies may need to smoke as a form of protection when they need to feel a greater sense of boundedness and separation. When we feel unboundaried and unprotected, we find substitute ways to defend ourselves if our environment feels threatening, incoherent, or overwhelming to us. However, smoking as a defence of course damages the physical body, and cuts the person off from a deeper sense of energetic aliveness and connectedness with others, as Moss describes.

The energy body is wholly interactive with the physical body; every energetic flow or blockage is reflected in the functioning of the bodymind, and each cell of the living body has an energetic counterpart. It is my own experience and observation that there are correlations between the condition of the membrane of the subtle body, the subjective experience of the skin and membranes of the physical body, the health of the immune system which is our primary system of internal defence, and the quality of psychological boundaries.

Skin

The skin is the body's largest organ. It wraps around and envelops the whole of us, defining the body's physical presence. As discussed earlier, it is the primary boundary, the first place of definition, of distinction between self and not self, and its importance in the development of a healthy sense of self is unquestionable. The skin is the interface and place of communication between inner and outer worlds, a place where transformations between those worlds take place. Earlier it was noted that the skin and the nervous system develop from the same layer of germinal tissue, the ectoderm. This intimate relationship connects the most exterior surfaces of the body with the deepest, the most interior surfaces of brain and spinal cord, and thus with the internal processes by which our whole being and doing in the world is mediated. As a sensory organ, the skin registers changes in contact, pressure, and heat; sensory nerves convey these impulses directly to the brain where they are transformed into perceptions of pleasure, pain, discomfort and so on. These perceptions inform our relationship to our self and our interactions with the external world. We learn about self and other as we brush against the world, meeting with both ourselves and another in each encounter we make.

A natural boundary, such as the skin, should be a place of meeting and interaction, a ground for the exploration of relationship, not an impenetrable barrier between separate worlds. But the skin may come to be experienced as a barrier separating us from the full experience of life around us. Such a relationship to our primary boundary may occur as a result of having been invaded in the past by contact we did not wish for or invite, whether physical, sexual, or emotional; but when the skin becomes defensive, it prohibits loving and nurturing contact as well as intrusive or abusive touch. A 'defensive' skin may also evolve because of a lack of nurturing touch in early childhood. The person must learn to 'hold' herself – a defensive boundary develops to hold herself together and protect against disintegration; opening to even loving touch may threaten the fragile coherence and integrity of the inner self.

On the other hand, the skin may be experienced as too insubstantial or permeable a boundary. I have witnessed this in clients who had in effect 'left' their bodies because of some deep hurt or trauma in their past. The dissociative state leaves them unable to embody the protective boundary that their skin affords, and thus renders them psychologically vulnerable and unprotected. In working with such a client somatically, it is common for awareness to be drawn immediately into the inner depths of the body, often directly to the organs. The experience of a too permeable skin may also be a consequence of inadequate holding, for it is through touch and holding that we develop the sense of a primary boundary; without it we cannot fully embody the sense of a distinct and boundaried self.

One client had felt 'invited' into an intimate sexual relationship where she felt held and was able to open to her childhood pain but was then abandoned by her partner. This left her feeling very vulnerable. She felt that she had lost her boundaries in this 'merging' contact with her lover and was afraid that if she contacted her deep feelings in therapy the same might happen there; she longed to be held but was afraid of becoming too vulnerable and dependent, losing her boundaries again. However, she wanted to explore this important issue; she knew that if she felt overwhelmed she would go 'out of her body', which left her more vulnerable, so she felt her task was to stay aware or notice when she was dissociating.

She chose to lie in a corner of the room with a blanket wrapped around her. I kept checking if my degree of closeness to her was all right, and asked if she wanted to be touched. This brought up the pain of separation, knowing the session would end soon and I would have to leave, so I did not touch but sat close to her while she talked about her need to be held as an infant. The front of her body needed contact, so she placed her own hand there to focus her attention on it, and cried deeply as she connected to her feelings of pain and grief. I was moved by her pain and felt a strong wish to hold her, but resisted it and simply witnessed her. She expressed a fear that I would not be able to sympathize with her feelings, and would judge her for being in this 'awful' state; it was important for her to know that this was not the case. Afterwards she felt relief at having contacted these feelings, and also surprise that she had not wanted the contact. It was more valuable for her at that moment to know that she could contact her deepest feelings and *not* lose her boundaries, which threatened to leave her too vulnerable. Only after this could she, in later sessions, receive and at times initiate contact safely.

Boundaries are about awareness. At the most fundamental level, the boundary is awareness of where I end and where you begin, but beyond that, awareness of what I need in order to maintain the integrity of my being, and how to meet that need in an ongoing way without violating the integrity of others. Relationship, in its myriad of manifestations, is the play in which we learn and develop awareness, and boundaries are the playground where we meet.

When working somatically with clients who need to explore their sense of boundaries, the skin may be the medium through which we first make contact. With the intention focused on the skin, different methods such as simple touch, stroking, or massage can be used to stimulate awareness in the skin. The therapist maintains some awareness of the tissues in her own body, which she is seeking to contact in her client; this both keeps her grounded in her own somatic experience, and enables her to 'resonate' or communicate information directly to the tissues under her hands (for a fuller description of the different body systems and principles of working with each somatically see Hartley, 1995). The process may involve dialogue about what the client experiences as contact is made, sometimes making and breaking contact several times as the client explores her experiences and personal meanings. This must be worked with sensitively, particularly when there is a history of abuse or trauma, so that the client's awareness, and thus her sense of personal boundary, can awaken gradually and according to her own timing.

Fat and subcutaneous connective tissue

Although the surface of the skin represents the primary physical boundary, other tissues of the body also provide protection, containment, and defence. If the skin does not offer an effective boundary, or indeed if it is open and receptive in a healthy way, our touch, when making contact, may settle or be drawn to deeper levels. The deepest layer of the skin contains connective tissue and fat, and this provides another level of protection. The connective tissue quite literally holds all of the body parts together; it is the major containing and supporting tissue of the body, and the superficial sheaths unite the body into one coherent and functioning whole. Fat acts as a shock absorber and insulator; it protects us, keeps us warm and comfortable, and also holds an immense amount of energy and power. Fat is a very disavowed part of the body in our Western culture, and some clients, especially women who feel they are overweight, may be confronted with deep anxieties, fear, and shame around their body image when focus is brought to this level. Somatic experience can be very different from body image, and my concern in working with fat is to support the client to experience it as a natural, life-supporting, warm, powerful, and pleasurable part of their being. Fat that is accepted can be explored, its energy, power, and the meanings it holds for the individual integrated, but so long as it is avoided the qualities it contains remain unembodied aspects of the personality.

Fat becomes problematic when its energy is held, static. As a second layer of protection, the fat may hold energy rather than allowing the energy to flow naturally through it; if people feel vulnerable they may hold energy in the fatty tissues as a protection against potentially harmful influences coming into them from outside, or the held energy of the fat may be used to stop their own feelings from flowing out. This may have a lot to do with why many women feel overweight in a society that expects them to be thin, requires them to be all things to all people, but discourages them from expressing their true feelings, especially their anger. In general, it is hormones that determine whether fat is held statically in the cells of the fatty tissues, or released to be used as energy, more than what the person eats or how much exercise they take. This means that the amount of fat the body holds onto in its static form is intimately connected to our emotional and mental states, as well as past conditioning, attitudes and beliefs, and hereditary factors, which are all woven into the unconscious neurohormonal processes of the body. Exploring how we hold onto or express our feelings, and how we deal with the emotions of the people around us may be helpful, when working with weight problems.

Immune system

Beneath the skin lies a network of very fine lymphatic vessels, which reach into the intercellular fluids of the body. They form part of the immune system that protects the body from infection and disease. The partially open ends of these vessels actively draw fluid into them, called lymph once it enters the vessels; the lymph flows with a slow sustained rhythm through the vessels towards the centre of the body. At certain points it passes through lymph nodes, specialized organs of the lymphatic system, where potentially harmful and toxic substances are broken down and depotentiated. The superficial vessels eventually join deeper channels, finally emptying their contents into major blood vessels near the heart. Once the lymph joins the blood flow, the waste products can be eliminated from the body, primarily via the kidneys as urine.

The lymphatic system operates in two distinct ways to maintain the health of the body. B-cells, which originate in the bone marrow, patrol the intercellular spaces and produce antibodies which protect the body from foreign 'invaders', such as toxins, bacteria, and viruses, before they cause disease. They are associated with 'antibody-mediated immunity'. T-cells mature in the thymus gland, and their function is to check cell membranes throughout the body for cells that are worn-out, damaged, or virus-infected; such cells are broken down and destroyed. This is called 'cellular immunity'. Thus the B-cells mediate protection from foreign bodies invading from outside, whilst the T-cells are concerned with the internal 'housekeeping', the removal of old and worn-out, infected or damaged self-structures (Baumgartner, 1995).

When the immune system is in good health, these two processes work together in balance, but under stress the balance is disrupted. Stress causes a heightening of sympathetic nervous system activity, which gears the organism towards 'fight or flight', towards an active engagement with the outer world. Sympathetic arousal also increases B-cell activity and decreases that of the T-cells, whilst parasympathetic arousal enhances the activity of the T-cells. Prolonged periods of stress and heightened sympathetic arousal which are not balanced by periods of parasympathetic rest and recuperation result in lowered T-cell activity and a failure of the processes of cellular immunity:

> Under the influence of stress the antibody-dependent immune responses are intensified, and the T-cell dependent immune responses are weakened. That means that in stress situations the defence against the intrusion of foreign living and inanimate material predominates over the internal 'clearing up' of cellular immunity.
>
> The concept of stress . . . states that the multiplicity of psychological, toxic, inflammatory and nutritional demands on the human organism all act towards enhancing performance related (fight or flight) metabolism, to the detriment of the recovery phases. Characteristic of reactions to each of the above stress factors is the dismantling of body reserves by switching the vegetative nervous system towards achievement, a process called sympathicotony. (Baumgartner, 1995: 6–7)

Similarly, in the area of psychological behaviour, we often see that under stress all of our reserves go towards fighting or fleeing from (or projecting onto) the enemy outside; we may be unable to pay attention to the 'housekeeping' work of maintaining our internal psychological health whilst all of the focus is upon defeating the enemy without. Under severe or prolonged stress the human being often resorts to a 'military' option, and loses contact with the natural processes of internal ecological balance, self-regulation, and healing.

Today we are collectively suffering a crisis in the areas of stress, immunity, and defence. Stresses of all kinds can adversely affect the balanced functioning of the immune system; poor nutrition, environmental pollution, drugs, tobacco and alcohol, emotional and mental stress all compromise the wellbeing of the human organism. On a global scale, the natural functioning of the human immune system has been further weakened by the widespread use of inoculations in childhood, and artificial means of attacking illness; the frequent use of drugs, such as antibiotics, weakens the body's natural immunity. Now we have complex diseases such as cancer, AIDS, and ME, all symptoms of a weakened immune response, for which we have no truly effective remedies. As new antibiotic-resistant viruses begin to threaten us, fear is now growing within medical circles that antibiotics may soon fail to provide the essential foundation of modern medicine.

I cannot help but wonder further about the relationship between our natural immunity, which has been so severely compromised by the stresses and excesses of the modern world, and the question of national and global defence. Governments are developing ever more remote, 'unnatural', and lethal weapons of war. Does this not bear some relationship to the fact that our natural physiological and psychological processes of protection are weakened and out of balance? As we lose our individual and collective ability to protect ourselves effectively, we come to depend more and more upon external and artificial means – the weapons of mass destruction, as well as the 'guns, knives, bombs, and chemical warfare' of invasive medical procedures. The focus of attack against an external enemy sometimes seems to obliterate the need to look within and attend to the internal disorder; projection onto the 'enemy' is felt to be easier. When our responses at the level of cellular and intrapsychic ecology are weakened, we may see only the option of fighting the enemy without, whether it be a virus or a neighbour threatening our territory. The virus only takes hold in the body if the immune system has been weakened by other stresses. We can only wonder if it is the same in the social and political arena; could it be that a state of internal balance and natural order might present a ground in which invasion could not so easily take hold? Is the condition of our collective immune response not reflecting the psychological and political realities of our world, and if so, what can we learn from our growing knowledge of psychoneuroimmunology, and our own bodymind processes, that could be applied to the political arena?

Finding balance

Working with clients with a weakened or imbalanced immune system necessitates paying attention to many areas simultaneously, with a focus on reducing the stress factors that are compromising their system; this usually involves somatic and psychological work simultaneously. Working somatically, I observe that stimulating a client's lymphatic system through focused touch or movement evokes a clearer presence, a more boundaried sense of self, and a feeling of empowerment. The feeling of clear boundaries can be embodied by allowing the presence of the lymphatic vessels and the slow sustained movement of lymph through them to support the body and its movement. Imagine simultaneously the active reaching outwards, from the centre of the body to its peripheries, of the fine lymphatic vessels; and the slow movement of the silvery lymph fluid through the vessels, towards the heart centre. The tension created by these counterbalancing flows creates a spatial tension between the centre and the peripheries of the body; we define our personal space, the limits of our kinosphere, whilst at the same time moving in towards the very centre, the heart centre of the self. The relationship between inner and outer is maintained in such a way that we can be aware of both simultaneously, equally. We see this balance most clearly in the movements of the master of aikido or t'ai chi ch'uan, martial arts which practise non-violent self-defence which respects both self and other equally. Such disciplines have a beneficial effect on the immune system, and also help us to understand that true defence is not about attacking and overcoming or destroying an opponent, but meeting and engaging fully with their energy in a way that neither party is hurt. We have much to learn from the wisdom of the ancient principles embodied in these practices.

To help bring the two processes of the immune system into harmony (the externally directed, 'yang' approach of the B-cells, and the internally focused, 'yin' approach of the T-cells), the sympathetic and parasympathetic branches of the autonomic nervous system must also be in balance. As we saw above, stress overactivates the sympathetic 'fight or flight' response, to the detriment of the processes of recuperation and cellular immunity associated with the parasympathetic branch, and the functioning of the T-cells. An immune system disorder requires that we support the body at the cellular level, encouraging an increased parasympathetic response that allows the natural healing processes of cellular immunity to be restored. Increased T-cell activity also enhances the function of B-cells, so periods of rest that allow the bodymind to return to its own rhythms can support both aspects of the immune system. Bodywork can be most effective in this respect, including all kinds of therapeutic touch and massage techniques, which aim to bring about relaxation, comfort, and a calming of the responses of the sympathetic nervous system.

Contacting the cells directly can be a profound way of supporting the natural healing processes of cellular immunity. The process of cellular breathing and cellular touch was discussed earlier in the chapter on foetal development. When we 'touch' the membranes of the cells with our awareness and a contact that is sensitive and focused, we bring energy to them. T'ai chi Master Liang puts it this way: 'When the mind moves, the mind intent is immediately aroused; when the intent is aroused, the 'ch'i' will immediately follow. So the heart (mind), the intent, and the 'ch'i' are closely connected like a circle' (Liang, 1977: 70).

Here we return to the correlation between the skin and the membranes of the cells as important boundaries, places of contact, communication, and choice, for it is at the membranes that certain 'decisions' are made that affect our health and wellbeing at all levels. The cellular membranes are involved in processes of actively accepting or rejecting, of drawing into the cell body or expelling, continuously making choices towards the health of the individual cell and the organism as a whole. The cellular membranes are acutely sensitive to chemical changes in their environment, which either support their healthy functioning or inhibit it, and these changes occur as a result of what we ingest – food, drugs, and so forth – hormones and neuropeptide messengers circulating in the blood stream, and other chemicals released by neurological and physiological activity. It is at the level of the cellular membranes that health or disease is ultimately decided, but the decision comes as a result of complex interactions between the nervous, endocrine, immune, and neuropeptide systems.

The cellular membranes form the primary internal boundaries of the bodymind, where the life process in its most fundamental form is contained, protected, and maintained. When the bodymind is out of balance, these internal boundaries are no longer able to function to support the health and integrity of the cell. As a result, the cell may be invaded by infectious or toxic substances; it may be 'rejected' or starved by the organism as a whole, and unable to take in the nutrients it needs to survive; or it may 'reject' the organism it is a part of and isolate itself in a process of cancerous growth. Disease may result when the healthy functioning of the cellular membranes is compromised, in the same way that psychological functioning can be impaired when psychological boundaries are weak, damaged, or overly defensive. To strengthen, soften, or clarify boundaries at all levels we can focus directly upon the cellular membranes, the skin, and the balance and healthy functioning of the immune system.

The sense of self in action

As we travel deeper into the interior landscape of the body we come to the muscles, and the connective tissue sheaths that wrap around the individual muscles and bundles of muscle fibres. The muscles are richly supplied with networks of blood vessels and nerves. The blood supplies the nutrients and oxygen necessary for the muscle cells to do their work, and removes the waste products of their metabolic processes. Sensory and motor nerves form a continuous feedback circuit between muscles and tendons, and the central nervous system. This constant flow of information enables us to act with intention, precision, and mastery. The neuromuscular system mediates agency, will, and the directives of the ego-self. On our planet earth, it is represented by the multitude of mobile and sentient life forms, which have the ability actively to meet their own needs or consciously manipulate and alter their environment. The way in which we use our muscles precisely reflects the habitual tendencies of the personality and the formation of character, as Reich and Lowen's work has so clearly demonstrated.

In the process of development, as described earlier, the motor nerves that serve the muscles mature before the sensory nerves; we move first, and information about this movement is then conveyed back to the central nervous system via the sensory pathways. This in turn stimulates more movement and new sensory impressions. Through movement we receive feedback and learn about ourselves, discover ourselves as embodied beings who can act upon and affect the world. I move myself, and thus feel myself. This has a fundamental implication for psychological development too; it supports the view that we are not a 'blank slate' at birth, or even in the womb, but that self-generated activity facilitates the embryonic development of self-awareness and psychoneurological growth.

A client needing to develop or strengthen her sense of a core self will need to feel her own muscular strength, her agency, her ability to direct her energy in a focused and intentional way that achieves the results she seeks. For one client this came during an authentic movement session. For some time she had been following her inner movement impulses, often experiencing a sense of disconnection between parts of her body, which engendered feelings of helplessness and frustration. On this occasion she found the strength in her arms to push her whole body backwards across the floor in a powerful, integrated, and harmonious movement; her movement evoked for me the image and feeling of a wild cat creeping backwards in preparation for attack. She described this movement as pushing herself out of a stuck place, finally finding the strength and physical connectedness to move out of an experience that had frustrated her for a long time. This came about when she was able to embody fully the musculature of her whole body in a coordinated and active expression of intent. Afterwards, it was important to her that she could see the tracks her hands had left on the carpet as she pushed powerfully backwards, a confirmation that she had moved as she had intended to do.

Muscular system

In work with people whose sense of self is very vulnerable and unformed, or those suffering psychotic conditions, the muscles are an important system to embody. Specific exercises or clear movement sequences which stimulate active muscular engagement and coordination, and are directed by the conscious ego, help to evoke the sense of self in action. The young child learns to master both self and the external environment through her physical interactions with the world; so, too, can a vulnerable client be helped to experience a sense of agency and mastery through movement that challenges her to engage her own strength, power, and physical ability in consciously directed muscular activity.

The muscles give us a sense of activity and vitality, of strength, competence, and confidence, or of lethargy, weakness, lack of interest and motivation, depending on how they are functioning. This, of course, is influenced by many complex factors, including biochemical, nutritional, psychological, and environmental conditions. In general, we tend to feel better both physically and mentally after exercising. As well as stimulating the movement of energy through the body and helping the process of detoxification, movement can also release emotional stress; an activated sympathetic nervous system and stimulated adrenal glands need channels of physical expression before balance can be regained.

How we use our muscles affects the way they function, and this influences the way we feel, which in turn affects the way we use the muscles; cycles develop which can be beneficial or limiting to different degrees. The muscles may be used with a passive quality, not fully involved in the task at hand and in life; in an aggressively attacking way; in a tense and withholding way; or in an actively engaged way. This affects the tone, the degree of readiness for action, of tightness, looseness, boundness, or flaccidity of the muscles. Different muscle areas may differ in their quality of tone, each expressing a particular attitude to life, though an individual body may also have an overall feeling of muscular quality, such as a muscle-bound, relaxed, tense, fluid, or weakened state.

These states, and the feelings and attitudes that the muscles embody, can be explored psychologically. We may discover subpersonalities living in different areas of our muscular being, with different voices, needs, and information for us. Muscular tension is not 'bad' in itself, and it is not always appropriate to release tensions. It may be more useful to explore the function of the tension. For example, is it helping to support us because there is not enough support in our life, or do we need the tension because we need to get more of a grip on our life, not release it? Until such issues are addressed at the level at which they need to be, and alternative sources of support contacted, releasing muscular holding patterns may not be useful.

Each muscle use evokes a corresponding state of mind and feeling. For example, muscles that are long and released tend to create and reflect a relatively open and unboundaried or expanded state of mind, whilst short, contracted muscles tend to make us feel more substantial, bound, or contained. Depending on whether a person would benefit from feeling more open and expansive, or more contained and substantial, exercise and somatic therapy can be focused to meet their individual needs. The Alexander technique, for example, will create length and sensations of space in the muscles and in the body generally. On the other hand, a workout at the gym is more likely to create compact muscles and produce feelings of strength and substance. Through conscious choice of exercise programmes we can affect the general state of the muscles, and influence corresponding feeling states and attitudes to life; this alters the sense of self and the quality of ego boundaries.

Working somatically with specific muscle areas, we can repattern the way the muscles are used, which may enable old outgrown habitual patterns of perception and behaviour to be released too (Hartley, 1995: 157-80). The nervous system works through patterns. Throughout our lives, from conception to death, we are constantly receiving sensory impressions, forming meaningful perceptions and interpretations of those impressions, and acting in response to what we have perceived. Patterns of response become more firmly established within the sensory-motor circuitry of the neuromuscular system the more frequently they are repeated. This encoding process is at its most active during the early formative years of life; the messages perceived and responses developed in infancy and early childhood form the basic patterns upon which all subsequent ones will be elaborated. Thus habits are formed, and become part of the subconscious encoding of the brain. It is usually not possible to alter the habits of our neural conditionings without bringing them into consciousness. Psychotherapy approaches this through the exploration of unconscious feelings, behaviour, belief systems, and relationship patterns. Somatic therapy seeks to make conscious the unconscious patterning at the level of neuromuscular use, and to introduce other possibilities that will support more efficient functioning. This may be done through combinations of focused touch, sensory awareness, mental imagery or directions, and consciously directed movement. The mind of the muscles, or their unconscious patterning, will only change when consciousness touches them, and a new way of responding can be felt and initiated.

Important in this is the balance between sensory and motor processing. Learned messages to 'see but don't touch', constant criticism or prohibition, demands to achieve, or lack of appropriate stimulation in the child's environment are a few of the ways in which imbalances in sensory-motor processing can be established. If the cycles of sensation-perception-motor response cannot be fulfilled adequately, enough of the time, then blocks in perception, motor ability, or emotional expression can result. Corresponding attitudes and beliefs evolve as the child matures, and are constantly reinforced by the underlying neurological patterning, unless significant alternative experiences can be introduced. The psyche, like the body, tends towards healing and wholeness when given the right conditions. It is these conditions that therapy, somatic or psychological, seeks to provide, so that the client's own self-healing and self-regulating processes can be activated.

Finding the inner ground

Bones

Bones are the earth, the bedrock of the body. Moving through the superficial and deep layers of muscle, our touch meets with the relative firmness and solidity of the bony tissues. The skeleton provides the internal structure and framework of the body which, together with the muscles and connective tissues, enables us to lift ourselves up out of gravity to stand and move across the surface of the earth. It is an incredible feat when we stop to think about what is actually involved.

The skeletal structure develops in utero as cartilaginous tissue and only gradually, during prenatal and postnatal life, does it change into bone; this occurs as minerals are deposited within the cartilage moulds, giving the bone its strong and relatively stable character. Bones are living tissue; they contain fluids, bone cells, blood vessels, nerves, and connective tissue, and like all living tissues they respond to the forces acting upon them and are continually renewed throughout life. But they also contain a high percentage of inorganic minerals that come originally from the earth's rocky substrata, connecting them intrinsically to the earth and to a sense of durability and ancient history. Of bones, Clarissa Pinkola Estes writes:

> In archetypal symbology, bones represent the indestructible force. They do not lend themselves to easy reduction. They are by their structure hard to burn, nearly impossible to pulverize. In myth and story, they represent the indestructible soul-spirit. We know the soul-spirit can be injured, even maimed, but it is nearly impossible to kill. (Estes, 1992: 35)

Because of their almost indestructible, immortal quality, bone has been associated in many religious cultures with death and rebirth, with new life springing from the old, with destruction, decay, and regeneration. Bones have been associated with the seeds of new life, that which survives death and destruction, since the beginnings of time. Estes describes how, like the ovaries, home of our female seeds, the bones yield:

> . . . Knowing from deep within the body, deep within the mind, deep within the soul. The symbols of seed and bone are very similar. If one has the root stock, the basis, the original part, if one has the seed corn, any havoc can be repaired, devastations can be resown, fields can be rested, hard seed can be soaked to soften it, to help it break open and thrive. (Estes, 1992: 33-4)

Connecting to the bones of our being connects us to that which is enduring, essential, ancient, grounding, and healing of soul and spirit. They connect us to life in its most fundamental, secure, and lasting form. When we feel lost, ungrounded, insecure, cut loose without an anchor, the bones can help to bring us home. They give us a basis, a root, a place to rest in and to move out from into new ventures, new life. Caroline Myss associates the bones with the first chakra of the body, which she describes as the 'tribal chakra'. This chakra is also connected to the spine, pelvis, feet, and the immune system, those parts that give us our grounding, our connection to the earth, and the ability to defend ourselves or 'stand our ground'. Describing the energy of the first chakra, Myss (1997: 103-4) writes:

> Archetypally the word 'tribal' connotes group identity, group force, group willpower, and group belief patterns. All of these meanings make up the energy content of our first chakra. The first chakra grounds us. It is our connection to traditional familial beliefs that support the formation of identity and a sense of belonging to a group of people in a geographic location.
> . . . The first chakra is the foundation of emotional and mental health. Emotional and psychological stability originate in the family unit and early social

environment. Various mental illnesses are generated out of family dysfunctions . . .
First chakra energy manifests in our need for logic, order, and structure. This
energy orients us in time and space and to our five senses.

We develop our sense of identity first through our relationship to our family
and cultural 'tribe', and in this process we internalize the beliefs,
superstitions, fears, strengths, and weaknesses carried by our group of
origin. Difficult issues relating to experiences within the familial and cultural
group as children bring people into therapy; here they can sift, sort, and
unravel the harmful effects of their conditioning, to establish a separate and
healthier identity of their own, based upon their own values and beliefs.
Work at the level of the first chakra usually forms the basis of psychotherapy,
and can be approached through the body as well as through explorations of
personal history, and the fears, limitations, and belief systems inherited from
the tribe. The health of the bones and the immune system is integral to first
chakra issues:

> Immune-related disorders, chronic pain, and other difficulties with the skeleton
> are energetically activated by weaknesses in personal tribal issues. Difficult tribal
> challenges cause us to lose power primarily from our first chakra, making us
> susceptible – should a challenge become an extreme stress – to immune-related
> diseases. (Myss, 1997: 106)

Embodying the bones

Just as energy can be brought to the skin as primary boundary, or the
lymphatic system of defence, by focusing attention and touch there, so too
with the bones. Embodying the bones through movement or touch helps us to
experience their supportive and grounding presence within us. In particular,
weight or compression passing through the bones stimulates proprioceptors
in the bones and joints so that awareness of their supportive potential is
awakened. The skeleton is meant to carry the weight of the body, being the
densest tissue, but also flexible and resilient to forces acting upon it. The
bones are felt most clearly when they are well aligned and weight passes
clearly through them, rather than through surrounding soft tissues such as
muscles or organs. Specific techniques and exercises can be used to facilitate
clear alignment at the joints; this might also include focus on the ligaments,
the periosteum – the connective tissue 'skin' that wraps around the bones – or
the marrow which fills and flows through the spaces within the bones.

Because their nature is so fundamental to psychological wellbeing and to
the developing senses of self, one can usefully work with bones in any
therapeutic situation. As a ground, structure, and container for the inner
processes of the bodymind, we can always benefit from being reminded of
their presence within us. In somatic work I often use the skeletal system as a
basis from which to explore other body systems. The clarity and relative
stability of the bones offers an anchor by which the energies of the more

fluid and mobile tissues of the body can be integrated. I also find it useful to align the joints when patterning the early developmental movement sequences, for without clear skeletal integration it is difficult to embody these movements with ease and a sense of internal connection. Focusing upon the skeletal system, aligning the bones and experiencing them as supportive structures within us usually facilitates release in surrounding tissues, such as muscles and organs. As the deep support of the skeleton is felt and embodied, it becomes possible to let go of holding in the soft tissues; almost as a byproduct of working with the bones, tensions can be released and muscle use repatterned.

A well-balanced skeletal structure creates a clear physical and energetic connection with the earth; when we align ourselves with the earth energy in this way, we feel supported, strengthened, integrally connected to and part of the great earth body which is our outer home and ground. And, as Marion Woodman points out, grounding in the root chakra and earth element is essential for spiritual opening, as well as psychological growth: 'The grounding of the life force in the lowest chakra has to be secure, open to the energies of the earth, before the radiance of the spirit can take up residence' (Woodman, 1990: 40).

Gut feelings and the wisdom of instinctual life

Deepening to the innermost spaces of the body we find the rich and varied terrain of the viscera, the internal organs and glands, whose work it is to ensure the continued survival of the physical body and of the species. They embody the vegetative processes of nature, attending to the creation, nurturance, repair, reproduction, growth, decay, and death of living tissue. The miraculous balance of plant and animal life, which sustains our planet and its myriad forms of life, is reflected in the complex life-sustaining processes of the organs of the body, and the harmonious interactions between them.

The organs are fully developed and some of them are fully functioning in the early stages of uterine life. Long before the cartilaginous framework of the skeleton has been transformed into bony tissue, and before the muscles are able to function in a coordinated and controlled way, the organs are carrying out their life-creating and life-preserving tasks. The organs are in constant motion, contracting, pulsing, changing form and position as they do their work. They may also move, shift their position, contract, slacken, or torque out of alignment as a result of emotional stresses, thought patterns, and habitual patterns of use. As the organs are functioning from such an early age, they are already being imprinted in the womb with the movement traces of psychosomatic life. We carry our emotional history in our organs, along with the attitudes and beliefs that our emotional experiences have led us to adopt (Cohen, 1993).

Organic process is constantly changing and evolving, as is our emotional life, and some of the tensions and torques we experience in the organs can be transitory phenomena, the natural expressions of a life force that is sentient and responsive. But there can also be more deep-seated imbalances that may have roots in earlier life experiences. Unwinding these torques and tensions requires mindful touch and movement, and awareness and integration of the feelings and attitudes that might have been held in the tissues. Each organ tells a unique story, holds particular feelings and attitudes, and may embody an aspect of the self, a subpersonality, with its own needs, behavioural patterns, and purpose to fulfil. In our internal world they interact and cooperate with greater or lesser degrees of harmony, towards the benefit of the whole organism.

Digestion

Through the organs and glands of the digestive system we receive nourishment from outside; digestion is a process of breaking down the plant, animal, and mineral substances ingested so that they become usable. Then the body chooses what it will assimilate into its own tissues and what it will let go of; thus a small part of the external world becomes an integral part of us as it is absorbed eventually into the cells of the body. At the most intimate level we are a part of the world we inhabit.

The process of digestion occurs on many levels – physical, emotional, social, intellectual, and spiritual. Our first nurturance is of the body, and our relationship to the process of feeding in the womb and as infants sets a 'template' for the way in which we will approach the processes of nourishment at other levels. How we accept or reject, digest, assimilate, make use of, and let go of what we do not need, in terms of emotional, social, mental, and spiritual 'food', can be profoundly affected by the way we were fed and received nourishment in early life. The organs of the digestive system embody attitudes and patterns of response in relation to nurturing and nourishment; they also hold the memory of feelings associated with past experiences in this area.

The heart

Feelings and attitudes associated with other life processes are also embodied in the organs. The heart circulates nourishment, energy, healing, and information around the body, and embodies the healing love and compassion that reaches out to others and enables growth and wellbeing. When its energy is blocked, it may express fear and withholding. The body cannot survive without the heart; if it ceases to beat, the cells do not receive oxygen and nutrients and cannot metabolize energy. Life is dependent on the constant receiving and outpouring of the heart. Similarly, emotional and social life is sustained by the bonds of love and compassion we feel for and from others. Without these, personal relationships and the whole fabric of society begin to disintegrate. The heart is associated with the fourth chakra, which Myss (1997: 197) describes as the chakra of emotional power:

> The fourth chakra is the central powerhouse of the human energy system. The middle chakra, it mediates between the body and spirit and determines their health and strength. Fourth chakra energy is emotional in nature and helps propel our emotional development. This chakra embodies the spiritual lesson that teaches us how to act out of love and compassion and recognize that the most powerful energy we have is love.

Respiratory system

The lungs and respiratory system mediate inspiration and expiration, the passage of the breath of life into and out of the body. They concern the process of birth and death as the ongoing moment to moment reality of life; breath, life energy, new ideas are inspired, they are absorbed and materialized, then released, expired, allowed to die. The natural processes of beginnings and endings, meetings and partings, births and deaths and how we relate to them may be expressed in our patterns of breathing; do we grasp for breath and life, try to hold onto it, or expel it too soon before it has fulfilled its creative potential. The lungs also relate to fourth chakra energy; feelings of grief, sorrow, and sympathy for others are embodied here, as expressions of our feelings about loss and letting go, and our sense of connectedness to other beings.

Reproductive organs

The reproductive organs are of course concerned with physical creativity and the continuation of the species, but energetically they are also associated with creativity that does not necessarily go into making new human beings. The energetic seeds of our creative ideas are formed in the ovaries or testes, and gestated into form in the womb, or released into the world through the penis, to be materialized there. Our creativity belongs to us, and we are responsible for it; it must be nurtured, attended to, given space for growth, whether it is a baby, a work of art, a beautiful garden, a business venture, or a scientific idea that is being created. Difficulties around our creativity and its expression in the world are often expressed in diseases of the reproductive organs; relationships, work, money, and home issues are all related to our creativity, and problems in these areas may also contribute to reproductive organ diseases. For women, issues around the giving and receiving of nurturing may also be expressed through problems in the breasts; the enormous increase in cases of breast cancer in recent decades indicates that this is an area that urgently needs attention (see Northrup, 1995, for an inspiring and practical exploration of women's health issues and the relationship between the female organs and psychosocial issues). Many women have never learned to nurture themselves or felt they were entitled to do so, and an exclusive focus on supporting others' lives and creativity can have detrimental consequences for a woman's health.

Urinary system

The body also systematically cleans up its wastes. As well as the process of elimination, which is the final stage of the digestive process, the urinary system is essential in this function. The kidneys are constantly filtering the blood and eliminating wastes and toxic substances through urine, which exits the body via the bladder. They monitor the constituency of the blood, checking that it contains the correct balance of water, nutrients, minerals, and chemical substances optimal for the healthy functioning of the body as a whole. If the kidneys break down, metabolic balance cannot be maintained and life is at risk. Ensuring that we do not have too much of something that could be harmful to the body is as important as ensuring we receive enough nourishment, for the biochemical balance of the body is very delicate indeed. The fact that many people today suffer from stress and exhaustion in their kidney area suggests that the kidneys are having to work overtime to keep our bodies in balance and free of toxic substances, in the face of an increasingly polluted environment and stressful lifestyle.

According to traditional Chinese medicine, the vital life force, or chi energy, is thought to reside in the kidneys. Stress and pollution in the internal and external environments weaken the life force and this puts the whole organism at greater risk of disease and breakdown. Together with the immune system, the kidneys' job is to ensure that the internal environment is free of life-threatening and toxic substances, and provide the delicate biochemical balance in which life can flourish. The health of the kidneys, as well as the immune system, is affected by our psychological state and the psychic ecology of the environment in which we live; both individual and collective psychic 'pollution' creates work for these organs of detoxification, and can put them under stress.

Endocrine glands

The glands of the endocrine system are also essential to the internal balance of the body. They form a major chemical messenger system of the body. In evolutionary development, the chemical processes of the endocrine system preceded the electrical processes of the nervous system. It is an older and slower means of communication, but it works in coordination with the nervous system, the immune system, and the neuropeptide system to regulate the many processes of metabolism, growth, reproduction, and repair. Endocrine glands secrete hormones directly into the bloodstream. The hormones target specific organs or tissues, causing their cells to respond in certain ways, but they also circulate through the blood and can influence us in a more general way as well. Every woman knows the monthly effects on her moods caused by the cyclical changes in hormonal activity. Men, too, have periodic cycles, although they tend to be less obvious than women's. Imbalances in hormone production can cause problems on many levels, from changes in weight, to depression or irritability, tiredness or hyperactivity, reproductive problems, and general metabolic disorders. Immune system functioning and autonomic nervous system activity are also affected.

Energetically the endocrine glands live close to the core of our being. They are thought to be one of the subtlest manifestations of energy in the physical body, forming a link between the physical body and the energy body through their close connection to the chakras (Bailey, 1975). Whilst the organs express the ongoing processes of psychoemotional life, the endocrine glands embody the archetypal energies associated with our deepest instincts, intuitions, and body wisdom. Energetically they pattern the functioning of other body systems, including organs, muscles, and skeletal alignment, and influence our perceptual processes. Highly sensitive to chemical and nervous stimulus, they also respond to and influence thought and feeling. Consciously making contact with the glands can bring us in touch with the archetypal world of instinct, image and the dreams of our collective cultural heritage. It is a world of rich creativity and intuitive knowing, which pulses between balance and chaos. The endocrine glands embody powerful energy centres, and could be likened to the 'sacred sites' of our earth-body, where according to ancient tradition people go to seek wisdom, knowledge, and healing. In therapy they can be contacted and dialogued with when information and insight is needed, and they can be given attention and healing when balance needs to be restored to the bodymind.

Communication and integration

It is impossible to explore the body without encountering those body systems which connect and integrate all of the interacting parts into a functioning whole. The connective tissue, blood, lymph, and nervous system have already been mentioned; together with other circulatory fluids, they form the networks of transportation and communication, and the fabric which gels the whole together. They represent our internal 'oceans, rivers, and streams', and the 'roads, railways, and telecommunication networks' that link our interior world into a functioning whole. Together they facilitate the ecological balance of the body through intricate and complex interactions.

Connective tissues

The connective tissue sheaths that wrap around every organ, tissue, vessel, and cell of the body, contain, differentiate, and connect them all together. Connective tissue functions as a tensile support system and is, in fact, one continuous sheath of tissue weaving throughout the whole body. Without this tissue, the skeleton would not be able to stand upright, and the body would not hold together in a coherent form (Juhan, 1987: Chapter 3). It also facilitates the passage of nutrients and waste into and out of the cells. The healthy condition of the connective tissue ensures optimal conditions for this exchange. Factors that can diminish its effectiveness include toxicity in the tissue, or excessive rigidity and 'gluing', which can result from lack of movement, stress, and poor postural patterns. Fortunately it is a tissue that is highly responsive, able to transform within a range from fluid to gel-like substance; movement, pressure, warmth, and the manipulations of the bodywork practitioner, directly influence the connective tissue and can have very beneficial effects, thus enhancing the potential for health of the whole body.

But there is more to it that than this. Research into cellular biology has revealed that the connective tissue matrix extends into the interior of the cells, forming the *cytoskeleton* or *cytoplasmic matrix,* and also into the nucleus of the cells where it forms the *nuclear matrix;* this supports the genetic material, the DNA. Molecular structures called *integrins* within the cellular membranes link the cytoplasmic matrix within the cells with the *extracellular matrix* without; the cytoplasmic matrix is understood to facilitate specific biological processes within the cells (Oschman, 2000: 45-8). These internal connections have enormous implications for the somatic therapist, as Oschman describes:

> Conceptually, these discoveries are profoundly important. The boundaries between the cell environment, the cell interior, and the genetic material are not as sharp or as impermeable as we once thought. As a hands-on therapist, what you touch is not merely the skin - you contact a continuous interconnected webwork that extends throughout the body. (Oschman, 2000: 47)

Indeed as we touch the skin, energetically we may directly touch the DNA within the very cells. Drawing upon the extensive scientific research into energy and healing phenomena, Oschman hypothesizes that electrical, electronic, magnetic, and other energetic flows from the practitioner's hands are conducted through the connective tissue network into the cell, cell nucleus, and DNA (Oschman, 2000: Chapter 7). This field of research has opened up enormous potential for understanding *how* hands-on therapies actually work. Furthermore, Oschman describes how *pizeoelectric* energy (electricity produced by the activity of the tissues) from the heart is conducted via the connective tissue matrix into the cells and their DNA; herein must lie an important connection between our feelings and the health of our bodies (Oschman J, 'Heart electronics', lecture given to the Zero-Balancing UK Conference, 'Worlds within worlds', London, May 2000).

Support, connectedness, and integration are all essential functions of the connective tissue network; embodying this system can support the experience of 'self-coherence', one of the four capacities necessary to the development of the sense of a core self (Stern). When feeling fragmented, or that energy and movement do not flow through parts of the body, we can bring our focus into the connective tissue. Focused touch and movement can help to release energy blocks in the tissue, enabling the flow of connection and communication to be felt again.

Body fluids

The connective tissue provides the ground for the passage and exchange of the various body fluids. The body is made up mostly of water – about 80% – reflecting our watery origins in the ocean. It is the medium in which all life processes occur, contained within the membrane of each cell of the body. Body fluid is essentially one fluid that is able to transform from one system to another as it passes through membranes and takes on a different balance of chemical, mineral, and other substances. From interstitial fluid, to cellular fluid, to blood, lymph, cerebrospinal fluid, synovial fluid, and the various secretions of the body, the fluid is constantly transforming, being renewed, replenished, and providing the medium in which life can grow. Nutrients and oxygen, wastes and toxic substances, antibodies, hormones and chemical messengers are all transported through the fluids. They also provide 'shock-absorbing' protection to vulnerable areas of the body, such as the brain and spinal cord, and the joints.

The different fluids thus embody processes of communication, transformation, nourishment, defence, and protection. Each flows with a different rhythm, and these rhythms underlie the rhythms of our movement expression. From the very slow sustained flow of the cerebrospinal fluid, to the active pulse of the arterial blood flow, to the still contained presence of the cellular fluid, the fluids also mediate the balance of rest and activity. Each embodies a different quality of movement, and of touch, and a different range of emotional expressions. For example, the arterial blood embodies emotional warmth, nurturing, lively contact, communication, and weightedness. The lymph, embodying boundaries and defence, can be felt to have clarity of intention, power, and focus.

Preferences in expression of the different body fluids reflect personality, and those that are not so easily expressed reflect aspects of the shadow, those parts of ourselves with which we are not identified. In therapy, an unexpressed fluid may be contacted when the client is ready to acknowledge an unknown part of herself. She may be supported in accessing the disavowed or unexpressed part of herself, and embodying the energies that this part holds. (This will be addressed more fully in the following chapters.)

Nervous system

The nervous system has also been mentioned in relation to other body systems. It consists of billions of nerve cells formed into brain, spinal cord, peripheral nerves, the special sense organs, and sensory receptors dispersed throughout the whole body. Its role is to regulate and coordinate all of the diverse functions of the other tissues, together with the chemical messages of the endocrine system. Most of its activity goes into regulating bodily processes through its highly specialized systems of sensory-motor interaction. The highly developed cortex of the human brain also enables us to be self-conscious and self-reflecting, to act as sentient beings with will, intention, and awareness, and to develop our cognitive, social, and creative capabilities. The nervous system is the supreme achievement of evolution so far; more primitive life forms depend upon the slower and less specific chemical messenger system alone. But together, the two interacting processes of chemical and electrical communication systems have created multitudinous complex life forms; of them all, the human being is perhaps the most uniquely creative, innovative, unpredictable, adaptable, and infinitely fascinating to study.

I do not hold the belief that the physiological processes of the brain and nervous system create consciousness itself, but they clearly do mediate it. Everything we do, think, feel, imagine, and intuit has a corresponding activity in the nervous system; all of our emotional experiences, as well as our thoughts, perceptions, and physiological processes, are registered in the brain. Complex neural pathways in the brain integrate incoming sensory information from within and without, with memories of past experiences; the new information is compared and sorted, and perceptions and judgements are made that are based on the storehouse of old perceptions and memories. The responses initiated may be based largely upon our feelings about those past experiences. The limbic system, the emotional centre of the brain, is centrally involved in this, and many of our actions are unconsciously controlled by the patterning of emotional response that may have been set up in the limbic system over a whole lifetime. Psychotherapy brings consciousness to bear by bringing into awareness the unconscious patterns of emotional response. Somatic therapy can facilitate this by helping to access unconscious material, as well as by introducing new sensations which may enable old beliefs and habits to be reevaluated and modified, or uprooted altogether.

Sensation is the food of the nervous system; without an adequate and ongoing supply of sensory stimulus, we may experience disorientation in time and space, and dissolution or loss of boundaries. In such states we are still conscious, but it is a consciousness that is not well grounded in material reality. Mystical practices induce such states of consciousness by turning the attention away from the outer world of sensory distractions and focusing upon the interior world. When the sense of self is healthy and stable, such states can be experienced as ecstatic, revelatory, and deeply healing, but for the unintegrated ego, intense anxiety, fear, and even disintegration can be the result. The sense of 'self-history', another of the capacities necessary for the development of the sense of a core self, is nurtured in the infant and the adult alike by the ongoing experience of sensory stimulation. If an integrated core does not fully develop it may be difficult to attend to and properly absorb these stimuli, or the child may grow into an adult who constantly seeks more and more sensory stimulation in an attempt to create the sense of a core self. Much of the noise and frenetic activity of modern life may be a result of too many people failing to develop and maintain a healthy sense of core self, and thus needing to continually reinforce the ego through ceaseless activity and the quest for new, often dangerous, and exciting sensory experiences.

The somatic nervous system integrates sensory stimuli with motor expression; it is the vehicle through which we act with conscious intention and control. But much of our activity and experience lies beyond the control and awareness of the conscious mind. The autonomic nervous system regulates those activities that are generally involuntary, and usually unconscious. Its connection to the immune system and cellular health has already been mentioned. The balance of the two branches of the autonomic nervous system, the sympathetic and parasympathetic, is crucial to physical and psychological health and wellbeing.

Autonomic nervous system

The sympathetic branch stimulates the fight-or-flight response to stress, excitement, or threat from the external environment. The parasympathetic branch facilitates digestion and aids processes of repair and recuperation. When the body is in balance, the two branches complement and support each other, stimulating and inhibiting particular functions according to the changing requirements of the moment. Imbalance and ill health result when we become stuck in one mode or the other, or when a 'reversal' occurs. For example, unable to express anger and defend herself, an individual's sympathetic drive might turn inwards to 'attack' herself; this can result in disturbances such as eating disorders, stomach ulcers, depression, anxiety, insomnia, and irritability. When unable to turn inwards and find a place of quiet rest and recuperation, the parasympathetic process then tends to turn outwards as if trying to find a safe place to digest feelings and experiences; endless laments and complaints, and an inability to contain and process feelings may be witnessed. Usually both branches of the autonomic nervous system 'reverse' simultaneously to some degree.

Rebalancing this condition can be complex, and requires attention to both aspects. The sympathetic drive needs to find a safe outlet of expression and release; the containment of the therapeutic setting may enable the release of strong emotions, so that a healthy feeling of power and the ability to deal with the external world can be restored. Physical exercise, and particularly competitive or skilled sports, can also be helpful, as they enable the energy of the sympathetic drive to be released in a safe and focused way.

It can be difficult for people to rebalance the parasympathetic branch without some outside help, for turning inwards confronts them with their reversed sympathetic drive and restlessness or depression may be experienced instead of rest and recuperation. In the beginning, somatic therapies such as massage and other forms of healing touch can be most beneficial; some people find tapes of relaxing music or meditations helpful. Once some degree of balance has been restored, there are many approaches to self-help that can be used, such as meditation, t'ai chi, yoga, or journal writing as a way to creatively 'digest' inner feelings and experiences.

Biodynamic massage therapy, developed by Gerda Boyesen, directly addresses the balance of the autonomic nervous system. The focus of this form of massage is to integrate the emotions through the fluids and digestive organs of the body. Boyesen discovered that 'undigested' emotions affected the fluid pressure of the body and could be 'digested' through the alimentary canal through the application of specific massage techniques. Biodynamic massage has also been developed into a body psychotherapy practice, integrating the perceptual and cognitive aspects as well as the physiological and emotional. Balancing of the two branches of the autonomic nervous system is central to biodynamic massage. In what is described as the upward phase of the 'emotional vasomotor cycle', the sympathetic branch is stimulated by the emotional charge, and blood supply to the skeletal muscles is increased, ready for action. Once the incident of heightened emotional charge is over, the downward phase begins and the parasympathetic branch takes over. This is the place for digestion, rest, and recuperation, as the digestive system is stimulated. Clover Southwell writes of this process:

> We try to get under the secondary personality, to help the client reach into the depths of the unconscious and contact the life-force bound in those depths, so that the emotional cycles interrupted in the past can now be completed. Regression and catharsis may occur in biodynamic therapy, but this is not an end in itself. In the biodynamic view, the healing lies in completing the emotional cycle, with special emphasis on the down-going, inward phase in which we digest and assimilate our experience. When the cycle is complete we can enjoy the full benefit of the life-force. (Southwell and Staff of the Gerda Boyesen International Institute, 1988)

Full and satisfactory expression of the sympathetic nervous system's drive can be as essential to health and fulfilment as the processes of digestion and recuperation, particularly for a person who by nature has a strong need to achieve goals in life. They are complementary processes that are kept in balance through the natural movement from one to the other, and the completion of each phase. Many people cannot rest, release emotional charge, and recuperate because of a frustrated, blocked, or inhibited drive towards expression in outwardly directed action or creative pursuits.

Psychologically the sympathetic nervous system expresses an outwardly focused, goal-oriented approach to life. As well as physiological and emotional release, the sympathetic drive can also be fulfilled through expression in creative and intellectual projects that challenge us to our full capacity. As adults, we are able to sublimate our emotions and the drive of adrenalin coursing through our system into projects that demand our attention, energy, and focus at many levels, and can give us a sense of achievement and satisfaction when completed. Frustrated creativity can be as damaging to health as any toxins we may ingest, or emotions we repress. But the completion of a creative project, or some other challenge in the outer world, can bring a great sense of wellbeing, relaxation, and integration of the body, mind, and spirit.

The inward focus of the parasympathetic nervous system, and its physiological function of stimulating digestive and recuperative processes, engenders an approach that is process oriented, concerned with being more than doing, with desire and feeling rather than achievement in the world. Culturally we are expected to be busy, constantly setting goals, achieving, accumulating; so it is no wonder that many people experience difficulty in accessing the recuperative and restful state associated with this branch of the nervous system. Internalized social demands and cultural judgements play a large part in the difficulty many people have in finding inner rest and peace, and the space to digest emotional experiences and heal ourselves from within. We may be thought to be lazy and 'not pulling our weight' if we surrender to our deep inner need for such space; but if we do not, stress and ill health are more likely to result. We need dynamic balance, not extremes – when we take the time to fully rest, digest, and recuperate, then we will be all the more effective and creative in our activities in the world. In a society that suffers from excessive activity it takes strength to stop and attend to our need for recuperation and healing.

CHAPTER 8

Towards a 'deep democracy' of the body

Microcosm and macrocosm

> One of the natural laws in Chinese philosophy is that patterns and sequences recur throughout nature - on all levels of reality. The movement of the planets in the heavens is similar to the movements of electrons within atoms. As above, so below. The macrocosm is reflected in the microcosm. (Smith, 1986: 181)

So too, in the subtle processes endlessly occurring within the membranous boundary of our skin, we find a microcosm of the universe, and also of the social and political systems existing within our world. Physiological processes, such as growth and decay, nourishment, reproduction, organization, transport and communication, defence, and the disposal of wastes all occur within our internal world just as they do within the structures and institutions of social and political life, as well as the intricate web of the ecological balance of our planet. Within the individual cell we also find a microcosm of the organism as a whole. The DNA of every cell carries the innate intelligence of the individual, and of the species – the information that will guide and underlie every choice and action we make; there is diversity, but in essence we are all very much the same. Each cell takes in nutrients and oxygen, processes these into energy, disposes of wastes, and communicates with surrounding fluids and tissues in a similar way. Besides this, the cells of specific tissues and organs carry out tasks particular to their role and the needs of the whole organism. Without diversity, nothing could flourish; each has its place, its purpose, and its unique contribution to the whole.

In body-mind centering practice the focus of touch is on the physical tissues of the body, and the mind that moves through them, connecting to them at the cellular level. We explore all of the tissues of the body, seeking to bring the different anatomical systems into a dynamic and balanced relationship to each other. The model is that of a 'community of cells', where each cell has its own function and purpose as a necessary part of the whole.

166

Each cell, each organ, and each tissue layer is different but equally important and necessary to the wellbeing of the whole; together they function through extraordinarily complex interactions to sustain life. We seek to integrate the shadow elements by bringing to consciousness, embodying, and expressing all body systems and movement potentials available to us.

So the cells of the skin, with its functions of containment, protection, communication, and boundary formation, or the cells of the stomach, with their work of breaking down food so that the body can be nourished, are both vital to our wellbeing and continued existence. We need our heart and blood to bring oxygen and nutrients to the cells of the body; we need our immune system to patrol the inner spaces for intruders and root out any potentially harmful substances; we need our muscles to move us from one place to another, and so on. Each body system and organ also has a psychological aspect, which reflects the physiological function, as described in the last chapter, and to be healthy, whole, we need access to the full range of emotional expressions, as well as physiological functions. In society, each individual person, and each group or nation has its own function and purpose, and to be whole as a global community each needs to be supported to function and express itself in its own unique way. Listening to the diverse expressions and needs of each part is as essential to the health of society as it is to the health of the individual person.

In a less than ideal world we are, of course, subjected to all kinds of inner and outer limitations, restrictions, and expectations that do not support, or directly interfere with the full development of our potential and our individual purpose in life. This begins with the socialization process that we all undergo during infancy, childhood, and adolescence, so when looking at the healing of the individual, social and environmental factors must be acknowledged. Mayland (1995) writes:

> The client's unconscious processes shape the body. In the socialisation process most people adopt roles, play games, wear masks, put up facades, and put barriers in the form of muscular tension between themselves and others. They feel and believe that their genuine or authentic self is unacceptable. The roles, games, masks, barriers, and facades develop subtly in response to unspoken demands and pressures from the child's caretakers, become structured in the body, and require muscular tension to maintain.
>
> Our bodies and our characters are shaped by the social forces at work as we mature. The attitudes taken on as a result of socialisation are carried and expressed in the body, forming habit patterns that are embodied as rigidity and restricted movement.

As Ian Grand describes, the somatic structuring of experience does not occur only during infancy and early childhood, but continues throughout life as social and cultural influences impact upon our somatic experience and expressions:

The somatic forming of the sense of self, the complexities of somatic representation of self and other, are not limited to the caregiver in infancy or to the family of
origin . . . It is also important to see how representations of gangs, employment
opportunity, and life expectancy impact the conduct of the flesh.
Developmental process is not linear. It is based on accretions of interactions and
feelings coming from the culture as well as the family of origin . . . We all learn - in
schools, from friends, in clubs and gangs, from the media - different messages and
images concerned with how to live and comport ourselves bodily. (Grand, in
Johnson and Grand, 1998: 182)

Thus hierarchies of overuse and abuse, oppression or neglect, are set up
within the person's inner psychosomatic world; the roots, which may go
back as far as early developmental experiences, will continue to be reflected
in the person's behaviour and relationships. Unique potential cannot develop
fully, authentic expression is denied, and the world is that much poorer as a
result. Explorations of our inner world, through somatic, psychotherapeutic,
and meditative practices, yield knowledge and healing. The next and
necessary step in the healing process is to address the relationship between
what we discover within us, and how that relates to, reflects, and helps to
create what is without and around us. We cannot be truly healed as
individuals so long as the world around us continues to manifest toxicity,
imbalance, and oppressive power structures. When we explore our inner
psychosomatic world with respectful attention, love, and care, we begin to
generate an attitude of respect and care towards others and the environment
around us, as we discover how we are interconnected and interdependent.
Thus somatic learning can bring us to an awareness of the social, political,
and ecological needs of our world today.

When I meditate upon my heart, I witness a powerful muscle that beats
constantly. This muscle wraps around four empty chambers, through which
blood is pumped. The blood flows to every cell of my body, providing food,
energy, healing, and information about the needs of the cells in other parts of
my body. I imagine the heart of the universe as a powerful force that
constantly pours out from the void at its centre a flow of energy,
nourishment, healing, and information about life in its totality; I call this love,
and a wise knowing of what is required to sustain the life of the whole. I
imagine the universe is within me, and that I am the universe. When I close
my heart, when I inhibit the full flow of lifeblood to every part, the universe
suffers.

It matters that I keep my heart open, and the flow of life and love through
it strong and clear. It matters that we support each other to embody our
potential and express our unique purpose on earth, just as it matters that
every cell and organ of the body supports and is supported by its community
of cells to do what it is meant to do. And it matters that a child is encouraged
to develop according to her own natural unfolding, as this is the foundation
for the expression of her unique creative potential throughout life.

The language of the bodymind

To move towards a deep democracy of the body where each part is acknowledged, each inner voice heard and heeded, we can begin by exploring the many diverse tissues and anatomical systems of the body, bringing each one into conscious awareness, listening to it, respecting its functions and needs, expressing its energy. Any aspect of our psychosomatic being that is unacknowledged and unexpressed remains hidden from us until we bring it into conscious expression; the body systems and tissues which we do not express or have access to represent the somatic aspect of our shadow.

In body-mind centering practice each body system and tissue layer, including skeletal, muscular, connective tissue, organ, endocrine, circulatory fluid and nervous systems, and the special sense organs are systematically studied and embodied through touch, movement, and focused awareness. Anatomical pictures and models are studied; then the structures are located within the body, using the visual information as a guide to contacting the actual tissues. Practice trains the sensory feedback mechanisms of the nervous system and the cells so that the presence, location, size, shape, density of energy, and quality of movement or stillness of the tissues can all be perceived with some accuracy.

We discover that the way the mind moves in a certain area of the body will be reflected in the quality of energy in the tissues. Energy may feel fluid and free moving, slow, heavy and sluggish, or diffuse and unfocused; there may be areas which feel dead, immobile, or dark and hard to access, and areas of high intensity where energy has been trapped within the tissues. Body tissues and structures may feel glued together where energy does not move through them easily, or they may feel disconnected where there is a lack of integration. Some conditions reflect momentary changes of focus and energy in the bodymind, but others may be deeply engrained patterns that have been established and repeatedly reinforced over long periods of time. The latter are difficult to change without bringing them into conscious awareness, as patterns of use and flow of information are established in the nervous system and unconsciously affect our functioning at many levels. The quality of energy in the body tissues may reflect innate personality, and we are not seeking to change this; but patterns of flow and restriction are also established as a result of conditioning experiences which limit us, and here support can be given to become aware of unconscious patterning, and make new, more healthful choices.

Writing about the flow of energy in the body, Gerda Boyesen observes:

> If all is well, the streamings or energy potential in the body should give natural growth and self-realization both psychologically and physically. Such energy should be available as a sort of reservoir to draw upon in emotional or emergency situations and also in ecstasy and delight. If a critical situation arises, the organism

has to draw from the reservoir the amount of energy needed to cope with the situation; but after this has been abreacted and the danger is over, the energy should be free to flow back to the reservoir and to circulate round the body giving the natural feeling of aliveness and well-being.

But if emotional expression is inhibited or stuck and the person is in a permanent situation of emotional provocation, the amount of energy in the reservoir is less because it is being used in the frustrated emotional block. This causes the organism to be exhausted or irritable and the natural feeling of euphoria disappears. But if the body is able to work out nervous energy, biochemical stress products are also released into the bloodstream and the organism can return to a free energy flow. (Boyesen in Boadella, 1976)

The bioenergetic approach

Like somatic therapies, body psychotherapy also seeks to free the flow of energy within the bodymind continuum, developing awareness of limiting postural patterns, and releasing bodily tensions and constrictions so that the individual may return to a fuller and freer way of being. Bioenergetics, developed by Alexander Lowen and John Pierrakos, is a development of Reich's early work in this area, and integrates Freudian analytic theory with Reich's understanding of the use of muscular tension to create 'character armour'. Character types are observed from body posture and the muscular armouring that creates and maintains that posture; muscular armouring is the embodiment of character. Lowen writes:

> In bioenergetics the different types of defenses are subsumed under the heading 'character structures.' Character is defined as a fixed pattern of behaviour, the typical way an individual handles his striving for pleasure. It is structured in the body in the form of chronic and generally unconscious muscular tensions that block or limit impulses to reach out. Character is also a psychic attitude which is buttressed by a system of denials, rationalizations and projections and geared to an ego ideal that affirms its value. The functional identity of psychic character and body structure or muscular attitude is the key to understanding personality, for it enables us to read the character from the body and to explain a body attitude by its psychic representations and vice versa. (Lowen, 1976a: 137)

There are five basic character types, observable through the structural and energetic appearance of the body, each relating to specific developmental traumas; they are the schizoid, oral, masochistic, psychopathic, and rigid character types (Lowen, 1976a: 151–73). These categories are based upon Freudian developmental theory, but as embodied manifestations of neuroses, they are worked upon directly through bodily experience. As Lowen makes clear, for a course of therapy to conclude successfully, body as well as mind must be addressed: 'It is an important thesis of bioenergetics that changes in personality are conditioned on changes in bodily function' (Lowen, 1976a: 115). He affirms that: 'The ego is not the person and does not function independently of the body. A dissociated ego and a dissociated intellectuality represents a loss of integrity in the personality' (Lowen, 1976a: 329).

Bioenergetic therapists 'read' the language of the body to ascertain the particular bodymind conflicts with which the individual is troubled. Posture, movement, and energy charge and distribution all give the therapist important cues as to where the energy of the body is blocked, and thus the nature of the client's fundamental psychic conflicts is also revealed. Freedom, in the form of the free flow and expression of energy, is sought. Lowen (1971: 15) writes:

> The character of the individual as it is manifested in his typical pattern of behaviour is also portrayed on the somatic level by the form and movement of the body. The sum total of the muscular tensions seen as a gestalt . . . constitutes the 'body expression' of the organism. The body expression is the somatic view of the typical emotional expression which is seen on the psychic level as 'character'.

John Pierrakos, through his investigations into the subtle energy body, also shows how each character structure manifests as a typical pattern of light, colour, and movement within the aura surrounding each person. The aura can reveal the person's whole life history, their past traumas, present condition, and their unique qualities and potentials which are expressions of their energetic core. Disturbances in the aura reflect organic dysfunction, blocked energy, and unhealthy patterns of thought and emotional expression or repression. Through both scientific and clinical investigation, Pierrakos has learned to recognize symptomatology within the appearance of the aura, and to use this as a diagnostic tool, together with observations of physical structure and behavioural patterns (Pierrakos, 1990: Chapter 9).

Keeping the particular character structure of the client as an overall context for its work, bioenergetic therapy uses exercises and body techniques to reduce muscular armouring, increase the connection to the ground through the legs, open breathing and feeling in the body, and thus help to free the body's energy to flow freely and vitally, a sign of wellbeing and integration in bioenergetic terms. Despite the usefulness of character analysis, however, Pierrakos reminds us of the essential point that each person is a unique and complex being, and should never be viewed as simply a character structure and collection of problems:

> . . . The defensive pattern does not define the person. The core does. A person in treatment is not a character type or structure or any other label. He or she is a human being whose functioning has gone awry, and whose soul has an inborn brilliance and beauty that the therapy is designed to release. (Pierrakos, 1990: 93)

In discussing bioenergetics and related therapies in his seminal book *Bodymind*, Dychtwald writes of:

> . . . How certain feelings affect the body in specific ways, and how, in turn, the structure and functions of the body predispose it to certain feeling states. For example, when shallow-breathing patterns are developed as a personal defense

against the experience of feeling, the muscles that surround the lungs, as well as the diaphragm, which rests below the lungs, begin to rigidify and contract, forming an inflexible band of tension around the lungs. This chronic muscular tension not only serves to further decrease the breathing capacity of the lungs but also works to encourage the state of low-grade anxiety and tension that often accompanies the shallow-breathing pattern. Shallow breathing can act as a personal defense against the experience of feeling, for to breathe is to feel; and conversely, to limit breathing is to limit feeling. (Dychtwald, 1977: 146)

Somatic therapies also address such cycles of interaction and work not only with tension in the muscles of the body. Stress, tension, weakness, hypertone or hypotone, sluggishness, and other energetic conditions can manifest in any body tissue; the focus might be on tension or torsion in the bones or connective tissues, inhibitions in the flow of the blood, tightness or lack of tone in the organs, holding or dispersion of energy at the joints, weakness or rigidity at the cellular boundaries, to name just a few of the many conditions that might be expressed through the bodymind. So a very subtle degree of differentiation between bodymind states may be accessed through somatic approaches, although the relationship to psychological process and character type is not generally as explicitly articulated as in the bioenergetic and neo Reichian therapies.

Traditionally bioenergetic therapists have worked explicitly with the observation of body structure, and the mapping of specific parts of the body with particular psychoemotional expressions. This can provide very useful reference points but it must be noted that different practitioners propose different associations in some cases, and these body mappings should therefore be used wisely as guidelines, and not as ultimate truths about an individual's bodymind expression. (Some examples of systems of body mapping can be found in Kurtz and Prestera, 1976; Lowen, 1976a; Keleman, 1985; Pierrakos, 1990.) Somatic therapies also work from observed structure and function but generally there is also a strong focus upon gathering information from direct, first-person sensory experience. In both bioenergetic and somatic therapies both approaches may be used to different degrees, depending on the practitioner and the therapy. To this extent, insight into psychological meaning is discovered by the client from within the depths of her own bodymind experience.

Reich's view of the healthy ideal was the free flow of sexual energy throughout the body, his focus upon genital character. Following his lead, bioenergetic therapists have proposed an 'ideal' posture to be acquired through the release of restrictive tensions and inhibitions; again they are not all in agreement as to what this ideal should be. Dychtwald takes the point of view that each positioning of a body part will predispose the person towards a certain way of being in the world, just as the way in which she or he deals with the psychophysiological functions associated with that body part will be reflected in the posture and movement of that area. Extreme misalignments and stress can produce imbalance within the whole organism, and it is obviously preferable to change such a condition if at all possible; but apart from this, Dychtwald's approach is to look at individuals and what they need in order to enhance their health and possibilities for growth and expression, rather than to seek an ideal of perfect posture (Dychtwald, 1977: 80-1). Most somatic therapies do not seek to create a particular 'ideal' posture, but to develop choice and the ability to balance dynamically the many forces - physical, psychological, social, environmental, and spiritual - acting from within and without.

The body-mind centering approach

In the somatic practice of body-mind centering, we work directly with the body tissues to effect changes in the quality and movement of energy within and through them. The aim is not to achieve a static state of balance in the body, but a dynamic, alert and fluid quality of mind by which we can adapt moment to moment to our internal and external environment out of free choice rather than habitual patterning. Bringing awareness into the body tissues through focused touch can itself be enough to support movement and change; as she touches her client's body, the practitioner centres her awareness in her own body, in the tissues she is seeking to contact in her client, and through a process of 'resonance' she helps her client to access this level in herself. Each tissue, each organ, each body system, evokes a different quality of touch. Allowing our hands to 'ride' on the subtle movements of energy we feel in the client's body, we are given information as to which system needs attention and what quality of touch will be most helpful. We make contact and wait to see which systems come into awareness.

Sometimes awakening awareness in the cells and tissues is all that is required; it allows the tissues to awaken to their own presence and creates a space for the body's own healing process to unfold. The practitioner may simply witness and follow the process in her client's body, giving subtle somatic feedback to the client through her mindful attention and focused touch; or she may feed in information and new sensations through the use of intentional touch and specific repatterning techniques, sensitive to the levels of tissue that are calling for attention, and the subtle movements of energy that are needing support in order to flow more freely. This opens up choices in movement and perception. With greater choice we are not tied to old pathways, but can find a fuller range of expression, access more of who we are.

As awareness shifts in the body we find that the quality of perception, attention, vocal, and movement expression also changes. Each body system, each fluid, and each individual organ of the body expresses a different quality of movement and a feeling tone, or mood, when attention is focused there and movement initiated with the mind in that tissue. We call this quality or feeling tone the 'mind' of the tissue or body system, and specific qualities have been identified as being associated with the specific systems. The 'mind' of the tissue is a reflection of its weight and density, its energetic vibration, the flow and rhythm of its movement, its physiological function, shape, texture and so on. For example, through the muscles we may find the expression of a 'mind' that is vital, active, and powerful, while in the bones a sense of inner structure, clarity in space, and a grounded lightness is often felt; the organs express volume, presence, and feeling, each organ expressing a different range of emotional states associated with its physiological function. Bonnie Bainbridge Cohen, the originator of body-mind centering, states:

> Our body moves as our mind moves. The qualities of any movement are a manifes-
> tation of how mind is expressing through the body at that moment. Changes in
> movement qualities indicate that the mind has shifted focus in the body.
> Conversely, when we direct the mind or attention to different areas of the body
> and initiate movement from those areas, we change the quality of our movement.
> (Cohen, 1993: 1)

Each body system reflects and expresses a different aspect of our psychological being, a different mind and feeling state, perceptual outlook, and quality of movement. The language of the body systems describes a physical basis for observing and evaluating personality styles. We each have 'preferences', qualities of expression that are closest to our nature, and others that are alien or less accessible. We seek to bring into conscious awareness, by embodying them through touch and movement, those systems that are less familiar. When we bring into expression a system that is usually unconscious, our familiar expressive systems can go 'unconscious' for a while. This allows them to rest and recuperate. Without this they may become exhausted from overuse. For example, a person who is very sensitive, aware, reflective, and perhaps introverted, and does not often allow herself to let go and move or play without self-conscious attention, is expressing primarily through the nervous system. To bring her systems into better balance she may need to rest at times in the fluids, in free and unselfconscious movement or play such as sports or expressive dance, in order to let the nervous system relax its vigilance and rest. Another person who is chaotically emotional might be expressing a lot of organ and fluid energy; she might benefit from finding the support and containment that the skeletal structure can give, in order to help clarify and channel into form her emotional energy.

The unembodied systems, those that are not expressed or are inaccessible to our awareness, are called the *shadow* systems. This has relationship to Jung's psychological concept of the shadow, as it relates to aspects of our being that are repressed, or that we are not conscious of or identified with. Accessing unfamiliar body systems and expressive qualities may be a support for integrating split-off aspects of the personality. Once a shadow system has been brought into awareness and expression, it is then allowed to go unconscious again, but once a system has become accessible in this way it becomes a *supporting* system for our usual expressive style, giving to that a fuller, more integrated quality. Hence the process can support us in expressing with more ease our basic nature, and in integrating aspects of our being with which we are not identified.

We frequently find that we are limited in our expression and have problems not because we lack something, but because we are stuck in a particular state, which blocks other options. Cohen states that our weaknesses are often our strengths, functions and qualities which have been overused and not been able to recuperate. We need to be able to move fluidly from one system to another, as inner and outer circumstances necessitate. Our range of expression can be increased when the mind is able to move freely through the body. Holding, resistance, inhibition, and lack of awareness at the cellular and tissue levels of the body are reflections of the way the mind moves, and also in turn influence the way the mind is able to move in the body. It is a cyclical process. As such it can be approached at any point in the cycle. We can work through the mind to affect the body, or work directly on the body tissues to affect the mind. The practice of *touch and movement repatterning* might use both approaches at different moments to enter the matrix of the bodymind. Ultimately both approaches merge when we contact the mind of the cells and tissues we are working with. It is just this that we seek to do, joining with the mind of the tissues under our hands, bringing it into conscious focus so that change can be effected. Overall the change we look for is to bring into awareness, support, and facilitate the natural function and flow of energy through the cells and tissues of the body. An understanding of healthy functioning is the model used to contextualize and guide the work, and this is a primary focus of study.

Somatic therapists have long understood this two-way process of communication between mind and body, but scientific research is now beginning to offer us evidence of the physiological basis for such intuitive assertions. As described earlier, information from the cerebral cortex is processed through the limbic-hypothalamic system, and from here messenger molecules carry information to all cells of the body via the channels of the autonomic nervous system, the endocrine and immune systems, and the neuropeptide network. Information in the form of feedback is constantly flowing to and fro between the cortical and sub-cortical centres of the brain, and the cells and tissues of the whole body. If we consider the other direction of the cortex-limbic-hypothalamic-cell-gene pathway, we can imagine that when the cells of the body tissues are touched with conscious awareness, this must surely introduce new information directly into the cells and genes. If a conscious intent, such as a message to relax, to open and breathe fully, or to feel contained by the cellular membrane, is directed towards the cells, it seems possible that the highly sensitive and intelligent system of neuropeptide communication may respond to this information by circulating new messages to the brain, nervous, endocrine, and immune systems. If this is the case, then we can understand how mental and emotional states, endocrine and immune functioning, and the balance of the autonomic nervous system can all be positively affected by focused and healing touch.

The splitting and reintegration of the body systems

During the first week of gestation, the multiplying cells of the embryo develop into three germinal layers, which later on differentiate into the different tissue layers of the body. The three layers are the endoderm (organs and glands), the mesoderm (bones, muscles, connective tissue, and blood), and the ectoderm (skin, nervous system, and sense organs). David Boadella describes how loss of the unity of the organism, which can occur at any stage of development, affects the integration of the three germinal layers of the body. When the integration of these layers is disturbed through trauma or through the 'civilizing' process to which we are all subjected, splitting occurs between the layers: 'The effect of this splitting is to cut action from thinking and feeling; emotion from movement and perception; understanding from movement and feeling' (Boadella, 1988).

This process of splitting relates directly to the concerns and practices of body-mind centering, where differentiation, embodiment, and integration of the different body tissues is a central focus. Whilst this somatic therapy and the body psychotherapy of biosynthesis, which Boadella developed, have grown from different roots, there appear to be many similarities. Both work from a cellular and embryological perspective; body-mind centering does not so explicitly address the psychophysiological causes of splitting but, following a model of natural and healthy functioning, it does offer an effective approach to reintegration.

The following response of a student, a dancer, gives an example of the process of reintegrating the tissue layers; she is discussing her experiences of embodying the skeletal system, a part of the mesoderm layer. She describes herself as experiencing a close connection between emotions and perceptions, or organs and sensory perception (endoderm and ectoderm), but in her experience the skeletal aspect of the mesoderm felt split off when she first began to explore it consciously:

> It wasn't really difficult to embody this (the skeletal) system, but it felt unfamiliar. This movement quality wasn't my favourite one. I would describe it in terms like: predictable, clear in the space, straight, short phrases and ways. In general I always preferred more fluid movement. This system gave me a sense of an overview and a kind of distant perception. It left my strong emotions outside. But I missed the pleasurable inner laughter, when moving with the focus on this system. Either I felt as if I was just a skeleton, or I felt the rest of my body, but I remember that I

didn't feel my bones inside of me. I didn't feel the bones surrounded by tissues.

For me, feeling and perceiving are normally strongly connected. Usually all my responses are coloured by emotions; it's not always a very strong emotional response, but I'm quickly touched by whatever I perceive: things, situations, people, thoughts, memories, stories etc. Working with the bones related to a symptom of often getting very lost in feelings, emotions and unknown inner and outer worlds.

My experience of working consciously with the bones is that of a frame and solid container for my immaterial being. It helps me stay in normal reality, or to come from distant unembodied places back into my body. Now I feel my bones present in my body, supporting me by their structure and mind not to give in too much.

Another wonderful experience is the old place of total peace inside my bones. Here I find rest and silence from all my running, falling, tumbling, searching, struggling and fighting. Now I can appreciate the unemotional mind and structure of the bones. They keep me upright and that is what they are supposed to do.

Body, emotional feeling, and mind

Different therapies and somatic practices focus on the integration of different aspects of this trinity of tissue layers, and of the action, feeling, and mental/perceptual processes to which they relate. For example, some somatic practices focus primarily on the integration of body and mind, of movement and awareness, action and perception, with less explicit attention given to emotional expression and psychological integration. The Alexander technique and Feldenkrais method are examples; body-mind centering also works in this way, although it is flexible in its application and can incorporate the conscious integration of emotional feelings and psychological process, depending on the practitioner's skill, training and experience. In discussing the fifth chakra of the subtle body, Dychtwald suggests that the Feldenkrais method (and other somatic practices) is particularly related to this chakra, and to its associated functions of reflective self-awareness and self-knowledge. He writes:

> With the heightened self-knowledge gained through self-experience and self-reflection, we can learn to construct our bodyminds and lives so as to allow the development of increased health, vitality, and consciousness. It is this human quality, the ability to mindfully reflect on one's own existence, and to generate change in that existence, that epitomizes the self-identifying aspects of the fifth Kundalini chakra. For as self-perceivers, we not only breathe air into our lungs, we also have the ability to breathe imagination into our thoughts and consciousness into our lives. (Dychtwald, 1977: 215)

In my experience and observation, such an approach helps to create a strong and integrated bodymind container. For some, the bodymind matrix is a natural ground from which to explore the inner self; for others who tend to be highly emotional, it can offer containment, emotional detachment, and focus. If taken to extremes, however, this way of working may serve to repress unintegrated emotions, which can result in an internal chaos of feelings. The effects of this kind of practice will depend on the individual's relationship between the trinity of mind, feelings, and body, and on the degree of splitting or integration between the tissue layers that embody thought, emotions, and action. In the language of the body systems we would say that an overemphasis on expression through the nervous system, through self-reflective somatic work, could for some people lead to suppression of the fluids, which are more closely associated with emotional expression. To rebalance this situation, the expression of the fluid systems in movement can be a helpful support.

In distinction to this focus of many somatic therapies, body psychotherapy places more emphasis on the integration of emotions with bodily expression, and to varying degrees with perceptual and cognitive processes too. Because of the greater focus on emotion in the body, it is likely to work primarily at the level of the first four chakras of the subtle body, although at times processes associated with the upper chakras can most definitely be directly involved as well.

For example, John Rowan (1988: 13) claims that primal integration therapy can work with almost the whole spectrum of Wilber's model of psychospiritual development (see Chapter 4). This approach evolved out of the pioneering work of Bill Swartley, Frank Lake, Stanislav Grof, and others; it has roots going back to Rank, Fodor, and Mott, and their insights into the importance of womb and perinatal experience in the creation of neurosis. Thus it addresses the effects of splitting at a very early stage of preverbal development, associated with the first 'root' chakra. A basic premise of this therapy is that early trauma is a primary cause of neurosis, and that beneath the defensive layers is the primal pain that was caused by the trauma. Primal integration therapy takes the client back to relive the trauma and release, through catharsis, the primal feelings that have been held since that time. Through releasing these feelings, the authentic self, hidden behind the protective armouring, can return to consciousness. The regression experience is then related to present circumstances, and integrated through opening to new choices and actions in daily life. Emotional release of primal feelings can be very powerful, as they relate to preverbal experience when emotional life was less differentiated and less inhibited, and cognitive awareness not yet developed. Primal integration stresses that the cognitive and behavioural levels must also be addressed, in order for the integration of primal regressions to be complete. (It should be noted that some would not see primal integration as a body psychotherapy because, in its original formulation, it was too based upon catharsis without attention to relational issues; however, more attention is now given to relationship within this approach.)

In working with perinatal and birth trauma, the transpersonal realm may also be accessed, evoking experiences of archetypal symbols, intuitions, feelings such as bliss, joy, or love, and connection to the deeper self. As we contact the authentic self, the core, by working through early trauma, a connection to the transpersonal self becomes possible; the personal self is considered to be a reflection of the transpersonal self, and therefore an opening towards it. The movement from personal to transpersonal self can be thought of as an ever-deepening movement towards the inner source of one's being.

Ron Kurtz, who developed the body psychotherapy called hakomi, also stresses that all levels must be involved in the therapeutic process:

> The work done must activate changes on physical, emotional, and mental levels, since each level affects the others . . .
>
> Deep change is much more than finding a comfortable role or playing better games. It is a true expansion of the self, a removal of self-imposed limits – restrictions grounded in irrational fears and childhood defeats. These fears must be contacted and reexperienced. The attitudes to which they give life must be brought into awareness, then examined, and the whole process enlightened with persistent self-discovery. A new base must be built up on physical vitality, realistic attitudes, emotional satisfaction, and the acceptance of life. By pursuing growth, by going deeper and deeper into our feelings, by seeking within ourselves the source and meaning of our lives, we can only come to find an unending spiritual reservoir – ineffable, mysterious, and yet the surest, truest ground of our existence. (Kurtz and Prestera, 1976: 10–11)

In contrast to the body-mind orientation of somatic therapy, and the body-feeling approach of some earlier forms of body psychotherapy, most approaches to psychotherapy and psychoanalysis focus primarily on the mind-feeling connection, and do not directly involve the body and somatic processes. Later developments in the field of body psychotherapy and *somatic psychotherapy,* which integrates somatic practice and psychotherapy, potentially address and seek to integrate all three levels of experience.

The level at which therapeutic work is focused should, of course, reflect the issues the client needs to integrate, and be related to which sense of self has suffered the primary disruption. Going back to Stern's work (Chapter 4), we remember that the emergent and core senses of self develop out of the ground of sensory-motor processing and activity, the subjective sense of self evolves with the subtle nuances of attunement to feeling in relationship, and the verbal sense of self develops as cognitive processes mature – the evolution of the trinity of body, feelings, and mind. However, we should always remember that no matter what level the problem is focused upon, we are always dealing with a whole person, and every level must be engaged.

> On the deepest level, change *always* involves the body. A new attitude means new perceptions, new feelings, and new muscular patterns. Psychological and physiological change go hand in hand. Since our deepest traumas are imbedded in our guts and muscles, to free ourselves we must free our bodies. Yet we are more than

just bodies. We are minds and spirits, feelings and imaginings. And though the body speaks, it must always be the whole person to whom we listen. (Kurtz and Prestera, 1976: 145)

Inner body dialogue

The intrapsychic dynamics – the conflicts, collusions, agreements, and other shifting arrangements – which exist within the complex inner world of the psyche always manifest somatically, whether in subtle or obvious ways. We may notice this when we suffer from tension, pain, or symptoms of ill health that respond directly to our changing attitudes, moods, feelings, or activity. But unless we are suffering from some physical pain or discomfort, we do not usually heed the more subtle messages that the body may be trying to communicate to us. It is usually only when something goes wrong that we begin to take note of the body's signals, and even then the doctor's prescription will be the preferred solution for many. But we do not have to wait until we are ill or in distress before attending to the body.

When we do pay attention to the body, listening inwardly, feeling, sensing its subtle activities, we may be surprised at how much information it can reveal to us. The body never lies; it has not learned the subtle tricks of the thinking mind to deceive us away from direct and authentic experience. When we listen to the body, it tells us stories; it tells the truth about our inner world, our conflicts, feelings, memories, hopes, losses. It opens us to knowledge and experiences we may have long ago forgotten, or never yet consciously encountered. It may reveal aspects of ourselves that we have disowned, never known, lost sight of, forgotten, or simply felt too shy to reveal. Our body, like our dreams, can reveal a treasure house of wisdom.

The inner body dialogue is a way of accessing the wisdom, the occluded intelligence, the instinctive knowledge carried within our cells and body tissues. It is a way of discovery, of exploration; we seek to discover how we truly are, what we truly long for and need, what we must avoid, in order that the inner self can be touched, nurtured, and cherished into fuller expression.

One way of entering the dialogue is through touch. The touch of another person focuses awareness, brings the wandering mind home into the body. When we touch another, first of all skin meets skin. We can rest with this awareness, witnessing what emerges into consciousness as the mind focuses on and is embodied in the skin. Sensations might be felt, or experienced as colour, as inner sound, or scent; an image might emerge – the primary boundary of the skin might be visualized as a wall, a mist, a soft blanket, an empty space, for example; feelings such as comfort, tenderness, fear, or confusion might arise; sometimes an auditory message, a voice, song, or spoken words, are heard within; or nothing might emerge at all. All of this yields information about our internal relationship to our skin as boundary, as place of definition, contact, protection, communication, and transformation between inner and outer worlds.

There might be a need to stop there and explore what has arisen: staying with a feeling, allowing it to deepen, dialoguing with an inner voice, drawing the image, allowing the process to unfold, expressing the feelings and the needs that have been contacted. Once a body process has been connected to, the process generally finds its own channel within which to unfold; attentive, compassionate witnessing, support, and encouragement underlie any techniques used.

Or the journey may continue, gathering information from ever deeper layers of the inner landscape, so that the relationships between the different tissues, and what they embody, can be explored. When there is a feeling of readiness and trust between client and therapist, we settle beneath the superficial layers of the skin, to touch the insulating layer of fatty tissue, the network of fine lymphatic vessels (part of the immune system), and superficial connective tissue sheaths which envelop and contain the whole body – the next layers of protection, containment, and defence. Again we listen, feel, witness whatever emerges as each tissue is touched, and may learn something about our relationship to the psychological processes embodied in these tissue layers.

Deepening further, we contact muscles and bones; we might also focus upon the fluid systems, such as the blood, deep lymph vessels, and interstitial fluids, or the nerves. Again we listen, feel, witness the messages the body yields. If it speaks to us, we may dialogue back in the language it has chosen - through sound, through imagery, through words, through movement.

As we deepen to the inner spaces of the body, the organs and endocrine glands are contacted. Each one expresses a unique story, holds feelings, memories, and knowledge; each with its unique function can reveal information about how we deal with nourishment, with taking in and letting go, with sorting and choosing, creating and destroying. Again we can witness, listen, and dialogue with the parts which are the embodiment of different aspects of our psyche, exploring the feelings, longings, needs, and qualities held within them. A relationship dynamic between two or more parts, embodied in specific organs or tissue layers, may emerge, and this can be explored through relationship work as if they were different characters living within us.

To explore and process this information, methods of inner dialogue used in some forms of psychotherapy to explore parts of the personality – subpersonalities – can be adapted. Appendix 2 gives an outline of the *inner body dialogue* I sometimes use, to give the reader an idea of how this approach to processing somatic material might work. This basic outline can be varied in many ways to suit each unique situation, but the general steps are useful to hold as guidelines. These steps involve embodying, or identifying with, a specific part - it may be a particular organ, a body system such as muscle or fat, or an area of the body holding tension or pain, for example. We 'become' this part, to experience more clearly the feelings, needs, attitudes and roles that have been somatized within it; we might speak, move, and express these feelings, in order to embody them more fully. Then we disidentify from the part again, to reemerge into a clearer sense of self in relation to this part and its needs. We may move back and forth as often as necessary until the dialogue is completed.

Body, feelings, mind, and the experience of self-identification

Cyclical interactions occur naturally between the body, feelings, and mind, and this can be used therapeutically. A mental image can alter both bodily and emotional feeling; a movement, posture, or gesture can affect feeling, awareness, and perception, and bring information to consciousness; a feeling has a profound effect upon the way we think and move and hold ourselves. Roberto Assagioli, founder of psychosynthesis, described many methods to work therapeutically with the interactive processes between body, feelings, and mind (Assagioli, 1975). He also observed that one or another aspect can be a shadow element; someone totally identified with their mind-as-self may be unconscious of most bodily sensations and emotional feelings, for example.

It is my observation that the way in which an individual organizes her personality, with respect to body, feelings, and mind, has some bearing on the way she most readily processes and integrates information and change. For some, mental understanding is essential to the discovery of insight, and the integration of new sensations, feelings, and behavioural patterns. Other people process primarily through their feelings, and change may not occur until there has been some emotional expression; once this has occurred this person might immediately feel clear and resolved about the issue in question, or come to some important realization or insight. A third group of people seem to process change most directly through the body; these people integrate most effectively in a non-verbal manner, through the direct experience of bodywork or movement.

It is helpful to understand a client's need with regard to such tendencies, as differing therapeutic approaches or methods may be called for. Arnold Mindell (1989a: 14-24) describes 'occupied' and 'unoccupied' channels of perception and expression, and has observed that unconscious information is most readily accessed through unoccupied channels, those with which we are least identified, whilst we integrate information most readily through the channels with which we are most identified (see Chapter 9). (In Mindell's theory of the dreambody there are six main channels of perception and expression: visual, auditory, proprioceptive, movement, relationship, and world channels. An 'occupied channel is one with which we tend to be more identified; an 'unocuppied' channel is one that is not identified with. Events are experienced as happening 'to us' through this channel and may be expressions of an unconscious process.) Such preferences may also provide information as to which sense of self has suffered primary disruption, or where trauma has caused splitting within the unity of the total organism. Ultimately, as Jung observed, change needs to be integrated at all levels – physical, emotional, mental, and spiritual – for true and lasting healing to take place, but each individual has a unique path towards this integration.

The inner body dialogue described above makes use of the interactive nature of the physical, emotional, and mental aspects of the personality, as it moves between proprioceptive, visual, auditory, movement, and relationship channels of perception and expression. It also uses the processes of identification and disidentification. All existential and humanistic therapies work towards the experience of self-identification, sometimes implicitly; Assagioli developed and defined this process, making it a central and explicit concern of psychosynthesis (Assagioli, 1975: 4–5). His approach cultivates the ability to disidentify from partial aspects of the personality and the *contents* of consciousness, and to identify with the core self; this is seen as essential to gaining psychological freedom and choice.

The issue of self-identification is not explicitly addressed in most approaches to somatic therapy. However, witnessing of and reflection on somatic process from the place of the centre of awareness enables us to integrate body issues into the whole personality; at the same time, the experience of self-identification, the sense of a core self, is also cultivated. There has been a need for this in body-mind centering practice. Cohen spoke of this need, and the dangers of not being able to disidentify from partial aspects of the body-self, during an early phase in the development of her work:

> . . . Often we, in this work, concentrate so much on the juggling of systems, whatever we happen to be studying, that we end up being sick a lot of the time. I think it has to do with some part of us identifying with the system or the imbalance that we're studying. So in fact we go from one unbalanced state to another. Certainly we become more well or potentially well by balancing all these different things, but what I'm exploring now is how we can come to some whole image, a whole state of mind that we would identify with. Then the exploration of each system would be a study, but we wouldn't attach our basic self with the study. Then I think we could become aware of the imbalances without becoming ill. (Cohen, 1993: 64)

This problem, particular to the practice of body-mind centering during the early years of intensive research and exploration, is now being addressed by teachers and practitioners in different ways. More recent theory and practice proposes that the 'mind' of cellular awareness represents that central core of awareness, 'a whole state of mind', which is all pervading and can also identify with specific parts. Training in psychotherapy, and also the practices of authentic movement and meditation, are other ways that I have sought personally to explore this issue. We are exploring a question, or perhaps a paradox: can we be one with the experience, not dissociated from it, and also not identified with it as if it were the self, the whole of us? This requires a meta-awareness – an ability to hold in awareness the part as well as the whole; it requires the development of a non-judgemental internal witness able to be present to subtle inner experiences without inhibiting their unfolding. This is an important kind of awareness for the student of personal and spiritual growth, as well as the therapist of any discipline, to develop.

Identification with, or groundedness in, the core self gives a greater perspective and the possibility to work with the bodymind in its wholeness. From here, we can choose to identify consciously with specific aspects of the personality, sometimes expressed through the body as symptoms of illness, injuries, body-felt sensations such as pain or tension, and so on, in order to explore them further. This can help us to experience the energy, feelings, needs, and qualities they embody, and so to understand and accept them more fully.

Extending awareness gained from the inner body dialogue we can also explore how the inner dynamics embodied within our cells and tissues reflect the relationship problems or world issues which concern us. We might enquire as to whether there are any similarities or connections between the inner and outer situation, and whether the information gained from the body also has meaning for the external situation. This may bring new insight into those areas of life which hold our deepest concerns and aspirations for the world.

Myra's story

Myra's process in therapy was very much about rebalancing the energy between different body systems, and integrating psychoemotional issues somatized into distressing bodily symptoms. She was suffering from a number of physical complaints, including digestive problems, headaches, back pain, and a scoliosis since childhood. In her early twenties she had suffered a nervous breakdown followed by a period of anorexia and bulimia, and was still troubled by a less severe eating disorder. She had also overindulged in alcohol and drugs during her late teens and early twenties, and spent over four years in a destructive relationship with a man suffering from a drug and alcohol addiction. At this point she 'touched bottom' and found the strength to begin to turn her life around. She began to receive bodywork treatments and later began to train as a somatic educator; she also left the relationship she was in and found another man who was more reliable and supportive of her.

Myra clearly showed a strong determination to heal herself but despite some success in creating a new, more healthful lifestyle and career, she still felt confused, depressed, and often overwhelmed by the complex of psychosomatic symptoms she suffered from. Her childhood had been difficult; she was the fourth of six children born in rural Italy into a family struggling economically. Her father suffered a serious accident when she was three, and was unable to work for the rest of his life. He took to alcohol and was diagnosed as schizophrenic. The family suffered great emotional and financial hardship as a result of this, and Myra was sent out to work in her holidays and spare time when she was only ten years old. Her mother disapproved of her playing or wasting time, and so she missed out on a great deal of her childhood. She believed that the pain and tension she was now suffering in her body was a result of doing heavy physical work when she was so young. She was told by her mother not to depend on men, and her father told her not to marry; her mother was also fiercely critical of her, and her father would shout at her if she could not do her schoolwork, so she learned from them that she had to work, struggle, and compete, but would never win. Despite winning a place at university, she had deeply internalized the message that 'to be poor means to be stupid'; she dropped out of university and still suffered from low self-esteem, criticizing herself sharply with regard to her intelligence and talents.

Myra described her relationship with her mother as 'bad'. She had been told that her mother was still breastfeeding her older brother until at least her third month of gestation, and Myra believed that this was the cause of her lack of prenatal chi (a term from traditional Chinese medicine). Throughout her life it seemed her mother never had enough energy for her, be it love, appreciation, emotional support, or money to pay for much needed health bills throughout her childhood. She described her mother as being a 'counsellor and healer to the whole community', but never having enough left for herself and the family. Lack of maternal care and nurturance seemed to be at the root of her emotional and psychosomatic problems; her decision to study somatic therapies appears to be a healthy choice in light of this, a way of giving her body some of the nurturing touch and non-judgemental care she did not receive as a young child. Without proper care and protection from her overstretched mother and a sick and disabled father, she was undoubtedly made vulnerable as a child. She was sexually abused by an older cousin at 9 years of age, and was attacked on two occasions as a young woman; fortunately she was able to 'fight for her life', and 'talk her way out of it' on the two latter occasions, a testimony to the inner strength she possesses, despite the difficulties she had endured.

My perception was that she had internalized many of the pressures and stresses of her early life and her family's beliefs and attitudes somatically. A central imbalance had manifested within her autonomic nervous system between the sympathetic and parasympathetic branches. As we saw earlier, the sympathetic branch mediates the outer-directed, goal-oriented, active energies associated with physical survival, emotional arousal, tension, competition, and achievement in the world. The parasympathetic branch is inner-directed and mediates digestive and recuperative processes, relaxation, rest, nurturance, meditation, and inner work.

Myra found it extremely difficult to access this restful and recuperative state and felt driven much of the time by inner pressures that manifested in bodily pain, or feelings of stress and inadequacy. During one session, she had described how she was unable to relax or bring her mind into her body. I invited her to see what happened when she tried to bring her mind into her body, and she said she could not feel her sacrum and pelvis. With her permission I very gently placed my hand on her sacrum; she experienced it as a pressure, as if being pushed, and connected this to the pressure from her mother to work. The message she carried in her body was 'you must work and not have fun, or something will spoil it all'. Myra had somatized this message as an overactive sympathetic nervous system that kept her constantly in a state of tension and arousal, unable to relax fully. The natural cycle of the autonomic nervous system is arousal of the sympathetic branch, discharge of energy in some externally directed expression such as physical activity, emotional discharge, or creative work, followed by a period of rest and recuperation. At this point the parasympathetic nervous system takes over, allowing full recovery of energy and a sense of wellbeing. When this cycle is interrupted, tensions build into stress, and vulnerable areas of the body may in time manifest pain or symptoms of disease.

Myra's overactive sympathetic nervous system was not finding a satisfactory way to release the stored up energy. On one occasion, a distressing situation with her addict boyfriend had led to an uncontrolled outburst of rage in which she had almost burned down the house, and attacked her boyfriend's friend with a knife. After this she was understandably afraid of expressing her anger and turned it inwards upon herself. This is an example of how the energies of the autonomic system can suffer 'reversals'; the active, life-preserving energy of the 'fight or flight' response turns inwards to 'attack' the inner world, when safe and satisfactory channels of release are unavailable or blocked. This manifested for Myra in feelings of depression when she turned her attention inwards, instead of feelings of rest and wellbeing; in an eating disorder, headaches, and back pain; and in a virulent inner critic and a 'pushy' subpersonality who, together, made her life miserable.

She came to recognize the positive life-affirming qualities of her critic, which she felt carried her strength and creative will. It had led her to escape her stifling family situation, and eventually took her into healing work, but she also recognized that it pushes her to the point where she feels overwhelmed, exhausted, upset, and unable to sleep.

Dialogue and movement work with these subpersonalities in their various manifestations allowed her to explore her deeper needs and the energy caught up in her body, and to begin to find safer channels through which to express her strength. She discovered a 'victim' within herself whose attitude was 'I can't, poor me', in conflict with the 'critic/rebel' which she experienced as a strong, creative force which would reply, 'you must'. Both had needs. She was more familiar with the critic/rebel and its constant striving to push her onwards, but the 'victim' also needed attention, and would constantly pull the other part of her back if this was not given.

To my understanding, it was more than a victim subpersonality that she was contacting; it was the vulnerable core of her being that needed loving care and attention. The kinaesthetic image she associated with this feeling state was of being ungrounded, standing on a cylinder that was collapsing and pulling her down into the earth, draining her of energy. It made her feel lonely, insubstantial, and tired. This reminded me of the lack of inner support of her organs, which would have given her the feeling of substance, fullness, and inner strength, and the lack of essential grounding of her physical and emotional being which her mother had been unable to give her. Lack of inner support through the digestive organs in particular relates to lack of parasympathetic support – the internal processes of nourishment and recuperation – and this was visible in her precisely held posture which was vulnerable to collapse if she did not consciously hold herself up. The unfulfilled parasympathetic energy also tended to 'reverse', to express in an external complaint about inner states and symptoms, with no means to creatively process the feelings; she lacked the boundaries to contain her inner world, and it would spill out, undigested, towards whoever would receive it. I had to be careful not to get drawn into her internal 'pressure-maker', colluding with her urgent need to have her problems sorted out immediately, to work too hard to 'fix' them for her.

To work with this kind of imbalance of the autonomic nervous system a two-way approach is needed, as one branch cannot come into balance without the other doing so too. Some of our earlier sessions focused on embodying the strength that was held in her muscular tensions, reversed expressions of sympathetic charge, giving them outward form that would support rather than imprison her. This was useful in giving some degree of containment, but she was still too vulnerable to be able to address her anger directly. We needed to pay attention to nurturing her vulnerable self first, so that she could access the inner support needed to deal with her very legitimate rage.

Bodywork was important in this respect, with the focus being on bringing her into her parasympathetic nervous system. Cellular touch helped to bring her back into her body, and into herself, as she described it. The most effective place to begin work was usually with her head and neck; freeing tensions in the brain tissues at the cellular level enabled her to come into her brain stem, where the cranial nerves of the parasympathetic system would be activated. This induces release of sympathetic activity and enables the recuperative and digestive processes of the parasympathetic nervous system to take over for a while. Sometimes many images of her past would come up and pass away as we did this work; she said she could simply 'digest' and let go of them. Focus on the organs and fluids also helped to ground her in her body, and release some of the muscular tension she was holding.

Myra was well attuned to her somatic processes, and was able to recognize several specific childhood issues that she had unconsciously somatized. For example, working to gently release muscular tensions held in her neck enabled her to see how she turned her anger in on herself and held it in her neck, which caused her pain and frequent headaches. The rigidity she felt in her neck reminded her of the rigidity she had witnessed in her father's disabled body, and she felt she had 'absorbed' his pain and the anger he felt about his life into her own body. By disidentifying from the somatized image of her sick father, she was able to dialogue with him, expressing some of her held-in feelings to him. After this she could experience some relief from the pain and heaviness she had been feeling in her body.

Through exploring and amplifying tension in her shoulders, she saw that she had developed this pattern as a child to protect herself when her father and mother were fighting. Her two brothers would run away when they fought but Myra would be paralysed and would hunch her shoulders in an attempt to hide, to disappear, so that she would not get into trouble too. Exploring this postural pattern further, she felt that she had experienced everyone as being 'a weight on her back'. This was literalized when she had to spend her summer holidays working at her relatives' farm, carrying heavy loads; she saw this as a metaphor for her life. Myra had learnt to fight to survive, there being no support for her feelings as a child, but it seemed that her unshed tears and grief at the loss of her childhood had been somatized as the pain and tensions from which she now suffered.

Before she could reconnect to her true inner strength, she needed to grieve, but her process demanded that we also pay attention to not weakening her too much in this process. Several sessions focused upon releasing body tensions and helping her to experience an inner core of support and integration. Work with the bones and organs was helpful in this respect; the bones also relate to the first root chakra, our fundamental ground and support and the place of physical incarnation and connection to the family or tribe. As so many of her issues were rooted in negative family and cultural beliefs and attitudes, it was important for her to experience her own base of support in order to be able to challenge those old attitudes from a more empowered place. Releasing tensions in the neck muscles and the cells of the brain, so that she could feel a connection through her whole spine to her tail bone, was one way she found to come into her body and her sense of self. Usually after this work she would feel some relief from her symptoms for a few days, but the effects did not last; the underlying issues still needed to be addressed, and the deep feelings of hurt and anger released. In Myra's case I saw the somatic therapy as both a support to help her to contain her feelings by discovering the strength bound into her muscular tensions, and as a way of receiving some of the physical and emotional nurturance that she had not received as a child.

During one session I was touching her head, and felt a pull in the back of her neck that connected to her solar plexus area. She cried a little but did not offer anything about what she was feeling; I was picking up anger but clearly she was not in a place to address this at the moment. I asked how she felt, and she replied very quietly, 'OK, I feel dead'. She looked pale and still, signs of dissociation, and I realized she may be contacting traumatic feelings that she was not able to process. It would be counterproductive for her to remain in this dissociated state; she needed to return her consciousness to her body and to the present moment. I shifted focus to more active work through her limbs, giving a sense of the bones and then of the blood and lymph flowing through the muscles and soft tissues with a substantial squeezing and massaging quality of touch, feeding the fluids back into her centre. The colour returned to her face, and she remarked that this felt good. The blood is a nourishing and communicating fluid and gives a sense of substance, warmth, aliveness, and flow; the lymph helps us to protect ourselves by creating and maintaining boundaries. These fluids proved to be a useful support for Myra to regain a sense of her embodied and boundaried self, if she dissociated from her body.

Myra's eating disorder was less severe than it had been in her early twenties, but was still a cause of great distress. It seemed to symbolize the difficulty she experienced in nurturing and taking care of her self; our physiological relationship to the food we eat has a direct connection to the way we receive, digest, assimilate, and release nourishment, ideas, and information at all levels – physical, emotional, mental, and spiritual. She recognized a negative cycle in which she would binge on food, especially sugar, when she felt depressed and anxious, and this would bring on headaches, making her feel generally unwell, heavy, and lethargic. She also tended to 'binge' on training courses, pushing herself to learn more and more, but could not digest and assimilate the information properly. Nutritional therapy had helped her food-related problems, but as she was sticking to her diet by willpower alone, and had not resolved the underlying emotional issues, she inevitably found it hard to stay on the diet for long.

During one session she was dialoguing with her stomach. The stomach told her it wanted her not to eat so much, so that it could rest. In a deep altered state she was able to take her attention to the inside of her stomach, and learned that the stomach felt abused by having taken in things that were bad for it and by the repeated vomiting in her past; the lining of the stomach felt damaged by this treatment and still needed some time to rest and heal. In the muscular wall of her stomach she felt tightness; as she expanded widthways, consciously using her breath to help her to release the muscular holding, she felt a pain shoot up along the stomach meridian, over her heart. This brought her attention to her heart. Her heart told her, 'something inside needs to be filled, so that you can fill your life', a clear message to pay attention to her inner needs rather than seek outside for what she felt she lacked in her life. With this she realized that she had been eating to try to fill the empty space within, connected to her heart. As she focused on her heart she shed a few tears and said that joy was missing in her life. She recalled more joyful and pleasurable times in her life, when she had a good job and a carefree, fun-filled life, but then remembered that she was also abusing herself with alcohol and drugs at this time. With the memory of pleasure also came the memory of misery, guilt, and self-criticism; this was exactly the message she inherited from her mother – that pleasure would lead to suffering. In her life, joy, pleasure, and freedom had become equated with self-abuse.

Courageously staying with her heart and these painful insights, Myra found an image emerging; it was of a small flame in the very centre of her heart. As she focused on the flame in her innermost heart, she felt at peace. After a while she emerged from the inner work looking open, relaxed, and calm. This was by no means the end of Myra's work on her eating disorder, rather a beginning. The emergence of an integrating image suggests that what she was seeking in order to fill her life with joy and pleasure is truly within her, in her own heart, and that she is able to access this. The image points to a potential, and can act as a guide as to the direction for growth and healing; the presence of a healing image arising spontaneously out of bodywork suggests to me that an inner healing process had in fact been activated.

Sometime after this session Myra's attention was diverted to other issues in her life, and she began to question her wish to continue in therapy at that time; she proposed taking some time off during the summer and maybe starting again at a later date. I imagine an edge had been reached that she was not yet ready to address fully, and readiness cannot be forced. She said she felt the need to take a break from therapy, and also a therapy training programme she had begun, to simply focus on bodywork for a while, and try to have some fun. The depth of the issues she was dealing with makes it understandable that she may have felt the need for time to integrate the work she had done so far; bodywork, *without* the focus on exploring underlying painful issues, would offer a safe and nurturing place to do this. Working with her within a psychological context, supporting her to connect to and explore her feelings, I may have been experienced at this point as the mother who pushed her to work too hard and stopped her from having fun. Some difficulties she had encountered in her therapy training group had also stirred up negative feelings, which she had been unable to resolve, and this had caused her to question the psychotherapeutic way of working. Whatever her true reasons for leaving therapy, Myra's own courage and determination to heal and grow, and the guiding image of the flame in her heart, gave me trust that she would find her way.

In our final session, she said that she had learned from our work together how to approach her self with more 'softness'; that this enabled her to go deeper, and through that to contact her strength. Through softening, her body had learned to yield to the ground, and from there she could find the core of strength within herself. She had recognized that she had been too 'hard and masculine' with herself before, and that now she was beginning to connect to her 'feminine' side. This also tells me that, at a physiological level, she was integrating the work on the autonomic nervous system; through softening and releasing into the parasympathetic mode, she found more inner support, and the two aspects of her being, experienced as a 'masculine', dynamic, pushy, and goal-oriented approach to life, and a 'feminine', softer, intuitive, and process-oriented way, were moving towards a more harmonious balance. Perhaps by projecting onto her therapist the mother who pushed her too hard, she was able to identify with her gentler more nurturing side. Although the therapy was not complete, by saying no to her therapist-mother for the time being, she was saying yes to, and affirming, herself and her own needs.

CHAPTER 9

Dancing with the shadow

When addressing the integration of unexpressed body systems through somatic movement therapy and bodywork we must inevitably grapple with the psychological shadow and the feelings that may arise when confronted with facing and owning the disavowed, unconscious, and repressed parts of ourselves. When we reach the limits of what we identify with as *self*, we may meet with resistance, fear, denial, and what Arnold Mindell calls *edge figures*, those dynamics within our own psyche that seek to prevent us from accessing the energies and the knowledge of the shadow. It is within this area of growth that psychological techniques and understanding are useful, if not essential, for the somatic therapist. In my own practice I draw primarily upon the techniques and perspectives of psychosynthesis and process-oriented psychology, with an awareness of psychodynamic and transference/ countertransference issues, as guides and supports for the intuitive approach I have evolved through somatic work. Other psychotherapies, of course, can also be integrated with somatic work; psychodynamic, Jungian, and Gestalt approaches are amongst those sometimes used by somatic therapists to process psychological material arising during somatic work.

Accessing non-verbal information

During an initial interview, or dialogue at the beginning of a session, the therapist seeking to integrate psychological process with somatic therapy will be observing, listening, and feeling on many levels. The relationship between conscious and unconscious processes is explored; what the client is intending to communicate, and her conscious attitude towards her problems, is heard against the background of the subtler messages coming from the unconscious. This information may be expressed through unintended or unexpected movements, the quality of movement, body posture and tone, the quality of the voice, or through the way the client addresses and relates to the therapist; it may also be expressed through dreams, images, synchronicities, disturbing relationship or world problems described by the

192

client. These communications can be thought of as information that is seeking to become conscious, and is already near to the borders of the client's conscious awareness but not yet fully perceived. Such information indicates the process that is attempting to unfold through the client at the moment; aspects of the shadow needing to be integrated frequently manifest in unconscious bodily expressions.

Important information can also be gathered when the therapist pays attention to her own body sensations, feelings, moods, posture, movements, fantasies, etc. in the presence of the client. The therapist's own person is the most powerful tool in the therapeutic relationship. Awareness of one's personal process in the presence of the client, and skilful use of this awareness to facilitate the client's process, is essential. Everything the therapist experiences is potentially related to the client's process in a meaningful way, as the two people are not only separate individuals but also exist within a shared field of energy and consciousness. The relationship between therapist and client may also manifest somatically.

Practices such as bodywork, t'ai chi ch'uan, yoga, meditation, and somatic movement therapy can help to train sensitivity to one's own and another's somatic and energetic processes. Body-mind centering trains practitioners to finely discriminate different states of awareness expressed through the body, and to resonate at a cellular level with the client. From a bodily point of view, I feel that much of the information we pick up from another when we are witnessing with sensitivity and openness happens at the cellular level, beyond conscious and unconscious nervous system processing. From a process viewpoint, we resonate with the unconscious signals of the client because we are part of the same *field,* and so can access information belonging to the whole field by paying attention to what is happening within us. This information contributes to what we call intuitive insights, which should not be reduced to purely imaginative guesswork; they are the results of integrating information that is processed beyond conscious sensory and cortical channels with information that is accessible to consciousness.

To understand the messages that the body reveals, the therapist must open herself fully to her experience of the other. Body psychotherapists Ron Kurtz and Hector Prestera, discussing how a person's way of being in the world is embodied in her muscular patterning, remind us of this:

> To see these patterns, and read the messages they contain, one needs a willingness to be affected by whatever is there. It is not only a matter of looking with the eyes; it is as much a sensing with the heart. It is a subtle sensing, of energies and vibrations not easily explainable. To the degree that we are open, unafraid, and consciously let ourselves be acted upon by another individual, to that degree we see his patterns, sense his energies, feel his pain, and know him. So: what the body reveals lies as much within us as within the someone we are trying to know.
> (Kurtz and Prestera, 1976: 4)

John Rowan writes about four levels of experience that are involved in the process of holistic listening. Drawing together experiences from a variety of practitioners he has developed a model that examines the four types of listening; they involve the mind, feelings, body, and soul or spirit of both the speaker and the listener. At the first stage we pay attention to the intellectual content of what is being said, and at the next level we also listen to the emotional expression; this is what we generally think of as empathic listening. Going further, we develop awareness of the non-verbal bodily messages, listening consciously to 'the body-feeling-thinking whole that is the talker' (Rowan, 1985: 277). Beyond this, in listening with our whole being to the whole being of the other, we include the soul or spirit, where:

> Instead of grasping and grabbing the world, we find ourselves allowing the world to come in to us, so that we can flow out and become that world, losing our usual boundaries . . . We can then suspend thinking and be aware of our experience in the ever-flowing present. This could be called holistic listening.
>
> But this is not all. If we can listen in this full way, our own psychic faculties can come into the picture. We can use our intuition in making remarkable leaps, leading to striking insights. We can use symbol and fantasy instead of words. We can tune in to the mythic aspects of what is being said. (Rowan, 1985: 278)

Rowan goes on to describe the processes of *countertransference* and *resonance,* using his four-fold model. In the case of countertransference, the listener pays attention to her own responses on each of these levels, as well as her client's communications, and uses them to inform the therapeutic interaction. Resonance goes one step deeper; it occurs when 'the listener sets up a model of the talker inside the listener'; she 'shares and attends to the talker's attentional centre and allows that centre to shift to inside the listener' (Rowan, 1985: 281–2). In this way the listener can experience and feel *with* the talker, which is the basis of the meaning of compassion. The ability to resonate with another is also cultivated through the discipline of witnessing in authentic movement, described earlier.

Whilst holding all of the information gathered through this multilayered process of listening, the therapist searches and waits, together with the client, for the emergence of the overall context of the work and the central themes which need to be addressed, not 'grasping and grabbing', but 'allowing the world to come in to us'. The relationship between the client's conscious awareness of her problems or symptoms, and the unconscious signals being expressed, gives important keys. For example, a client talks energetically, jumping from one topic to another in a somewhat chaotic but wholehearted and passionate manner, gesturing expressively with her hands and moving her body a lot as she speaks. In contrast to this, she holds her neck stiffly. As awareness is brought to this and it is explored, she realises that she is holding her neck in an attempt to feel a sense of stability and security. A focus for her work emerges as a need for more inner stability, centredness, and containment, all qualities that she was not able to develop in her home environment as a child. This is reflected in a recent dream image of a white foal frolicking in the sunlight, contained by a white rope that encircles a wide corral. She describes her feeling within the dream as joyful, as the foal could move freely within the security of the boundaried space. She understands from this that she needs an internalized sense of boundary in order to express herself more safely and fully. The tension in her neck could then be recognized as an unconscious attempt to provide the containment and sense of security she had not experienced in her childhood.

Applications of somatic therapy to psychological process

There are several ways in which bodywork and somatic movement therapy may be used to access, explore, unfold, and integrate the client's process. In practice these avenues often overlap, but I will attempt here to differentiate some main approaches.

Observation of movements and other bodily expressions in the client, and the therapist's own somatic responses to the client, give information that may indicate a starting place for the work, or directions to pursue. In the simplest form, bodywork may involve asking the client to pay attention to body sensations, breathing, or impulses to move; or if an emotional feeling is present, the client may be asked to become aware of how she experiences this feeling in her body. This information might be explored through imagery, for example, if the client describes an image in relation to the body process. Various techniques of active imagination and inner dialogue can be used. If the client's description of her experience has a strong movement content, the movement that she uses to describe the feeling may be explored, sometimes evolving into dance. Embodying a body sensation or feeling through movement helps to amplify it and draw out the energy and meaning behind the symptom. This can be further integrated through dialogue, or perhaps through creative work such as drawing, dance, song, or storytelling. The client's process will indicate the way.

When the client's description is primarily in terms of body sensation, hands-on bodywork might be indicated. In making choices about how to enter and support the client's process through touch, the therapist is informed by the relationship between psychological issues and physical symptoms, and choices are made within the overall context of the client's process. Body-mind centering offers a language for bodymind experience that I find both profound and embracing. As described in earlier chapters, specific movement patterns and body tissues embody particular emotions, perceptions, and qualities of awareness; this information offers guidelines as to which level of body tissue, or what kind of movement patterning, we need to work with. Although body-mind centering gives a detailed analysis of body-mind relationships, I feel that it is important that the client makes her own connections to the work we do. Rather than making interpretations, I allow the client to discover her own meaning, holding knowledge about generalized experience only as 'background information' that may guide the work but is not imposed upon the client's experiences. What the client discovers is her own relationship to the function and qualities which a body system or movement patterning embodies, and the meaning of the experience will be unique to each person. Often a body symptom or emotional disturbance will not change until the personal (and sometimes collective) meaning behind the symptom has been understood, embodied, and integrated into awareness and life.

Various touch and movement repatterning techniques, which have the potential to work at different levels, can be used. At one level, they can be effective in repatterning neuromuscular coordination, and integrating the mind and body in movement and vocal expression. This approach does not directly address the psychoemotional aspect of symptoms and body experiences but most certainly affects them, and should be related to the overall process of the client. It works primarily through the nervous system on the various body tissues. If emotional responses come up through this work, or insight is gained into psychological patterns, various psychotherapeutic or counselling techniques may be used to help unfold and integrate the process.

Another approach is to begin in a receptive state, witnessing and accessing information directly from the client's body through the hands. A dialogue evolves as the client's awareness is deepened to unconscious information held in the body; the dialogue may take place verbally, or it may take place directly through the body with a combination of touch and movement. Usually both verbal and somatic dialogue are used, so that we move between the conscious and unconscious, and open channels of communication between them. Without conscious acknowledgement and integration of awareness accessed through the body, the information may slip back into unconsciousness: symptoms may remain unchanged, or return once the immediate effects of the bodywork session have worn off. However, it is important not to try to analyse and understand a body process too soon, as the direct experience can be lost through premature intellectualization, and the process aborted. It is also important to remember that the nervous system needs time, repetition, and support to integrate new experiences, especially when they relate to deep and old patterning.

Bodywork and movement may also be used to support and integrate a psychological process, or an emerging quality or energy, which has been explored through other channels. Through specific qualities of touch, repatterning, or movement expression, we can support the energetic and psychological process that is unfolding. For example, during one session a client was exploring difficulties she experienced in standing her own ground in the face of others' criticisms, and her need for external affirmation and support in following her own path. She found an inner wise figure who could both protect and support her, and embodied this figure in her own posture and energetic presence. After drawing and dialoguing with this figure, we came back to the body. Something was attempting to express through her arms and hands. Responding to the movements she was beginning to make, I invited her to explore with me a dance of pushing against each other's hands. It related to an early movement pattern where the infant is establishing her physical and psychological boundaries, and sense of a core self; in this movement the infant learns to push up onto the support of her arms, and face the world for the first time from this new upright and *human* perspective. This stage of development has deep implications for the development of our ability to stand our ground, fend for ourselves, develop and express our strength, and maintain physical and psychological boundaries.

This client realized that she was generally unaware of the strength of her arms, and as a child tended to pull her energy into the muscles between her shoulder blades to defend herself from ridicule. She also felt she had never been encouraged to grow up or taught the skills to deal with adult responsibilities; her family preferred to keep her as the 'baby'. Finding strength and integration in her arms related to developing the ability to support herself and her own vision in the world. In the previous session we had begun to explore her relationship to her hands and arms through bodywork, and I had been reminded of the story of 'the handless maiden' as especially appropriate to her situation (Estes, 1992: 387–455). Women's feelings of disempowerment and worldly ineffectiveness in a patriarchal culture are often expressed through weakness in the hands, arms, and shoulder area; this story offers a map for women's healing and reempowerment. For this client, the actual embodiment of this area of her body through touch and movement brought greater insight and integration of the qualities accessed in her visualization and dialogue process.

The use of touch in psychotherapy

There are a number of benefits that the use of touch in therapy can elicit, as we have explored in previous chapters. To summarize, for clients who may have received inadequate or invasive touch in childhood, it may offer an experience of nurturance, comfort, and safety, which can help heal the wounds of early life, and support the development of the sense of a core self. Nurturance of the core creates the condition which Keleman describes as *grounding*:

> Almost universally, we have made a separation between what we call our selves and our bodily processes and feelings. We are like trees uprooted from the earth; we have lost our nourishment, support, and ability to grow. In my language, we are not grounded.
>
> To me, grounding means being anchored in our physical-psychic growth processes . . . Grounding means being rooted in and partaking of the essence of the human animal function. (Keleman, 1976: 192)

Physical touch and holding can also give a sense of *containment* that helps to strengthen body-ego boundaries when there is insufficient integration, and enables a client to contain overwhelming feelings. Keleman describes containment as:

> . . . The development of the ability to hold, allow, and be transformed by feelings. By living with and from our feelings, by allowing them to change us and growing with them, greater possibilities for love and expression are progressively revealed to us. (Keleman, 1976: 198)

Touch also stimulates vital physiological processes, as well as nurturing the ability to bond and relate to another. Montagu (1971: Chapters 1 and 4) describes the importance of touch for both infant and mother, whether human or animal, immediately after birth and during early life. The efficiency of important functions such as respiration, digestion and elimination, and immunology depends upon appropriate contact between mother and child. For adults, too, nurturing touch can have a healing, reparative effect, as described earlier.

Touch and bodywork can also be used to access memories stored in the body, to explore and resolve emotional experiences, to reduce tension and body armouring, and to experience the core of inner strength and support in the body. It can help create a more positive relationship to one's own body, and a healthy self-image. In the process of the psychologically maturing adult, integrating bodily sensation, emotion, and awareness enables us to heal the splits between body, feelings, mind, and spirit and cultivate the integrated bodymind described by Wilber as *centauric consciousness.*

Contraindications to touch

Somatic therapies can help in all of these areas. However, there are times when touch is not helpful and may be counterproductive or even damaging to the client, or the client-therapist relationship. Moving along the developmental continuum, at some point in the therapeutic process a client needs to move out of the preverbal, merger-like states that touch and somatic therapy can support. She will need to separate from the therapist who may be embodying the 'good mother', to develop her sense of being an independent and assertive individual, as well as learning to experience genuine and intimate relationship with another as an adult. Her anger may need to be expressed and her sexuality included. When these issues are dominant in the therapeutic process, bodywork involving primarily gentle, nurturing touch is generally not helpful and may inhibit appropriate development.

A somatic therapist may not have enough awareness of these changing psychological needs. What frequently happens is that a client simply leaves therapy if her need for a different approach has not been recognized; if the therapist is not aware of the psychological needs, the issue and the reasons for termination will probably remain unconscious. Or the client and therapist may collude in maintaining a symbiotic relationship to avoid anger, hostility, or the ending of their work together. The client can remain stuck at an early stage of development and may become addicted to the therapy and the therapeutic relationship. That is certainly not to say that long-term somatic therapy is always a negatively collusive enterprise; a client who is psychologically mature, or who receives psychotherapy elsewhere, may simply need to receive nurturing and healing touch on an ongoing basis, and may grow from the insight she gains from it. However, without relevant training the somatic therapist may not be able to differentiate her clients' psychological needs clearly.

Hunter and Struve explore the use of touch in psychotherapy, describing the many benefits of touch and the ways that it can remain safe and ethical. The use of touch in verbal psychotherapy has traditionally been prohibited. As it is not an expected and generally accepted element of psychotherapy, its inclusion needs to be approached with care. In the somatic therapies, touch is usually an expected part of therapy. However, the issues raised in their book, *The Ethical Use of Touch in Psychotherapy*, are also relevant to the somatic therapist, who may be unaware of underlying psychological issues such as abuse or trauma, transference and countertransference, and the power of the client-therapist relationship.

Sexual contact with a client is never ethical. A somatic therapist is highly trained in the use of touch and the different qualities of touch, and should be able to provide touch that is clearly non-erotic. If this is not the case, and they are unable to differentiate sexual and non-sexual touch, they clearly should not be practising a therapy that involves the use of touch. A psychotherapist may not have such a clearly differentiated sense of touch; in general, it would be advisable not to use touch as an intervention within psychotherapy without some training and personal experience in this modality. If the therapist is uncomfortable or insecure with touch, this will be communicated to the client and interpreted variably; her own fear, anxiety, unclarity about touching, unmet touch needs, or lack of body-mind integration may all influence the way touch is received by a client. So much is communicated by even the simplest gesture of touch that it is a subject all therapists would benefit from exploring further.

Despite the enormous complexity of the use of touch in psychotherapy, and the possible dangers of it being misused, the benefits are also too great to ignore. As Hunter and Struve (1998: 8) write:

> The primary objection to therapist-client contact results from extreme cases in which a therapist has violated professional standards and has, consequently, become sexual with clients. Any psychological technique – touch, talk, testing, research – can be done in an unethical manner by a particular therapist. The unethical use of any technique ought to be the cause for an indictment not of

the technique but rather of the clinician who misused it. Touch is too valuable a
tool in the service of human healing to deny its use to the psychotherapist.

Eiden (1999: 5) describes how the 'no touch' rule evolved from a mistaken
view that all touch is sexualizing, based on the psychoanalytic view that
the sexual drive was primary and all other physical needs evolved from it.
Now there is much more understanding within the body psychotherapy
field of the difference between nurturing and sexual touch, and these old
rules need to be reassessed in the light of new knowledge. It can even be
argued that not to use such a valuable tool as touch is unethical, for it may
deprive clients of exactly what they need for their healing and growth and
reenact a dynamic of touch deprivation, isolation, or neglect that is at the
source of their difficulties. It should also be remembered that not touching
will give messages to the client as much as touching will, and can equally
well create transference.

Despite the healing potential for the therapeutic use of touch, it is
clearly not appropriate in every therapeutic situation. A client who has
been physically or sexually abused, for example, may feel very threatened
by even the most gentle and caring touch and the use of touch must be
approached with great caution in such cases. Such a client can easily feel
revictimized by the therapist's touch and therapy may create more damage
than it heals. However, at the right moment, and in the right way, touch
can be very healing for clients who have suffered abuse or inappropriate
touching in the past.

One client would frequently request bodywork but invariably fall asleep
the moment he was touched. When questioned about this, he replied that
he was very tired, and that it was good for him to be able to let go enough to
fall asleep. Whilst I am sure there was some truth in this it happened so
consistently that I had to consider whether it was a form of defence. We
focused more specifically on his awareness of what he experienced at the
moment he was touched, maintaining contact for only very brief moments
then dialoguing about his responses. He was eventually able to stay
conscious throughout the touch encounter and he came to experience a
sense of safety he had not experienced before; he later affirmed that it had
been very important for him to experience being touched without any
demands being made upon him. The recognition of this need led to a greater
level of trust and respect in his relationship to me as a female therapist.
Some positive changes in his relationship with his wife also followed. The
feelings evoked in me when I worked somatically with this client suggested
that he had suffered from inappropriate handling as a small child and from
invasive maternal attention and expectations that he could not live up to.
Falling asleep during sessions was a way of shutting out this information and
defending himself from his therapist-mother's demands and expectations,
including the expectation that he become more conscious, which would
also entail taking more responsibility for himself.

It may sometimes be necessary to suspend the use of touch, at least temporarily, for example if negative or sexual transference and countertransference issues have arisen, or when verbal and Oedipal stages of development are dominant in the therapy. Similarly, when traumatic material emerges during the course of therapy, or when a traumatized client comes into therapy, the use of touch and other somatic techniques must be addressed with great care and understanding, to avoid retraumatization.

Hunter and Struve (1998: 10-11) remind us that the age at which traumatic or wounding events have occurred may determine the way in which they are stored by the bodymind. Until the age of 3 or 4 years, touch is the more dominant sense for children, and experiences related to this age may be stored somatically through the tactile sense. Beyond this age vision tends to become more important and memories may be stored visually. They also describe how children spend much of their time in trance-like altered states of consciousness. When confronted with confusing or distressing experiences children cope by entering an altered state; whilst in such states, memories of traumatic events are stored through the process of *state-dependent learning* (Van der Kolk and Van der Hart, 1989: 1530-40). As described in Chapter 2, certain neuropeptides are released into the body at the same time as memory is being laid down. Later experiences in some way replicating the original trauma will trigger the rerelease of the same neuropeptides, causing the person to enter again an altered state of consciousness in which memories of the original event may be vividly recalled and relived. Only when people *safely* have access to these highly charged states can their responses to such stimuli be altered, and the original trauma resolved (Hunter and Struve, 1998: 10-11). Without adequate safety, a client will almost inevitably feel retraumatized if such a state is reconstellated within the therapeutic work.

Because of the close connection between the tactile sense, childhood development, and altered states of consciousness, touch within a therapeutic context holds an immense power to both heal and harm. Therapists using touch, as well as visual techniques such as guided imagery, should be aware of the potential to retraumatize a client during the induction of an altered state of consciousness, and be able to recognize the symptoms of shock trauma so as to avoid this danger. (Levine, 1997, and Rothschild, 2000, give excellent descriptions of a safe and effective approach to healing trauma.)

Transference, countertransference, and the body

Somatic therapies are most distinct from body psychotherapy in their approach to the client-therapist relationship. Like other psychotherapies, body psychotherapy focuses upon the relationship, which is understood as the 'crucible of transformation'. In distinction to this, as Bernd Eiden (1999: 12-14) writes: 'Although a holistic model of the client is common to all approaches involving the body, most body therapies need to rely on a quasi-medical "expert" relationship to the patient whom they treat.'

To the degree that a quasi-medical model is used, the client may feel disempowered or dependent, and the model does not traditionally allow for these dynamics to be addressed. I have met many somatic therapists of different disciplines who, through their own personalities and sensitivity, empower their clients and engage them actively in the healing process; a spectrum of different attitudes and approaches will be found within this field, as all others, which are dependent at least as much upon personal qualities as professional training and approach. However, the client-therapist relationship and the dynamics of transference and countertransference are not explicitly addressed within the somatic therapies and it is in this area that body psychotherapy significantly differs and can usefully inform somatic practice.

The unconscious aspects of the relationship between therapist and client are expressed through the transference and countertransference. The phenomenon of transference was first discovered by Freud and his colleagues, and consciously working through the transference became a central technique in psychoanalytic practice. Will Davis (1989: 10) summarizes the view that is generally held within psychoanalytic schools: 'Transference is generally understood to be a process whereby the patient transfers his feelings and wishes onto the person of the therapist who has come to represent someone from the patient's past.'

The therapist may be experienced and related to as the 'good mother' the client never had, or the abusive father who tyrannized her childhood, or perhaps a teacher who judged and criticized her, for example. Bringing consciousness to the historical roots of transferential material is a central element of psychoanalysis and many forms of psychotherapy. However, since the time of Freud, various understandings and definitions of transference have evolved, and a clear and generally accepted definition tends to elude us.

Davis (1989: 10) suggests that, whilst being an actual phenomenon, it is also 'merely a "form" and a "tool" created by the client to "manifest and work through deeper unconscious processes".' He also believes that defining it as the substitution of the therapist for someone in the client's past limits its use by viewing it from a purely psychological perspective; the real roots of transference as an *energetic* phenomenon, as it was first understood by Freud, are obscured by this narrow view. For Freud, and Reich too, transference was seen as a natural process, present in healthy as well as neurotic individuals. In their view, it entails the radiation of libido outwards from the core, towards another; this enables the formation of object-attachment, and is the basis of all relationship. It is 'an energetic function that manifests in the psychic realm' (Davis, 1989: 12). Working psychologically through the repressed emotions associated with a transference is necessary but will not completely resolve a client's problem; she must also learn to take responsibility, in the present, for her libidinal impulses, her needs and desires, and to make appropriate choices which will bring her the love and fulfilment she is seeking in her adult life. However, Reich believed that until latent negative transference has been worked through, *genuine* transference, as a natural and healthy libidinal process, cannot occur. In the views of Freud and Reich, genuine (Reich) or positive (Freud) transference comes energetically from the very core of the person. Davis affirms that 'genuine transference must occur for the work to be successful' (Davis, 1989: 17).

The distinction between 'transference as a natural organismic process and transference neurosis' is further explored by Jacob Stattman (1988: 27). He believes that:

> The energetic psychodynamic underlying the transference mechanism is a natural function of the growth process in the very beginning of life itself, commencing before birth and at its most effective, in the first two years of life. The transference neurosis associated with the onset of the Oedipal period is a later development of the selfsame patterns which arise in the first two years. This Oedipal process is more easily seen and understood in part because there is memory to some degree in the client, and because it takes place in the verbal phase of growth. It can be spoken about . . . The transference of the first two years is natural, essentially somatic, non-verbal and preverbal. It is due to these points that transference remains a life-long phenomena in relationship constantly energized by the character structure embedded in the body itself and unavailable to the conscious, verbal, and rational aspects of mind alone. (Stattman, 1988: 28)

The origins of identity formation in the infant are rooted in the infant-mother relationship, experienced somatically in the earliest symbiotic stages of development. Through her mother's body the infant experiences and learns about her own; the mother's body is her ground and a necessary mirror for the development of the infant's own embodied sense of being. Through processes of somatic imitation, she gradually evolves her own embodied identity in the likeness of her mother. The mother can only transfer somatically to her child what she is herself, and so 'whatever is missing or distorted in mother's body is also mirrored in the developing body/self of the infant' (Stattman, 1988: 29). The failure of organic transference, of the ability to transfer the sense of embodied being, and the full range of human experience to the child, becomes a cause for a transference neurosis to develop; throughout life, such an individual will then be impelled to seek from significant others what she finds lacking in herself, that which was not nurtured into being by the maternal somatic matrix, in order to complete herself.

Stattman therefore considers that the development of character structures, and the dynamics of the relationships a person forms with partners or therapist, are indicative of the primary transference and the primary transference neurosis. The analysis of character through the developmental and Oedipal stages is a secondary model that will be founded upon the primary one. The frustration of needs leads the infant to contract and withdraw from the mother, breaking or weakening the transference; defensive behaviours develop which are the basis of the formation of neurotic character structures, embodied resistances to one's own libidinal nature, to the free flow of energy to and from the core:

> Life-affirmative vitality has been rejected due to an incapacity to live out the dynamics of the natural transference between two living beings. Every relationship from this point forward will contain a healthy impulse for transference and the elements of the transference neurosis. (Stattman, 1988: 31)

> The movement towards individuation is supported by a person as child to the degree the transference relation provides the resources required. Whatever is blocked by the transference neurosis also blocks an authentic individuation process. (Stattman, 1988: 35)

In therapy, the transference and transference neurosis are intensified. As with the mother-infant relationship, the therapist communicates to the client through her bodily presence and expressions, in such a way that she presents a mirror for the client to see her own reflection in; gradually the mirror will dissolve until it is no longer needed, and the merged can now exist as two separate beings, each a witness to the other. According to Stattman:

> The transference is thus transformation in its fullness. Reality is disclosed in all its aspects. The client will change according to the quality of the transference, NOT according to the quality of work on and reaction to the transference neurosis by itself. Where there is transference, the resistance decreases, energy increases, and relationship replaces the symbiosis according to organic principles universal in nature . . . When we are humanly present, the transference neurosis is fully disclosed, and loses its force to distort the transference, in life and in therapy. (Stattman, 1988: 40)

David Boadella (1980: 1) uses the terms *interference* and *resonance* to describe these different levels in the therapeutic relationship. For him, a resonance pattern is the natural state of bonding between the child and parent, or between two adults, when a healthy relationship allows energy to flow freely from the core of each person. Transference and countertransference are reflections of early interference patterns that arise when resonance is disturbed; the disturbance can be on the part of the client or the therapist, respectively. Transference and countertransference are seen as disturbances in bonding.

Boadella uses Reich's model of the three layers of the personality to elucidate his theory. The superficial layer is the mask, the defensive character structure that is presented to the world. Beneath lies the secondary layer of the shadow where distorted or repressed energy, and negative emotions such as anger, fear, tension, anxiety, and stress reside. The primary and deepest layer is the core, where authentic positive feelings have their source. He suggests that resonance occurs when both partners are in touch with and relating from their core. Relationship from the superficial layer can manifest positive transference and countertransference; the secondary layer may evoke negative transference and countertransference. Therapy must lead the client beyond the transference, both positive and negative, to the core, so that a state of resonance can be created; only then, according to Boadella, can meaningful work be done, and bonding and genuine relationship occur. It is also essential that the therapist can meet the client from her own core process, and not from the more superficial layers, in order for therapy to be successful (Boadella, 1980: 2-3).

Davis makes the point that what Boadella is calling resonance is not equivalent to Reich's genuine positive transference. For Reich, a false positive transference must be overcome before the core can be reached; but genuine transference is something qualitatively different, an energetic expression from the core, a libidinal radiation and reaching out towards another which is a natural and healthy process throughout life. Davis agrees that resonance is a vital process in therapeutic work, but differentiates it from genuine transference, which must be present in order for resonance to occur:

> As Reich describes it, after Freud, transference is a spontaneous, energetic reaching out that happens regardless of the response. It is primary. The response from the desired object will affect what comes of this, but transference is an internally motivated, unstoppable happening. The response and rapport that follows will affect the psychic structure of the individual and the therapeutic relationship and both will determine the quality of the resonance. Transference, therefore, is a spontaneous, core originated process – a movement out by the individual into the world, while resonance is the vibrational harmonizing between two or more organisms psychically and/or somatically once this initial process has occurred. Transference, in its initial impulse, is essentially intra-psychic. Resonance is always inter-psychic, interpersonal. Both are required for successful work, but resonance is a consequence of Reich's genuine transference or Freud's positive transference. (Davis, 1989: 15)

Davis goes on to describe how traditional therapeutic approaches seek to influence the client from without, through an interpsychic, relational process; in doing this, they will inevitably encounter the defensive layers of the transference neurosis, as they seek to contact the inner core of the client. The transference must be worked through for therapy to be successful; ego defences and resistance must be encountered, broken down and overcome. However, when the focus is on energetic and intrapsychic process, the work comes from within the client and moves outwards; the therapist is primarily in a supportive role. In this approach, as energy begins to flow from within outwards, we might again expect to encounter the defences of the transference neurosis. However, Davis affirms that energy flowing outwards from the core is not necessarily obstructed by the ego defence system; when this system is not activated, energy can and does flow outward freely: 'In fact, there *is* no battle, so the energetic forces respond naturally: transferring, flowing outward, seeking contact, attachment, and eventually, response' (Davis, 1989: 20).

Somatic therapies focus on energetic work from within, encouraging and supporting the free flow of energy from the inner core of the client, outwards. The somatic therapist has many ways to access the client's core energy; in body-mind centering practice, a key access may be through a specific organ system, the body fluids, or a developmental movement pattern, for example – the route of access will be unique for each client, and it is the therapist's task to help discover and contact this place of access. Once contacted, core energy is supported to flow freely and express the impulse that emanates from the core. For this reason, a somatic therapist may be able to facilitate significant change in some clients, without specific attention to transference issues – provided, of course, that she too is in touch with her own core, and can offer an authentic response from there to her client's radiating energy.

Somatic resonance

Stanley Keleman first introduced the term *somatic resonance* to signify that this responsive rapport is sourced in the biological and energetic core of each partner in the relationship. We are always, inevitably but usually unconsciously, receiving somatic messages from others. Our own bodies respond to what we unconsciously feel and perceive – adapting, mirroring, internalizing, defending – and in this way our environment helps shape our ongoing experience of ourselves. The somatic and body psychotherapist develops conscious awareness of the somatic as well as emotional responses she has to her client. Being able to feel and respond to another's somatic expression enables us to contact her core experience, and somatic resonance then becomes possible. Boadella writes:

> In work on transforming blocked patterns of feeling and expression, the most essential tool is the responsive life of another human being. Reich called this 'vegetative identification', the ability to sense in our own body the blocked patterns of expression that are constricting another. Stanley Keleman used the term 'somatic resonance' for the biological rapport between two people. (Boadella, 1987: xv)

The term *somatic countertransference* is used to refer to the bodily feelings and sensations which are evoked in the therapist by the client's presence, process, and transferential material. This phenomenon has been noted previously as an important tool for the body-oriented therapist, who gathers subtle information regarding the client's unconscious process by paying attention to her own somatic responses to the client. Traditionally, somatic countertransference has been viewed less positively. As Michael Soth writes:

. . . The term 'somatic countertransference' is generally used [to refer] to interactions which we think of as involving primitive processes of projective identification. The danger with this specific and rather restricted use of the term is that we can easily forget that any countertransference experience is bound to also have a somatic aspect . . .

In this sense the term 'somatic countertransference' owes more to psychotherapy's traditional focus on the therapist's thinking (as opposed to feeling and sensation) than to clinical accuracy and coherence. In other words: the term is still more a symptom of the return of the counsellor's own repressed body than an expression of its integration. From an holistic perspective, 'somatic countertransference' is like saying a 'swimming fish'.

But having said that, the term can retain some clinical usefulness if we're clear that the main feature is not the somatic nature of the experience, but the degree to which the body can be experienced as alien. This alienness is a function of the client's body/mind split, i.e. their internal sense of dissociation, which can indeed communicate itself to the counsellor through projective identification. The intensity of the counsellor's somatic experience is then a measure of the client's dissociation from it. (Soth, 1999a: 15-17)

Maarten Aalberse explores further the somatic process involved in countertransference and projective identification. Drawing upon Thomas Ogden's understanding of projective identification, Aalberse (1994: 59-60) summarizes its four stages:

- Essentially, one person (the client) tries to rid herself of an unwanted or intolerable feeling, impulse, or self-image by projecting or depositing it onto another (the therapist), who functions as container for the projected content. It may be an aspect of herself that is felt to be negative and dangerous, or something too precious to keep safely within herself.
- The sender must be sure that it has been received. To this end, she will put pressure on the receiver so that the receiver is induced to feel or behave in a way that accords with the projected content; if the receiver shows signs, usually non-verbally, that she has received and felt the content of the projection, the sender will feel some reassurance, and the bond between them will be enhanced.
- The third stage of the process involves the receiver's ability to process the content so that it becomes less toxic, more bearable, possibly even enjoyable. If this can be done, the sender learns that the projected feelings can be tolerated, and some healing may occur. If the receiver cannot accept and process the feelings and impulses, they are taken back and experienced as even worse, less tolerable than before, by the sender.
- In the fourth stage, the sender reassimilates the projected content, together with the receiver's feelings about it and her ways of transforming it, internalizing the receiver's responses into her own way of being.

Aalberse points out that this process may occur not simply as a means for the sender to get rid of intolerable feelings, but in order that she may be more fully understood. And the assimilation of the projected content by the receiver may be a natural and healthy process by one who seeks to understand:

> It may also be that these induced feelings are not precisely intended to be dumped in a container outside the self. The subject may 'only' want to make himself understood effectively, without necessarily wanting to 'dump' his feelings and impulses. And the object (parent or therapist) may want to understand the subject (baby or client) so deeply that he opens himself for all the non-verbal messages that the subject involuntarily sends out. Reich has labelled this process of tuning into deep somatic processes of another person 'vegetative identification'. As a result of close observation and vegetative identification the mother figure or therapist feels in his own body vegetative rhythms that are closely similar to those of the child or client. And by making sense of these rhythms, one becomes able to understand what the other is experiencing. (Aalberse, 1994: 64)

The therapist can make a conscious and voluntary effort to identify or resonate with the client but this also commonly occurs involuntarily via the process of organic transference described by Stattman. When seeking contact with another person, we tend to take on that person's breathing pattern, posture, tension or movement patterns, which causes us to feel to some extent the way the other person feels. Aalberse believes that much of the induced countertransference that occurs in therapy can be explained in this way. Depending on the therapist's degree of conscious awareness and ability to transform projected contents, the client may experience healing or further toxification.

The therapist's responsibility

It is the therapist's responsibility to be aware of the nature of a transference that has arisen in the client, and to determine appropriate responses. She must also develop an ongoing awareness as to how the client's material affects her, and the ways in which she may unconsciously respond and defend herself against the feelings and conflicts evoked in herself by the client. At each level that transference may arise in the client, so too may countertransference be evoked in the therapist. This too can be seen as an inevitable process, and not a failure of the therapy, so long as the therapist is conscious of her responses to the client, and is able to deal with them appropriately. The therapist must always strive to use the counter-transferential feelings evoked in her to the benefit of the client, and not to further her own agenda or personal needs. A constant reflection upon the personal issues evoked in the therapist by the client's process and transference is required, to safeguard the client from revictimization, abuse, collusive gratification, or other problems potential in the therapeutic relationship.

In discussing the ethical use of touch in psychotherapy, Hunter and Struve (1998: 246) write:

> We do not subscribe to theoretical orientations that define transference within the paradigm of client resistance, nor do we believe that countertransference is indicative of therapist incompetence or misjudgment. To the contrary, transference and countertransference are inherently present in all human transactions and, therefore, they are natural and expected within any therapeutic relationship. Furthermore, we believe that dealing with these complexities openly and directly – particularly when touch has become a consideration in the therapist-client relationship – is one of the most prudent strategies to ensure that the psychotherapy remains ethical.

They go on to describe several forms of transference (in the sense of interference patterns, or false positive and negative transferences, as described above) that can be expected to emerge, which might be particularly intensified when touch is used in the psychotherapeutic relationship, such as the therapist as 'perpetrator', as 'nurturant figure', as 'ideal figure', as 'good partner', and as 'object of developmental' transference. Similarly, some of the counter-transferences which can be predicted are 'perpetrator', 'victim', 'authoritarian', 'therapist as client', and 'sexual and voyeuristic' counter-transference (Hunter and Struve, 1998: 248–52). The occurrence of such transference and countertransference issues need not be seen as a defect in the relationship, but as providing valuable information for the therapist to use within a therapeutic context.

Despite the natural occurrence of transference and countertransference dynamics, Hunter and Struve suggest that touch should not be used when a perpetrator, authoritarian, or sexual countertransference has been evoked, or when a negative or sexual transference has arisen in the client, as an abusive dynamic may evolve. Even with the clearest intention and quality of touch, a client may interpret a therapist's touch in various ways, for example sexualizing, feeling attacked, or feeling oppressed by a contact that was intended otherwise. They affirm that these occurrences can become useful, however, when discussed in an open way, and held within the context of the transference. The body psychotherapist, trained to use touch in psychotherapy, develops the awareness and technique to integrate the body into work with such material.

The personality embodied

Personality is embodied somatically, as we have been exploring. A primary goal of somatic and body psychotherapy is to integrate the personality and the sense of a core self through attention to these somatic embodiments. To this end the therapist may integrate psychological theory and methods with somatic practice. Below are a few models of the psyche which have a direct relationship to issues of embodiment, and can be applied to somatic processes.

Subpersonalities

The model of *subpersonalities*, already mentioned, can be usefully applied to the processing of somatized psychoemotional issues. Subpersonalities are constellations of specific energies, thoughts, feelings, behavioural patterns, attitudes, and beliefs (Assagioli, 1975: 74-7, 121). Each reflects a partial aspect of the personality; they evolve out of childhood experience as the personality is developing, and have their roots deep within the unconscious.

They often appear to the imagination in the form of human characters, animals, fairytale figures, or images of ourselves at a younger age. They continue to change and transform throughout life. Their formation is a normal part of personality development and organization but can become problematic when we unconsciously identify with one whilst denying the existence of others, or when one dominates with behaviour that is oppressive or abusive to other aspects of the self. Subpersonalities can be embodied in particular areas of the body, in specific body systems, organs, or movement qualities; as described earlier a variety of psychotherapeutic techniques, such as guided imagery, inner dialogue, embodied enactment of relationship dynamics, drawing, and creative movement, can be used to explore, process, and integrate subpersonalities emerging through somatic work.

For example, a student in a class on the organ system found within her large intestines a large, fat, jolly character who stomped and rolled and roared in deep guttural tones. As she 'danced' this character, he gave her a feeling of weight, and great freedom in being clumsy, gross, and infinitely humorous. For the woman, physically small and delicately boned, there was great joy and laughter in discovering this hidden aspect of herself. The shadow is not always something to be feared, but just as often as dark secrets, we discover light, joy, and humour which was forbidden and repressed long ago.

In another training group, we were again focusing upon the organ system. This group had developed a culture of taking care of each other, being sensitive to others' needs and offering support and acceptance. This, however, led them to experience difficulty in confronting each other directly, and in expressing clearly any feelings of anger or assertiveness; thus, whilst a conscious process of loving care evolved, the dynamics of power were largely unacknowledged shadow elements within this group. (This is a common phenomenon in somatic training groups, where the cultivation of sensitivity, empathy, and a caring and non-judgmental attitude is intrinsic to the work.)

During the work on the organs I could feel tension growing within the group, but members were reticent to express their feelings openly. They were then invited to embody the 'characters' of each organ, and to express them freely in improvised movement and sound. This tentative group was suddenly stamping and roaring, pushing, yelling, and asserting, but all in a spirit of playfulness which made safe the expression of the repressed shadow of the group. The permission to give voice and form to powerful inner impulses and the unspoken shadow of the group, by identifying with the different organs as subpersonalities within them and within the group as a whole, allowed a liberating and powerful experience to unfold. Grounding experience in the physical sensations of the body contained and made safe the emotional release.

Love and power

Another psychological dynamic that is ever-present in the personality is the relationship between the archetypes of *love and power.* So much of our experience falls within this polarity; desire and aversion, attachment and rejection, bonding and defence, hurt and anger, caring and assertion, are all expressions of these essential dynamics. When issues related to either love or power are the subject of a person's conscious concern, a more fundamental but unconscious issue related to its counterpart usually underlies the client's problem. A conscious focus on power issues, for example, might be hiding a deeper, underlying, and less conscious issue concerning love; a dominant concern with the expression of power, self-assertion, or rebelliousness often masks feelings of vulnerability, sadness, the need to love and be loved, or unresolved grief. All of these processes are relegated to the shadows. The reverse is also true; when love matters and vulnerable feelings are the primary focus of a person's attention, the issue of power lies in the shadow, and may be expressed in covert and manipulative ways.

The dynamics of love and power, and all their permutations, are frequently witnessed in somatic work as areas of softness or weakness, and tension or strength in the body, or in movement where one body part moves aggressively or powerfully, and another with gentleness, for example. Unexpected and unintentional movements that are not congruent with the person's general style of expression may also signify an unconscious process seeking attention; for example, a single fast and sharp movement during a long sequence of slow and gentle motions might be an interesting signal to explore.

A wide range of body symptoms and postural or movement expressions can be sourced back to the dynamics of love and power - their distortion, repression, denial, or frustration. Through the basic perinatal matrix (Grof) explored earlier, we saw how the archetypes of love and power are embodied in the physical experience of birth; our relationship to these energies influences our experience of the second and third stages of the birth passage respectively, and the subsequent organization of basic patterns within the personality. These personality patterns will have somatic counterparts, such as areas of muscular or organic tension or weakness, and idiosyncratic postural and movement patterns.

Buddhist psychology also holds that desire and aversion (expressions of the love and power archetypes) are fundamental to all of our suffering. They are founded on a fundamental delusion, an ignorance of our true nature, of reality as it is rather than as it seems to be. In our development, our process of coming into the world, this basic ignorance begins to coalesce during the first stages of intrauterine life – also the first stage of the basic perinatal matrix. Trauma at this stage can result in dissociative states of consciousness, a turning away from the immediate experience of pain and fear; and our basic ignorance of reality, of life as it truly is, may also be somatized in areas of the body that we do not feel, are ignorant of, or dissociated from. Thus from our earliest days, the essential energies that shape our experience of life begin to imprint themselves upon our bodymind and shape our growing form and sense of self.

Will, surrender, and embodiment

We also saw earlier how the birth process relates to the development of the *will*. Assagioli (1984) described the will as the active, expressive function of the self, and developed a method to train it to organize and direct skilfully the various elements of the personality towards greater health and wholeness. The will is directly connected to the body. Every willed action involves the body; all of our activity in the world is an expression of embodied will. The skilful training of the will is a useful and necessary part of psychological and spiritual development; however, the equally necessary process of surrendering the will to unconscious bodily and energetic processes is not addressed in Assagioli's method. It is here that the somatic therapist has much to offer. Somatic work supports this surrender, which allows the client to enter the 'healing state'; here insight, transformation, healing, and wisdom can be accessed.

Assagioli described the unconscious psyche as a hierarchy of *lower, middle, and higher unconscious.* He describes the lower unconscious as the seat of emotions, bodily instincts, and destructive forces which are base and inferior (Assagioli, 1984: 17, 21); in his view, spiritual experiences and states of awareness can be accessed only through the higher unconscious. But, as John Firman (1991: 86–90) argues, self can be experienced at all levels of consciousness; spiritual growth can be realized as readily through experiences of pain and disintegration, or through the mundane and everyday, as through the so-called 'higher' states of consciousness.

Experience also shows that spiritual experiences can be, and often are, accessed or evoked through the body. This knowledge has been understood and applied in many different forms, from ancient yogic practices to modern bodywork techniques. In Assagioli's description of the unconscious, autonomic bodily processes are associated with the lower unconscious, and are to be transcended on the path towards spiritual liberation. However, this view can encourage a process of transcendence that is hierarchical and *masculine* in orientation, and could result in a dissociative splitting of mind from body (Firman, 1991). Consciously embodied experience, a *feminine* path of descent into matter, of immanent spirituality, is a necessary complement to the masculine way of ascent and transcendence, and must also be included. Surrender to the deep impulses of the body can open us to the most sublime of experiences, as the stirrings of spirit are embodied and expressed. Authentic movement offers a wonderful vehicle for this exploration, as do many other movement practices; and therapeutic bodywork also has the potential to evoke profoundly healing and integrating moments through its invitation to surrender to bodily-felt sensation and the flow of energy within and through us.

The dreambody

The practice of process-oriented psychology, or process work, most explicitly seeks encounter with the unknown and the irrational side of life. Process theory views what bubbles up from the unconscious as meaningful, and appreciates symptoms and disturbances of any sort, not as pathologies to be healed or transcended or somehow got rid of, but as expressions of the very thing we need for our further growth, happiness, or enlightenment. The change of focus from symptoms as problems, to symptoms as potentials holding the seeds of healing and growth, marks a major turning point in twentieth century psychological thought. Process work turns psychology into an adventure where the unexpected is the guide. It approaches therapy not from an analysis of the client's past, but from analysis of the totality of expression in the present moment, and utilises methods drawn from many fields of practice, according to the need of each unique situation.

Process-oriented psychology and the theory of the *dreambody* were developed by Arnold Mindell, a Jungian analyst and physicist. His work has been influenced by the new paradigm of modern physics, Taoist philosophy, and shamanism, as well as Jungian psychology and Reichian bodywork. It seeks to bring together the transpersonal and body-oriented approaches evolved by these two earlier pioneers. Mindell perceived relationships between dream images, body symptoms, unconscious or unintentional movements, relationship problems, and world issues, which he developed into a theoretical and practical approach to working with symptoms through many channels of perception and expression. The dreambody is the name he gave to the dynamic and purposeful force which underlies the manifestation of all living phenomena and life processes.

In her introduction to *Dreambody*, Marie-Louise von Franz (in her introduction to Mindell, 1982: xi) describes the concept of the dreamingbody as 'a re-formulation of the age-old idea of a "subtle body"'. Mindell (1982: 5) also likens it to the Eastern and ancient ideas of shakti, kundalini, mercury, and chi, to the shaman's concept of the 'double' (Mindell, 1993: 135), and to our Western idea of 'soul' (Mindell, 1982: 29). In dreambody work the movements, postures, and inner experiences that arise spontaneously sometimes mirror the movements of sacred dances, or traditional yoga postures, or healing and meditation experiences known to ancient cultures and traditional practices. This suggests that experiences which are universal to humankind, crossing the boundaries of space and time, express through physiological as well as psychological channels. Archetypes, as Jung had come to understand, have a physiological basis as well as a psychic representation.

Mindell writes: 'I would define the real body as a result of objective physiological measurements, and the dreambody as the individual experience of the body' (Mindell, 1982: 11). This distinction is useful in the practice of somatic therapy, where the therapist is engaged simultaneously with her relatively objective perceptions of the client's physiological body, as well as the client's own subjective experience of her body (Dowd, 1991, explores the simultaneous perceptions of somatic therapist and client).

Mindell developed Jung's methods of working with archetypal processes through dreams and active imagination and applied them to working with body symptoms and movement as well. Dreambody work explores the archetypal processes behind illness and other disturbances, and offers practical methods for accessing the healing power which lies within the symptoms:

> Whereas medicine might see different diseases existing in the body at one time in terms of different causes, in dreams and body work all physiological processes appear to be governed by single gestalts and their archetypal processes. These processes seem to choose any and all available signals or unstable organs for expression. (Mindell, 1982: 14)

> Just as Jung sees the psyche as a collection of complexes, each possessing an 'energetic charge', 'luminosity' and consciousness, so we are now discovering a dreambody picture consisting of energy vortices which possess archetypal experiences. In other words, the Jungian concept of the psyche may be applied to the dreambody. *The dreambody is a collection of energy vortices held together by the total personality.* (Mindell, 1982: 32)

Channels of perception

The aim of process work is to analyse, follow, and support the unfolding process of the dreambody as it manifests through various channels. A channel, in this context, refers to a 'mode of perception'; the main channels used in process work are the visual, auditory, proprioceptive, movement, relationship, and world channels. The dreambody sends out signals through the various channels in the form of dream images or fantasies; inner or outer sounds, voices, or dialogue; body sensations such as pain, heat, cramps, or tension; unexpected or unintentional movements and gestures; relationship problems; and events in the external world which touch upon our inner experience in a meaningful or synchronistic way.

Information may be sent through several channels until it reaches awareness, can unfold and reveal its message. Physical illness, relationship problems, accidents, and so on, are seen as processes which are incomplete. The process worker seeks to uncover the underlying process which is trying to complete itself, or 'dream itself into being' (Mindell, 1982: 184) at any given moment, and support this unfolding through whichever channel is indicated. The signals may be amplified through whichever channel the dreambody is using at a given moment. By amplifying a signal, we can experience it more fully, and the meaning of the signal can be embodied and 'digested', integrated at a psycho-physiological level.

Primary and secondary processes

Determining which signals to work with, and which channels to work in, requires training in awareness of signals and analysis of process structure. A process structure consists of 'primary' and 'secondary' processes. In Mindell's theory, a primary process is that which we are most identified with, and that which we intend. However, this is not always fully conscious, so it would be incorrect to equate primary and secondary processes with consciousness and the unconscious. The secondary process is what we do not identify with, control, or intend; it manifests through dreams, body symptoms, unintentional movements, relationship problems, and so on, in its attempt to integrate into consciousness the unknown and unexpressed aspects of the total personality. All problems and symptoms are therefore seen as useful and meaningful. The process worker does not try to alleviate or cure symptoms, or resolve problems, but helps the client to explore the signals and so discover the archetypal energy, the meaning or message, trying to express through them. Mindell writes:

> All the figures of the psychic pantheon – the gods, snakes, animals, the anima, animus and Self – have physiological counterparts. From the viewpoint of body awareness, the images of dreams and fairy tales are symbols of psychological as well as physiological processes. The physiological corollary of the Self, the organizing power behind psycho-physical processes, is the dreambody. This power, restlessly yearning for development, appears in illnesses, body symptoms, compulsions and 'doings'. (Mindell, 1982: 161)

When we are wholly engaged in our primary intended activity, then the primary and secondary signals appear 'congruent'; there is not some part of us that is expressing something contrary to what we intend. For example, when engaged in a conversation and our tone of voice, body posture, level of energy and gestures all fit with the message we are consciously trying to communicate, then we would appear congruent to the one we are speaking to. However, there is often a secondary process going on that interferes with our clear and direct communication; an unconscious relationship issue, an uncomfortable body symptom, a disturbing dream that still haunts us, or an unacknowledged need to be doing something other than we are doing, might create secondary signals such as a tone of voice, gesture, or body posture which is not congruent with our conscious intentions to communicate with this person. These *double signals* can create confusion and tension in relationships, and undermine our intended action (Mindell, 1989a: 12–13; 1989b: 60–1). The process worker would amplify and follow the secondary, unintended signals to discover what the dreambody is trying to express. Thus the private and disavowed aspects of our inner self (Stern) may come into conscious expression.

Occupied and unoccupied channels

We each tend to be more identified with certain channels, whilst there may be others from which we tend to be dissociated. In our modern Western culture the auditory and visual channels tend to dominate; for many people the proprioceptive and movement channels of the body are what Mindell would call *unoccupied:* 'In terms of the basic channels, visual types may have no proprioception, they do not occupy the proprioceptive channel. As a result phenomena happen in this channel as if they were occurring outside the personality of the visual type. He experiences body problems as occurring to him, as strokes of fate or as accidents' (Mindell, 1989a: 24).

Unoccupied channels open the most direct access to secondary dreambody processes, and it is in these channels that the most powerful and also irrational and uncontrolled experiences are likely to occur. The primary *occupied* channels are the ones in which secondary processes can best be integrated; they also offer a safe and familiar ground to return to. According to this theory, we can see that working through the body can evoke powerful experiences, and that the body holds potential for the greatest change for many people in our mentally-oriented culture. Language or image may be important integrating channels for such people.

Edges and edge figures

At the borders of what we accept as self we meet with our growing edges, the places where shadow elements impinge upon consciousness through signals such as body symptoms, dreams, and relationship problems. Here at the edge we meet our challenges to grow, by integrating the shadow elements that are calling for attention through the disturbances and symptoms we experience. An edge marks the limits of what we identify with and the borders of our conscious awareness. The anxiety and fear often encountered when facing an edge can be great, and *edge figures*, subpersonalities that obstruct us from crossing the edge, will be encountered. We may dialogue with, plead with, fight with, or reeducate our edge figures. Sometimes a great deal of time must first be spent just living near the edge, getting to know the edge figure and the feelings associated with it, before a step beyond it can be made. At other times we may leap first, and then look back; integration of the edge issues may come later. A somatic therapy session can stimulate changes that allow the client to go over an edge and embody a previously unacknowledged aspect of herself; however, if the feelings encountered around making such a step are not consciously integrated but 'jumped over', it is likely that the change will not last and the experience of going beyond the edge may eventually be lost to consciousness.

We step into the unknown when we go over an edge, and what happens here cannot be predicted. Thus process work does not follow prescribed techniques, for it deals with and must be open to the unexpected and unpredictable, although it may draw upon techniques from many disciplines, such as gestalt, psychodrama, Reichian bodywork, dance movement therapy, and subpersonality work. Awareness and analysis of the process structure indicates which channels to work through and which secondary signals to follow; the analysis of information according to process theory also offers a theoretical foundation for the choices we may intuitively arrive at through the subliminal processing of information. Once engaged, the process itself determines the methods to be followed, and the process worker learns to follow the positive and negative feedback of the client, using this to guide the work. 'A governing paradigm of process work is that the process which presents itself in the moment contains all the elements necessary for its own solution' (Mindell, 1989a: 25).

Individual and collective process

As well as working with the dreams and body symptoms of the individual, dreambody work also explores relationship, family, and group processes, applying the same methods of amplification of signals through different channels to the dynamics of a collective situation. Jung's collective unconscious, and the field theories of new physics have influenced the development of methods to resolve interpersonal, social, and global conflicts. The model is holographic. Just as the individual psyche is composed of many elements organised by a central archetypal core, the Self, and its psycho-physiological counterpart, the dreambody, so too is a couple, a family system, group, or nation made up of separate elements organised by a collective dreambody. Mindell (1992: 3) believes that the collective dreaming process plays a decisive role in binding people together in relationships and groups.

The role of the sick or disturbed individual or group in society is also explored as a part of the universal dreambody. The sick, the marginal, the socially excluded members of society are seen to embody, through their illness or social problems, not only their own secondary processes, but those of the collective in which they live. Sometimes individuals are suffering from the world's sickness. Healing means bringing the secondary process back into the collective, and in some way changing the collective, as well as the individual, through integrating the shadow aspect of the collective dreambody process (Mindell, 1991).

Thus dreambody work offers an holistic and embodied approach to working with personal and collective issues, drawing together many strands of somatic, psychotherapeutic, social, and spiritual disciplines.

Working at the edge

The following is an example of work with edges and secondary process, applied to somatic practice. It is an account offered by a student, Janis. The experiences that initiated this process occurred during a five-day training seminar held with a group of advanced students, and her process continued over several days and through various channels. This account will include my own comments about what the group was working on, what I observed in this student's process, and her own descriptions of what she experienced. As this process occurred during a group teaching situation, I did not have access to all the details of her experiences; much of the work was done with a fellow trainee (whom I will call her 'partner').

The group had been exploring the body fluids through movement and touch, facilitating partners to access the feelings, energy, and movement qualities of the different fluids. They had been asked to choose a fluid that was less accessible to them, and to explore this with a partner's help. At some point in the work they were asked to find an image for an edge figure, an intrapsychic presence which prevented them from fully embodying their shadow fluid.

Janis was not sure whether to work on the blood or cerebrospinal fluid, both of which felt unfamiliar to her. With the blood came an image and body feeling that frightened her, and so she resisted exploring this further, choosing instead to work with the other fluid which evoked a less threatening image. After some movement exploration she drew the first image very quickly, then went to the second, safer one. The image that frightened her was a dark figure lying on the floor, unable to move; along with the image, there was a place in her belly which felt threatened and hurt. She feared it would say something about sexual abuse and she did not want to look at this. Her partner and I both offered support but also respected her fear and her need to say 'no' to this image at the moment. She had reached an edge, and beyond it was something unknown that she feared to face at the moment. The psyche has its own timing, and the individual's unreadiness to confront something difficult must be respected.

The next day she spoke to her partner and myself about the image. The figure made her think of an uncle who, when she was a child, would touch her in a sexual way that she did not want; she felt that this was part of the truth behind the image but not all of it. That night she had a dream that she later saw was directly connected to her experiences with the movement work, and the image and body feeling that had come out of it. In her dream a small child ran up to her and embraced her, saying 'mammy, I love you'. She felt a great love for the child, but then ran away and began to cry. The boy turned around and said to her 'I will come every Tuesday into your dreams.' On awaking she felt sad, but did not see the connection to her earlier work until speaking about it at breakfast; then she realized that the figure unable to move, and the hurt place in her belly, related to an abortion she had had many years earlier. The feelings around this incident had been of her body being sexually violated and abused, and much of the physical memory and pain had been held unconsciously in her body tissues, until the work with the blood had reawakened feeling at this level.

We continued to explore the fluids and edges that day; she describes how at one point she began to feel nauseous, and eventually her body feeling 'took over'. She shook and sobbed for some time as the energy bound up in this trauma began to release. Gradually the image of the blond four-year-old boy of her dream returned, and she could begin to talk about and process the feelings of violation around her abortion. I trusted my own intuitive feeling that some higher guidance was both needed and available to her and asked if there was anyone who could help her in her distress. Immediately she found the image of a wise guardian figure, which helped her to reintegrate after the powerful emotional release.

As she continued to work with the dark figure over the next few days, it became less threatening; however, there was also some disappointment in this, as it held a great power and fascination, and she felt she might lose this power. A week later, on a Tuesday night, she had another dream about a male figure who was 'both fascinating and evil'. He said to her, 'you can't choose with whom you go to hell', and she replied, 'no, you can't choose with whom you go to heaven'. The elevator they were in began to rush down, and she knew she was going to die, but he held her hand and she felt so loved by him that she did not mind. The first dream had given her insight about her abortion and the feelings of violation held in her body which related to this; the second dream she felt completed the cycle, integrating the transformed dark male figure into her psyche as a loving and powerful presence.

The numbing of painful feeling in the body was happening, in her case, through the blood. The dark edge figure, discovered as she brought conscious awareness to the flow of blood, stood at the borders of consciousness, at the edge of what she could feel and own and identify with at the moment; it kept the bodily memory of trauma and violation unconscious until such time as she was ready to experience the painful feelings. As she did this she could also begin to connect more fully to the qualities connected with the blood – the rich, warm, heartful, healing, and nurturing system of the body. The full embodiment of the qualities of the blood would also, to some extent, be part of her secondary process, not fully expressed and identified with until that edge could be crossed. The second dream suggests that the direction of her process was indeed towards the integration of an element of her shadow, and the loving and healing qualities it contained. My impression of her in the days and months that followed was of a deepening of emotional expression, a greater openness, tenderness, and wonder, and also an increased capacity to be with and support others' emotional feelings.

In the interview she spoke of her journey through three days of bodywork, coming to an edge and her mind not wanting to look at the image that had come up. Then going one step further where a dream took over, telling her the truth; her mind still wanted to reject it, but her body then took over. Then her mind was ready to look at the issue and process it more consciously. Finally another dream completed the cycle. This woman strongly occupies her visual channel and is fluent in dream work, so it is not surprising that it was primarily through her dreams and images that she was able to gain insight and integrate her powerful and at times frightening proprioceptive experiences.

The feelings that came up in relation to the abortion were of being powerless and unable to move. She said she had worked on this incident with her mind, but not through her body, and was surprised at how powerful it was to connect to a source so deep in her body and to the knowledge that body and soul had both been abused by her treatment during the abortion. She experienced a great relief after going over this edge and processing her feelings and body reactions. Now she feels she has clarity; previously she had wondered if she had experienced actual sexual abuse and this made her watch certain family members with suspicion. Whilst her earlier statements show that there was abuse in the form of inappropriate touching from her uncle, she now feels clear that the actual feelings of violation and the depth of physical trauma in her body related to the abortion. It was a relief to be able to stop the suspicious watching of her family members and it has made space for her to be able to think of making certain changes in her life.

CHAPTER 10

The body in relationship

In the therapeutic relationship, as in all relationships, most of what we communicate to each other occurs non-verbally, beyond the reaches of conscious awareness, through our posture, unconscious movements and gestures, the tone of our voice, and other subtle bodily signals of which we are usually quite unaware. In fact it is said that only 10% of what we communicate is conveyed through the words we speak. Relationship encompasses a mysterious world of energetic exchanges, chemical messages, unconscious gestures and movement impulses, postural and facial expressions, glances or shifts of the eyes, vocal innuendoes, and the projection of our own thoughts and feelings onto the other. At times we speak and act congruently, words and bodily gestures communicating with a common intent. More frequently we are at odds with ourselves, or unaware of what we really feel, need, or desire, and communicate through conflicting 'double messages'.

It is in this rich world of non-verbal relating that the therapist must immerse herself. If we do not value the client's storytelling, and her own meanings, we risk abandoning her in a solitary world of suffering; but if we do not take into account the realms of non-verbal communication then the therapeutic experience will be that much poorer, and the client will at times be left high and dry in the disembodied world of language, when she needs to be deeply immersed in the fluid transformations of bodily process.

When meeting a client for the first time, the somatic or body psychotherapist engages herself in a multilayered task of listening, feeling, sensing, observing, and imagining, whilst witnessing her own responses to the client's multilayered communications. Careful attention is given to the client's account of her problems, and to her telling of her story; this information is essential to the building of a context for the therapeutic work, and to the development of the therapist's understanding. Being heard clearly, with care and without judgement, may allow the client to begin to trust the therapist, and a healing relationship to start to grow. The ability to empathize with the client's feelings also helps to plant the seed of trust, and enables the therapist to begin to enter into the client's world; empathic relating allows therapists to open their hearts in the presence of clients, and shows clients that they are not completely alone – they are being met by another in a place where they hurt, or are afraid, or full of shame.

At the same time as she pays attention to her client's story and expressions of feeling, the therapist opens her awareness to the non-verbal messages she is receiving. In my own approach, this is done primarily in a receptive and intuitive rather than analytical way, holding theoretical concerns in the background of awareness as a loose framework against which to assess what the client presents; information can be analysed later. Most therapists will use both intuitive and analytical modes of assessment to differing degrees. (Arnold Mindell's process work analyses verbal and non-verbal communications, as described in the previous chapter, and offers a theoretical foundation for understanding intuitive insight.) Observing posture, movement and gestural expressions, changes in the quality of the voice and of speaking style, facial expressions, and energetic shifts, I attempt not to jump to hasty interpretations, but to simply hold all of this information lightly, together with the client's verbal communications, waiting for all of the separate pieces to begin to coalesce into a more complete picture, or pattern, or central issue. By waiting, staying in the unknown, together client and therapist hold the creative tension for long enough to begin to allow a bigger picture to emerge. This bigger picture may include future as well as past and present. Appropriate questions help the client to reflect on her problems in a new way, and possibly begin to see them from a new perspective; thus a context may evolve that includes the transpersonal, soul, and spiritual dimensions of the client's life, her unexpressed potentials needing to unfold, as well as the pain and limitations of her past.

The practice of witnessing, as articulated by Janet Adler (see Chapter 3 on authentic movement), is a metaskill that can be applied at all times to verbal communication and unconscious non-verbal signalling, as well as within the discipline of authentic movement. Whilst listening to a client and witnessing her bodily and energetic communications, I also seek to be open to my own responses to her presence and her stories, as she describes them. It is a lifelong practice, like a meditative discipline, to learn to witness one's own responses to another clearly; I seek to notice as best I can the thoughts, feelings, images, fantasies, body sensations, and energetic processes that are evoked in me by the presence of the client and her story. In this approach I acknowledge that the judgments, interpretations, and projections which emerge in my mind are my own; the feelings, images, fantasies, and physical sensations evoked also belong to my own experience. They may well have relevance to the client and are often evoked by or transmitted from her, but in witnessing I first claim ownership of my own responses to the client's communications, and in so doing, allow her the space to accept or reject their relevance for her. By first owning my experience, I learn to see myself more clearly, and thus create a space within which the client can also begin to see herself more clearly and discover the truth of her own reality.

Whilst the therapist acknowledges her own process, evoked by the client's presence, she also understands that what happens between them is a relationship between two unique people. It is not solely the product of the client's psychology; nor do the therapist's own initiatives or theoretical agendas determine it. The two engage in an intimate relationship, and it is largely upon the quality of this relationship that the success of therapy depends. The practice of clear, non-judgemental witnessing is the ground upon which transferential and countertransferential issues can be held, reflected upon, and resolved. It enables the therapist to monitor her own responses to the client constantly; the more the therapist becomes conscious, the clearer the boundaries become, and thus a contained space is created within which the client can come to know herself more deeply.

The somatic and body psychotherapist is also engaged directly with questions such as 'what is the client's body telling me about her unconscious process?' 'Where do unconscious bodily signals interface with the story being told?' 'Where are they in conflict?' 'What is the embodied expression of the issue being presented?' 'What kind of support is needed to help the process unfold?' 'How is our relationship being embodied somatically?' 'How does she embody relationships in general through her physical symptoms and movement patterns?' These questions are ongoing, and guide the therapeutic work.

Choices as to which mode of therapy is appropriate are continually being made; the process may move between verbal dialogue, relationship work, exploration of dreams or imagery, movement, bodywork, and artwork, and the therapist needs to be flexible and creative in guiding the work through the most effective channels. At times the client's verbal descriptions point clearly to one mode or another. For example, if she uses active expressions such as 'pushing', 'dragging', 'crushing', 'whirling' to describe her experience, or if she uses very specific movements and gestures as she speaks, movement work might be indicated; description of feelings in terms of imagery might indicate inner work with the image, or if experience is described in terms of bodily sensations, then some form of body awareness work might be appropriate in that moment. The client's verbal and non-verbal signals generally suggest the channel in which the process needs to be explored. There are many ways in which a process, a feeling, a part of the body, or a subpersonality may ask to be given attention when it is needed.

As described earlier, somatic work can serve various purposes in therapy, and the different therapeutic modes are each appropriate to specific developmental issues. Therefore choices as to when somatic work is indicated, and when verbal approaches are more relevant, will be related to the developmental process of the client, and the primary issues being addressed at different stages of the therapy. The emphasis on somatic or verbal therapy generally changes during the course of therapy and will vary with each client. To briefly summarize, with reference to Stern's model of the development of the senses of self: issues relating to the emerging and core senses of self, before, during and immediately after birth, can be addressed effectively through somatic therapy, with cognitive work to contextualize and integrate experiences; the intersubjective stage requires attunement and empathic relationship, which may be experienced through the witnessing of dance movement and other creative arts, as well as through the therapist's ability to respond empathically to the client's verbal and emotional expression; issues relating to the development of the sense of a verbal self require a verbal approach, with other methods being used to access split-off experience in the non-verbal realm, as there is a need to integrate and give language to the experience of the body-as-shadow. When dealing with Oedipal material, bodywork involving touch may be contraindicated during phases of the work; due to the sensitive nature of the relationship dynamics between client and therapist-as-parent, touch might be felt to be invasive, abusive, seductive, or in some other way confusing or overwhelming to the client, until she is able to differentiate her sense of self from the internalized parental conflict.

In order to give an example of this work in practice, the therapeutic process of one client will be presented in some detail, showing the interweaving of psychological and somatic work through various channels and developmental issues. The examples will be referred back to theoretical concerns mentioned in previous chapters. This client suffered from an illness manifesting in clearly interrelated psychological and somatic symptoms, so her process is especially relevant to this study.

Arlene's story

When Arlene first came to see me she was 29 years old, in a long-term relationship with a man she was soon to marry, and had been unable to work for some time because of illness. She had worked as a secretary and personal assistant in law and advertising until the onset of ME (myalgic encephalomyelitis) 5 years previously had forced her to stop. She felt her illness was due to her 'not being true to herself', living a lifestyle and doing work that were not right for her, and she was seeking to find her own truth and sense of purpose in life. A crisis which involved both emotional and physical trauma seemed to precipitate the illness: Arlene learnt that her father was having an affair with her cousin Sandra, at the same moment that she was involved in an accident, together with her mother, father, and cousin. Before this event she felt as if she had been 'sleeping'; the knowledge of her father's incestuous affair woke her out of her 'innocent trust' in the security of her family, and plunged her into a disturbing world that she felt ill-equipped to deal with.

Arlene had also suffered previous physical trauma, all concerned with falling. At the age of 6 months she had fallen down a flight of stairs; she had hit her head on a radiator before losing consciousness and suffered a broken leg. As a young adult she had fallen from a horse. And in the accident with her family, they had been enjoying a trip in a hot-air balloon; the balloon landed badly and Arlene was thrown to the floor and injured her spine. The experience of falling suggests to me 'coming down to earth' from a height; it could indicate a lack of support, either internal or external, or both, and a loss of ground within. In working with Arlene it became clear that all of this was true for her. Work with this multiple trauma had to be woven carefully into the therapeutic process.

Over the 5 years of illness she had received various alternative therapies, and her health was considerably better by the time she came to see me, although she still suffered many symptoms. She had also been in psychotherapy for a period of time, and said this had been helpful, but it was terminated prematurely when the therapist moved away. Whilst she did train and work for a while as an aromatherapist, she had to stop this work as it was draining her; she felt she still 'needed something for herself' first. A deeper level of healing was being called for.

Arlene was the youngest of three children and felt that she had always been treated as the 'baby' of the family; because of this she felt she had never been supported to do things for herself, and now, with the betrayal of her trust in her father's goodness and omnipotence, she felt unable to cope with the demands of life. The betrayal of her 'godlike' father had also adversely affected her relationship with her own spirituality, and her experience of the divine was infused with threats, judgements, and injunctions to suffer. She was still holding a lot of anger towards her father on account of his affair, and was unable to find a way to deal with these strong feelings. Her internalized, now untrustworthy, father was very powerful, consuming, and seemed to be eating away at her core in an onslaught of painful criticism and judgement. The symptoms of her illness could be, in part, an expression of this debilitating psychological dynamic.

Her mother was strong, overprotective, and sometimes overwhelming to Arlene in her warmth and enthusiasm. Arlene was very close to her mother and clearly loved her, but Arlene also felt that her mother treated her more as a friend, and sometimes mother, than daughter. She felt she could not look to her mother for emotional support and was often put in the role of confidante or mediator between her parents; in this way she had been required to help her mother deal with her father's affair, and had found no support for her own feelings. During her childhood she had been exposed to her parents' relationship issues and sexuality in ways that were inappropriate for a child and invasive of her boundaries. She had a close relationship with both parents, but was still bound to each in ways that were undermining her own sense of self-worth, authority, and autonomy, and needed to separate. Her deep need was to develop clear boundaries within which to nurture a sense of security in her inner self.

One way in which her boundary issues had manifested was in a relationship with a male therapist who had touched and kissed her in a sexual way. She was unable to respond clearly; she felt it was a loving relationship and did not want to disturb this by objecting to his behaviour, so she simply left and said nothing about it. Her inability to resolve her feelings around her father's sexuality would have left her vulnerable to this kind of professional abuse; the therapist's betrayal, reflective of her father's, might have offered her an opportunity to reestablish her boundaries, but she was unable to at the time, and instead dissociated in order to protect herself from further hurt.

When she came into therapy Arlene felt a need to connect more deeply to herself as a woman. She held very negative judgements about her female body, about being a woman, and about womanhood in general; she had difficulty in accepting life on earth, in a human body, and struggled with the feeling of not fully wishing to be here. Incarnating, embodying herself fully, accepting the suffering of human life, and learning to love her body and herself as a woman were central issues in our work together.

My first impressions of Arlene were of a very pleasant and open personality; she was always willing to communicate and explore, and an easy rapport and mutual liking was quickly established between us. I experienced a sense of lightness in her presence that belied her own feelings of pain and discomfort in her body; her usually cheerful manner was also in contradiction to the extreme emotional states she frequently suffered. As I generally felt a sense of ease, spontaneity, and freedom in her presence, I imagine I was resonating with her secondary process, in Mindell's terminology – that is, the aspect of her process with which she was not primarily identified, but which was attempting to emerge and find expression. In this instance it manifested through the relationship channel, causing me to experience the qualities which she was not identifying with at the moment. Later experience seemed to verify this; on a number of occasions, by working with her symptoms Arlene was able to access feelings of lightness, spontaneity, freedom, and fun which were qualities she needed to embody and express.

The light, slightly giddy feelings I experienced in Arlene's presence suggested that energy was moving upwards and the centre of gravity located in the chest, head, and at times outside of the body altogether; this can be an indication of a tendency to dissociate. These sensations drew my attention to the nervous and endocrine systems, and in fact it emerged through our work that these systems were highly sensitive and vulnerable to disturbance; imbalances within the neuroendocrine system were associated with the roots of many of her physical symptoms and emotional patterns.

This is in keeping with current information about the symptoms of ME. For a long time dismissed as 'all in the mind' and not taken seriously by the medical profession at large, more recent research has revealed that the various manifestations of ME, or chronic fatigue syndrome, show dysfunctioning of the central nervous system, and in particular the hypothalamus (Smith, 1995: 13, 24-5). The hypothalamus is a part of the old forebrain which is intrinsic to the central nervous system's regulation of physiological, perceptual, and emotional function, and it also directly influences and regulates the secretions of the pituitary and other endocrine glands. Thus it affects virtually every aspect of bodymind functioning.

In Arlene's case, the mental stress of working in an environment and a job that did not suit her, the physical injury to her spine caused by the series of accidents, and the emotional trauma of learning of her father's affair may all have been precipitating factors in her illness. A constitutional sensitivity may have also played a part in the development of an illness so clearly associated with imbalances within the central nervous system. Factors of conditioning, upbringing, and learned patterns of behaviour and response might also have predisposed her to this particular condition and the symptoms she presented. Imbalanced functioning of the immune system, with its intimate relationship to the neuroendocrine system, is also central to the illness. This client had experienced confusion and violation of boundaries in various ways; psychological boundaries, as we saw in earlier chapters, can be related to the integrity of the cellular membranes and to the immune system. Recent research into CFS and ME is giving us a picture of a damaged boundary and faulty filtering system, which allows toxic substances to enter and poison core structures of the body, in particular the brain and central nervous system, and the cellular membranes (see Appendix 3). This seems to me a remarkably accurate reflection of what happens to the psyche when psychological boundaries are breached. One way in which I experienced her boundary issues in our relationship was in being easily drawn in to identify with her experience; her openness seemed to invite this, and perhaps it reflected her lack of appropriate separation from her mother who she felt would often 'take away her experience' and make it her own. Continual awareness was called for on my part to remain centred in my own experience, even as I witnessed and empathized with hers, in order that she could begin to form clearer boundaries herself, and take full ownership of her own experience.

Whatever the multiple causes of Arlene's illness and emotional problems, it was clear that both somatic and psychotherapeutic work were required. My premise was that, as psychological factors were clearly indicated in the onset of her illness, psychological work might help facilitate the restoration of balance in neurophysiological as well as psychological functioning; and that somatic therapy could also help to reduce stress, rebalance bodymind functioning, and contribute to the cultivation of a healthy sense of self. Fortunately she viewed her illness as a call to grow and become more fully herself, and could appreciate the connection between mind, feelings, and bodily symptoms, so she was very amenable to this holistic approach.

Creating a strong container

One of the experiences of people suffering from ME is the loss of a clear sense of self, which might be expected from a situation where boundaries are damaged and the core is invaded by toxic material. This can create or exacerbate symptoms of anxiety, and vicious cycles are set up whereby the stress that was a precipitating factor in the illness is increased by attempts to alleviate the anxiety. Arlene suffered many distressing symptoms that were her body's attempts to control powerful feelings that she feared and was unable to process. Without a clear and boundaried sense of self she could find no stable inner ground from which to deal with her feelings, and felt overwhelmed by their toxicity; she seemed to be battling against herself in self-destructive attempts to find relief, often exhausting herself in these efforts. This could also be a reflection of an autoimmune disturbance that causes internal physiological boundaries to be breached.

Our early work together focused largely upon developing clearer boundaries and strengthening her sense of a core self; by creating a stronger psychological core, and reducing the cycles of stress within her central nervous system, it was to be hoped that the biochemical dysfunction would also be positively affected. This was approached through work on relationships with the people close to her, and bodywork that helped to bring her awareness more fully into her body and experience it as a strong, safe, and containing place. She was also able to access awareness as to how she was somatizing emotional issues and destructive psychological patterns. Arlene had suffered emotional and physical trauma, and this would need to be addressed, but first safety and trust, both in her own resources and in the therapeutic relationship, would have to be cultivated. My approach to bodywork seemed to allow her to develop a transference onto me as a 'good mother' who gave her support, affirmation, and nurturing touch, whilst also allowing enough space for her to digest her own experiences. In order to address trauma within an ongoing therapeutic relationship, a genuine positive transference is essential; the client will almost inevitably feel retraumatized by the therapist when sensitive material arises if a negative transference, or countertransference, has been constellated.

In one body awareness exploration, I placed my hands lightly over areas of her body, and invited her to take her awareness through the tissue layers, which she was able to do, in order to access information about her symptoms and patterns. Coming into the organs, she felt vulnerable in her solar plexus area, and began to cry; the area felt tight, like a fist. It was a feeling she knew well and described as a 'defensiveness', but said she did not know how or when to use this quality to protect herself; her self-protective instinct was damaged. As she simply stayed with the feeling and image, the fist began to loosen until it could rest, open, like the hand I had placed over the area. She could then sense the presence of something within her that needed love, and noticed her breathing had become fuller by simply allowing space for the feelings held there. Her attention was then drawn to her throat, where she felt a stuckness, a distressing strangled feeling. She could sense energy moving upwards through her body and getting blocked here. At this point she connected to anger, but was afraid of expressing it as it might destroy; she imagined it as a monster with a lid over it to keep it under control. She did not know how to deal with it. I asked how she usually dealt with her anger, and she spoke of different things she had done; sometimes she would beat cushions, but this did not help and caused her to bleed from her vagina. Seeing that a discharge of these strong feelings was not appropriate, I suggested she draw the image; this enabled her to disidentify so that she could begin to explore her anger from a place of safety. As we witnessed her drawing together, she came to see that the 'lid' that covered her monster might be serving a function and needed to be respected; time and care were needed before it could be safely removed. Her uncontained attempts to release the tension were self-defeating and even harmful, and contributed to her stress.

Endless outpourings of grief, such as Arlene frequently suffered, or angry beating of cushions with no relief, occur when trauma is activated but cannot be resolved. Careful work around reintegrating the core self needs to occur before the hurt of past injuries can be safely experienced and released somatically, as well as emotionally.

In another session she began moving, following inner impulses to see what would emerge through her body from the unconscious. She very quickly began to cry, and dropped to her knees. She talked of wanting to move with a flexible spine but felt stiff and tense; it was hard for her to stay in her body with its pains and limitations, but on this occasion she did and felt the pain of this. We then worked together with a movement exercise that would help bring more awareness and flexibility to her spine, as well as giving her a sense of containment for her feelings, and she noticed how the energy was blocked between her shoulder blades so that it could not descend in her body. She amplified the sensation into a movement where her arms were held tightly behind her back.

At this point I had a choice to encourage her to explore this movement and what it might mean to her, or to offer bodywork that would follow the movement at a subtle tissue level. I chose the latter, as this has the additional focus of reeducating the tissues to give her an alternative experience to her habitual holding pattern; bodywork can also reduce sympathetic nervous system activity and thus help to address her general difficulty with managing stress. Until she was able to assess her limitations and regulate her autonomic nervous system, it was necessary for me to set boundaries for her in such a situation, and guide the work into channels that would not overstimulate sympathetic arousal. To amplify the tension pattern at this point might have led her deeper into activity that would cause further stress and be counterproductive. Because Arlene tended to be a very willing and compliant client, it was important to constantly check her unconscious bodily signals for feedback, when deciding how far to go or in which direction to take the work. However, so eager was she to experience everything and hopefully grow and heal through this, and so trusting, that at times unconscious feedback signals were not apparent. I also needed to be aware of my own subjective responses and intuitive feelings when guiding the work, in order to check whether her willingness to engage with a process was an expression of a failure to recognize the boundaries of what she could safely contain.

As I worked to bring more freedom into the muscles around her scapulae, she could feel her arms more clearly and realized that she does not usually feel them at all; energy was locked into the muscles of the upper back, and with this the flow of feeling into her arms was blocked. We finished with a movement where she used her arms and elbows to support herself, and she realized that the only pattern her upper body had known was to pull in; this was an ineffective use that did not support her. Previously she had thought that her tension pattern was caused by having to be strong and carry her hurt because there was no support for her feelings. Now she accessed a deeper level of truth that was the fear of being ridiculed; this, and accompanying feelings of rejection and shame, stopped her from facing the world in a direct and self-supported way.

This was followed in the next session by a dialogue with an inner figure who could give her the approval and affirmation she needed in order to stand up for herself. As she embodied this wise inner figure, she made a dance with her arms flowing freely and strongly. It was new to feel strength in her arms, and this enabled her to explore a dance of pushing against my hands. The phrase 'just back off' came up as she worked with this movement; her ability to protect her own space was tentatively emerging, and through the form of the dance she was able, in that moment, to create a strong boundary against a potentially invading presence. I hoped that being able to playfully push her therapist would enable her to internalize permission to say 'no' to me too, if necessary. And indeed, she did gradually come to know her needs and her limits more clearly, and learnt to make her own choices about what was appropriate for her.

After this session she described 'finding her centre for the first time'. This was the beginning rather than the completion of integrating the sense of a core self; it laid the ground for her to begin to explore her boundaries in relationships, and issues with various family members were brought in to subsequent sessions. She began to integrate projected aspects of her shadow; for example, she felt hurt by her sister-in-law, whom she experienced as 'unhearing, immovable, unchanging, unforgiving'. An image of a nasty, old giant-woman living in a castle emerged. Identifying with this image gave Arlene the sense of being protected, immovable, not taking in everything from those around her, and she realized that the qualities she disliked in her relative were not only disowned parts of herself, but also the very qualities she needed at the moment to strengthen her own boundaries and create the space she needed for herself. After this session she described 'standing up to' her father for the first time.

Arlene had been very occupied with family conflicts during this period, and felt a lack of support from them for her upcoming wedding plans. It became necessary for her to create space for herself, as the role-play with her sister-in-law had suggested, so that she could turn her focus inwards and look at her own feelings about the wedding. Two dreams at this time seemed to confirm this. In one she was wearing a veil over her eyes, a perennial symbol for the bride entering into the ritual of marriage, and also an indication of the need to turn the attention within (see Leonard, 1986, for a discussion of the symbology of the veil). In the other she dreamed of being dismembered, cooked, and eaten. These are archetypal symbols of initiation (see Eliade, 1975, for descriptions of ancient shamanic initiation rites), rites of passage through the death of an old self-identity into a new life, and as Johnson describes, marriage is a death to the old self for a woman in a way that it is not for the man (Johnson, 1977: 23–4). Through her marriage and through her healing journey she was in fact embarking upon a process of initiation into womanhood, a deepening to herself as woman, fully embodied and human, and all the suffering and joy entailed in that.

Dreams can have meaning at many levels, and Arlene's second dream also suggested to me a reversal of the autonomic nervous system. In such a situation, the outwardly focused expression of the sympathetic nervous system tends to turn inward to 'attack' the inner world; this can manifest in digestive problems, auto-immune and allergic reactions, destructive self-criticism, and harming oneself through addictions, self-abuse, or pushing oneself beyond healthy limits. The person suffering in this way may find no peace in their inner world; turning inwards can result in depression and despair, rather than relaxation, recuperation, and self-awareness. Simultaneously, the parasympathetic nervous system turns outwards, inappropriately trying to 'digest' inner processes in the outer world; this might be recognized in a tendency to pour emotions out inappropriately, to constantly talk about problems without being able to properly process and digest them, or to project the inner world outwards and be unable to differentiate these projections from reality. Most of us suffer from such imbalances and reversals at some time, to some degree; the crucial factor is learning how to rebalance the system so as not to become locked into such a pattern. Arlene's first dream seemed to suggest she was now ready and able to look within in a way that could heal this tendency.

Rebalancing the autonomic nervous system was an important aspect of Arlene's work, and required several approaches. Somatic therapy was particularly important. Dealing with her inner critic and judge, and learning to be gentler on herself were issues that needed much attention. Finding a safe inner space, learning to accept her limitations, and regulate her rest and activity were necessary. She began to learn that it is not appropriate to be always open and share everything with everyone, an injunction probably forced upon her by her parents' openness about their relationship and sexuality, and reinforced by an ill-informed popular psychological culture. Arlene needed to learn to discriminate when and with whom it was safe to open herself. And she needed to look at how she wanted to work and express herself in life – what were appropriately challenging and rewarding activities into which she could channel her creative energies.

Somatic work to calm the sympathetic arousal might focus upon bringing her into her organs to experience the substance of her body, and allow space for internal digestion of her experience. She arrived at one session feeling unable to cope with her emotional feelings and the stress she felt under. Her father was in hospital and this led her to fearing the death of someone close. Her body felt so tense it was 'driving her crazy'. She was able to track the sequence of symptoms in her body that resulted in this state of high tension: it began with an emotional feeling like a 'cannon-ball' hitting her belly, then pain shooting up her body from her right leg, and her right leg feeling disconnected. The right leg is thought to be associated with the father and the masculine side, so these sensations were possibly an expression of the difficulties with her father and her fiancé that she was preoccupied with at the moment. The disconnection of her leg then created tension and immobility in her lower back, and her belly swelled up. Structurally and energetically there is a close relationship between the spine and back of the body, and the organs in front (also associated with masculine and feminine respectively); if they are not integrated and mutually supportive, tension in one area might coexist with lack of tone in the other. Both back pain and digestive disorders frequently result from this patterning and lack of lower back support. In Arlene's case, the inability to ground the emotional onslaught and process her feelings left her without ground, energy dammed up in the middle of her body, and this lack of support put stress on her lower back. From the swelling in her belly, she would then feel nauseous, which caused stress and tension in her neck – probably an attempt to try to control the emotional feelings and distressing physical sensations. The muscles in her neck felt as hard as bone to her; this degree of tension in the neck would block the flow of energy, again escalating the feeling of loss of ground, and increasing the distressing accumulation of energy in her head. On one occasion she described feeling so much energy in her head she wanted 'to rip it off'. (The sensation of excessive energy in the head is a common symptom of ME.)

Somatic work with such symptoms was woven into our therapeutic work over a long period of time. On this particular occasion we chose to begin by addressing the swelling in her belly, as addressing the 'cannon-ball' of emotion in her solar plexus was too much for her at that moment. She said that usually when she experiences this swelling she ignores it; she normally does not give her belly or the 'feminine parts of her body' attention, and does not feel them I helped her to bring awareness to the organs of her lower body - her ovaries, uterus, and intestines - in order to gain some sense of their volume and substance within her, focusing on somatic sensation rather than the exploration of emotional feelings. We then explored the relationship between her spine and small intestines through the connecting mesentery, and the support of the intestines from the lower pelvic organs. She responded well and sensitively to this work and experienced her uterus, which normally felt empty, as full of rich earth colours. In this way, her concept of her embodied female self could begin to change. Standing after this work, she felt relaxed and connected to her feet and to the ground; feelings of support, grounding, and connection to her feminine ground emerged from this experience.

Embodying feminine ground

Arlene's struggle to accept her womanhood and being in her body were key issues that slowly unravelled throughout our work together, as she began to focus on the inner dynamics of her relationship with her parents. She was very critical of herself as a woman, and also rejected the roles that society traditionally gave to women. She feared becoming a 'normal' housewife after her marriage, and was critical of female relatives and friends who seemed, in her eyes, to have bought into a limited existence as overworked wives and mothers. She wanted something more for herself, but did not feel her partner's full support of this.

After her marriage Arlene had to face the truth that her husband Mark could not fill an absence she felt inside, as she had hoped. She must look deeper within. The crisis her marriage precipitated plunged her into a deeper level of feeling. Stories of her childhood and early family relationships began to emerge. She saw how she had always lived with her father's worry and anxiety, and had internalized this so that now, as an adult, she still seemed to go from one crisis to another, her internal father worrying and pushing her beyond her limits. Many dialogues were enacted with inner figures who related to this dynamic; her father was associated with her inner critic and judge, with the parts of her that would not let her rest but pushed her on to be busy in the world, to do and achieve, but whatever she did it was never good enough and she ended up feeling guilty, ashamed, and defeated. She saw how much this internal figure ruled her, like a harsh taskmaster who was never satisfied and could not appreciate her sensitivity and vulnerability. He left her no space to simply be, to surrender to the impulses of her inner life, to discover who she truly was. His judgements of her feelings and her tears made it impossible for her to fully accept her pain and move through it. He was the drive behind her overcharged nervous system responses, and much of her psychological work revolved around confronting him in various forms, and reclaiming her inner space from his clutches.

Arriving at one session with a sore throat that made it difficult to speak, she chose to work through movement. She came to the floor and curled up like a baby, where she could finally let go and feel her grief. She cried a little but did not need to for long, and was able to continue moving and processing her feelings; the support of the floor seemed to help her to carry her grief, so that she did not fall into her familiar pattern of endless crying. My presence as witness to her grief served as another form of support and containment, both ground and therapist-witness giving her an experience of the early maternal holding she still needed to receive. After moving she talked about what had come up for her; she remembered how her mother had not wanted her during the pregnancy, and she thought that when she was born her father was having an affair. He showed a great lack of respect for both his wife and child in this. Arlene felt that her mother also suffered from a lack of self-esteem, unable to value herself as a woman and not receiving the affirmation she needed at this vulnerable time from her husband. So her mother, not fully supported and loved herself, could not be fully there to accept, love, and support Arlene. Her father had frequent affairs, and Arlene took on the role of mediator between her father and mother. As a small child she was loved by all; her cheerfulness was a distraction which helped the family avoid dealing with their problems. At 18 months she seemed to say no to this false situation, and became a 'cantankerous' child; when she was not pleasing them they had to face their problems, and she seemed to lose their love. This painful situation left no room for Arlene's own sense of beingness, and she succumbed to the pressures to achieve in order to please her father, or become ill in order to gain her mother's full attention.

She arrived at the following session feeling anger towards her father; she was also suffering symptoms of burning and stabbing caused by an injury to her left foot, and painful haemorrhoids. To me these symptoms suggested concerns with the support of her feminine side, and her root chakra, the place of embodiment and embeddedness in the maternal matrix. She felt embarrassed to express her burning anger in front of me, in case she looked foolish; she spoke of 'women's secret anger – all women have it but don't show it'. She smiles at this thought, and thinks of the talk of raucous and obscene women; the image of a Mediterranean women with big breasts and hips, powerful in her anger and able to laugh with it too, appears. Stepping into this character, she is able to find the strength to stab and beat a cushion, embodying her secondary process as the 'symptom-maker', which is stabbing and burning her. This time she is able to express her anger in a way that is contained and not hurtful to herself, as she embodies the subpersonality of the powerful Mediterranean women. She comments, 'all men need this now and then, to know women are powerful', then stops and remarks that her father would probably have enjoyed this.

This spontaneous comment causes her to reflect on the sexuality in her relationship with her father. She clearly sensed inappropriate sexuality, and knows now that he views children as 'sexual beings', so must assume he also viewed her in this way when she was a child. At puberty he distanced himself from her, unable to deal with her emerging sexuality, and she found this separation deeply hurtful. She had no memory of sexual relations being overtly acted out between them, but her father's feelings and behaviour towards her had clearly been confusing, and her own boundaries and her identity as a woman were damaged. Dealing with this kind of covert violation of sexual boundaries, and the anxiety it tends to engender, can be very difficult as there may be no clear and tangible events to focus upon. However, uncovering and talking about her fears and fantasies, and releasing some of her anger towards her father, brought some relief.

Through our work together Arlene was beginning to appreciate how her usual pattern of trying to analyse and work hard to *get rid of* her pain was not serving her; she was coming to see that by being with it, experiencing it directly, she could work *with* it in a more fluid and organic way. Her symptoms, she was beginning to discover, offered a way to contact her self and her own wisdom, and she could reframe her goals as not getting rid of her problems completely, but rather being able to deal with them differently, and maintain a sense of wellbeing even though things were not perfect. She was starting to get a hint of what it might feel like to be free of old patterns; she sensed herself to be in a transition where old patterns were beginning to lose their power, but the new ways, her new sense of self, was not yet clear.

At the beginning of our work Arlene had felt trapped in a victim mode. She felt victim to her emotions and to her painful body symptoms, and spent great amounts of energy trying to get rid of them. In her relationships, too, she felt victim to other people's perceptions and expectations of her, and attempts to empower herself usually failed; she suffered from feelings of being rejected and betrayed. She was caught in an unconscious identification with victimhood, which at a conscious level she tried energetically to avoid. In terms of Grof's basic perinatal matrix, Arlene sought the peace and harmony of a return to the first stage as an escape from the pain and limitations of the second, when contractions and labour begin. She frequently used a rebellious fighting mode associated with an unintegrated third stage to try to achieve this; this only served to hurt her, as expressions of her assertiveness and power through angry tirades were not grounded in her source, and were thus ineffective. Unable to accept her pain and the suffering of human life fully, she was caught in a conflict where her tendency to dissociate from her body when life felt difficult was answered through her body's creation of debilitating tension and pain, as if her symptoms were calling her to return home to her body.

In order to grow, Arlene needed to consciously own her experiences of pain, betrayal, and the limitations of being human. She needed to fully embody herself and accept her suffering in order to integrate the issues associated with the second stage of the basic perinatal matrix, and thus be able to move on and connect to her power, assertiveness, and will in an effective way. In order to do this she needed to experience the ground of trust in a holding environment that would not reject or betray her. At this point, about a year into her therapy, it was clear that Arlene was beginning to do this; she was able to stay with her emotional feelings and painful body symptoms, accept and process them, and with that she was beginning to feel more grounded, stronger, more 'adult', and more able to value herself as a woman. As her core self strengthened, she also found herself more able to stand her ground in relationship conflicts. Her psychological work was not yet complete and she was still troubled by distressing body symptoms, but she was able to descend safely into deeper feeling and begin to address early issues and trauma from a more stable and embodied sense of self.

Continuing menstrual difficulties brought Arlene to explore her relationship to her female body further. Blocked energy in her womb, which stopped the flow of blood and the flow of energy into her legs, evoked a male voice that said 'she's unclean, disgusting, imperfect'. From the tight womb, like a fist, emerged the message 'if I don't move no-one will see me'. Although her mind now held more positive views about her womanhood, her body had clearly internalized and somatized these negative messages; she felt that they originated both from the culture and from her father. Focusing on her belly area, she could not bring awareness to her womb because of the layer of fat covering it, which she tended to disown. Gentle touch to facilitate movement of energy in the fatty tissues in this area of her body, together with embodiment of a subpersonality she called Fatima - discovered in a previous session, who was a 'disgusting and rather crude, fat lady who loves who she is and isn't concerned with what others think of her' - helped her to loosen and mobilize the repressed energy held in the fat tissue. This enabled her to connect to movement through her womb and legs in a beautiful dance reminiscent of Arabic 'belly dancing'. Feeling her body move in this way, she could begin to change her somatically held beliefs about her woman-self, but she also needed to understand more deeply, and somatically, the origins of these beliefs.

Arlene arrived at one session feeling hurt and betrayed by a woman friend, as if her friend were punishing her for something, but she did not know what it was. This was a familiar feeling for Arlene, and as she focused on this feeling, she felt very small and 'foetal'. Following her process in movement, she curled up with some cushions, and felt an intense pain in her neck and head. I held her head, allowing her to rest for some time like this, where she felt soothed and comforted. She was able to relax deeply and began to access the sense of being in a state of shock in the womb, frozen and unable to move; she remembered her mother not really wanting her, and how this made her feel as if she were being punished for simply being there. Later on in life she developed patterns of overworking to justify her existence. Whatever had frozen inside of her at this very early stage of life, she now needed to rest, be soothed, held, and witnessed in that hurt place, in order to begin to unfreeze the places were she was stuck and immobilized.

Work at this level needs to use non-verbal channels, for at this stage of development there are no words or concepts. In the following session Arlene continued to explore her process through her body. She was feeling pain in her chest area, and was also dealing with boundary issues – what was and was not hers to deal with? We began by focusing on the skin as boundary, and I first touched her arms and legs with this focus in mind; this felt good to her. Going to her chest area, the skin felt very thin and the muscles 'mangled and tired'; the bones did not feel very present. Her organs felt as if 'spattered against the body walls'. She was not used to letting her organs move freely, holding tension at this level, so I held and gently moved her organs, giving a feeling of fluidity; she reported the image of an egg emerging from this feeling, which began to 'bob about' as her organs softened. The image was reminiscent of the work in the previous session, and perhaps also suggested something embryonic trying to birth in her now.

Arlene was still trying to intellectualize her body symptoms, but her analyses of what she needed tended to lead her into exhaustion. An incongruency of felt experience and verbal representations indicated that she was also trying to resolve a disruption in the sense of verbal self; it was necessary to keep encouraging her to pay attention to her direct experience, and to bring this into language so as to make sense of her inner world and the symptoms rooted in early life experiences.

In a following session menstrual problems and a kidney infection brought us to focus on her kidneys. The right kidney felt ripped and scarred, as if with old wounds, and she imagined acid coming out of it; both were aching, but the left one looked pinker and healthier in her mind's eye, so she focused upon the right side. Paying attention to what it needed, she connected to sweetness and warmth. She could imagine the acid flowing out through her pores; this allowed her to rest and the sweetness and warmth to flow in. I then gave a light touch along the pathways of the nerves running through her pelvis, where she was also feeling pain, and tension there released. After this work she felt free of pain, and could appreciate that the qualities of sweetness and warmth are actually part of her. She admitted that she was felt by her family to be sweet and warm as a small child, but when expected to be like this all the time for others' benefit, she rebelled; she associated the acidity with her subsequent criticism of her self, and denial of her own sweetness.

The association of acidic and sweet milk also came up. Since our previous sessions, she had talked with her mother about her birth and prenatal time. Her mother was 28 and just regaining her sense of her sexual attractiveness after the birth of Arlene's older brother; it was Arlene's father who wanted her to have another child, against her own wish. She complied but was ill throughout the pregnancy. It can be imagined that her emotional conflict, particularly in the light of her husband's affair, would have affected Arlene; acid would be a fitting analogy for an emotional state infused with jealousy and resentment, and her mother's inability to fully value herself as a woman would have communicated subtle messages to Arlene about her own femaleness.

Following this, Arlene felt a qualitative change, like a state of 'grace', and expressed feeling connected to her body, to herself as a woman, and liking herself as a woman now. She had an image of a witchlike figure leaving her. She felt she had been possessed by this figure all her life, prevented from touching and experiencing life; now she felt as if she was fully in it. This suggested that some level of trauma and dissociation had been resolved. The witch was connected with guilt and the fundamental sense of badness that she had always carried with her. Purging the acidity of the witch and absorbing the sweet milk, she could experience herself as good, and no longer destroyed by the acid of her internal critic. The critic was still there, and still needed to be dialogued with, confronted, educated, and challenged at times, but the fundamental and psychologically debilitating sense of badness had lifted.

Addressing trauma in the body

At this point in her therapy Arlene began to feel she was ready to end her work. She felt more able to deal with her life, and expressed seeing me more as a person. Release from the witchlike figure indicated a level of separation from her mother that enabled her to simultaneously feel more separate from her therapist. Several dialogues ensued between the part of herself that wanted to be independent, and believed that she should be able to support herself, and the fearful 'child' who needed safety, understanding, and time to grow at her own pace. Having established that both parts could be present in her therapy, and that she did not have to leave immediately in order to separate, she decided to continue. As separation was an important issue for her, it needed to be addressed *within* therapy, and might require a longer period of time. After this decision was made, Arlene's renewed commitment seemed to allow her to work more deeply with her trauma; and in keeping with including her 'independent self', she was able to take more charge of the direction of the therapy, being clear about what she needed and how far she was able to go.

In a series of sessions Arlene began to address the fall she had at 6 months of age. The pattern of symptoms connected with her early fall were easily triggered by stress, and the knowledge that her body and the ground could let her down evoked anxiety and fear. When we suffer a trauma that we are unable to process, beliefs are established deep in the unconscious mind, in an attempt to avoid further hurt. In the event of early trauma, the beliefs are embodied somatically, together with memories and associated feelings. Arlene came to believe that being in her body equalled death, and so she had never felt able to fully embody herself. Whilst it is likely that the accidents engendered this belief, she also realized that the physical pain they caused also brought her *into* her body, and thus could be seen to be trying to serve her in a way. An even earlier reluctance to fully embody herself, probably originating in her lack of wholly positive holding in the womb, may have been at the root of her fears and beliefs about her body. The pain caused by the accidents could be seen to be opportunities to address the issue of fully incarnating, accepting life on earth and the limitations, as well as pleasures, of being in a human body.

Arlene was experiencing pain and swelling in her left foot; her left tibia had been broken when she fell down the stairs at 6 months, and she spent some time with her left leg and foot in a cast. (At this period of development she should have been practising the crawling movements which would articulate the feet and integrate them into the spine; missing out on this experience would leave her spine without an essential grounding and support.) She and her husband were also living temporarily with her parents at this time, and she was finding her mother's 'big character' too much for her; she was unable to find her own space, and perhaps the inflammation of the left foot reflected this and the lack of appropriate support from and for her feminine side. As she talked about this, I noticed she was alternately stroking and prodding the foot. She said she was trying to dig out and get rid of the pain, and also trying to soothe it. I invited her to take her awareness into the foot and imagine how the foot was feeling; it felt like something sensitive and finely tuned that had a lot of pressure put on it. The bones felt brittle and the whole foot inflexible, with the muscles gripping the bones. It needed flexibility so that it could bend and not snap with the pressure; this was a clear description of how a part of Arlene frequently felt, embodied in this instance in her foot.

Using her imagery as guidance, I traced the bones of her foot and worked to open the joint spaces, bringing some fluidity to both bone tissue and joints; a lot of heat was released and more freedom was gained between the tarsals. She was then able to move her foot more freely. This release stimulated a need to yawn, but the full breath was blocked in her upper chest. I placed my hand there and very gently amplified the movement of the exhalation, and her body began to shake slightly. With encouragement, she was able to release the shaking through her whole body; the muscles around her shoulders relaxed and she felt energized after this, also laughing and perhaps on the edge of excitement, I thought. She said it was a new experience for her to let her body shake without being in control of it, and was very impressed by this experience.

Subsequently her mother told her that after her fall down the stairs she had gasped for breath, her body shook, then she passed out. She was still experiencing fear of feeling pain, and her foot, although much better after the session, was hurting again after too much activity. More general bodywork to give her a feeling of safety enabled her body to integrate the first release, before we addressed the pain in the foot again. This time I worked more specifically on the periosteum of the bone and the actual bone tissue, allowing some unwinding in these tissues. Focused articulation of the bones brought new sensations and movements that she had not felt before, and changes in her breathing occurred.

We came to the centre of the pain, where she found an image of fire; it felt as if something were jabbing into the painful joint and turning inside it. Becoming the symptom-maker (Mindell), she enacted the movement of jabbing and turning with her finger into a cushion, and discovered that she was trying to remove something that looked like a black bullet that had grown long roots into her foot and got lodged there. She tried various things but could not extract the roots. We dialogued with the image and were informed that it was there because 'someone kicked me'. There had always been a question in Arlene's mind as to how she had been left in a situation, at 6 months old, where she could fall down a flight of stairs; why was no one watching over her? She had been left with two older children, and it is not impossible that she was accidentally (or purposefully) kicked, and fell as a result. She will probably never know this, and it is not necessary to her healing to know, but her body seemed to suggest that, whether literally or metaphorically, she felt kicked, prodded, and pushed; by enacting the symptom-maker she could see how she was also prodding, pushing and hurting herself in her attempts to heal. Through inner dialogue she learned that the area where the bullet was lodged was in need of attention and care, and she related it to the hurt part of herself in need of loving attention. She tended to judge this part as 'pathetic', and tried in different ways to get rid of it, pushing herself in her efforts; she was now being asked to be gentler, to own, accept and take care of her hurt inner child. She saw that she needed the pain, in the image of the bullet, to be there as a reminder to accept and heal her wounds.

With the evocation of the wounded child, Arlene's fear of being unheld and of falling was very present. She told me that the tension in her neck was connected to a fear that her head would fall off, so vulnerable did her neck feel. The focus of attention on her neck problems suggested she was ready to explore this area of vulnerability. I worked with her head and neck in this and many subsequent sessions, cradling her head in my hands and very gently facilitating small movements in the tissues, which allowed deep levels of release and integration through the central nervous system and the spine. She told me that I was only the third person whom she had allowed to touch her neck, so vulnerable did it feel; this was an affirmation that she trusted me enough to share the most wounded parts of herself and to feel held as she let go into her most vulnerable and undefended states.

The fear and tension locked into her neck led her to enter into the experience of the wounded child, who feared the world and wanted to hide from it, and who sometimes did not want to stay here at all. Connecting to her, Arlene cried deeply, then was able to see herself as a little girl hiding in a corner, covering herself to get away from people's demands and expectations. The child seemed very alone. The adult Arlene was now ready to take care of her inner child, and imagined taking her onto her lap and listening to her. Through inner dialogue she learnt that the child did not want to be here, and felt that home was in another place, a spirit world; she felt very homesick. Arlene feared the child would 'return to her spirit home', and to protect herself from this loss, she generally disconnected from both her inner child and her own spiritual life. Now she could feel the presence of the 'spirits' who told her that the child is here to bring light into the world; she needs to stay, as the world needs her light. In order to be here she needed Arlene to hold and protect her, and Arlene needed the child to make her life meaningful and connect her to spirit, and to the guidance of her spirit.

Around this time Arlene began to talk of her accidents and other problems differently; her language suggested that she was becoming more identified with the power behind the symptom-maker, rather than the weakness of the victim. She became more focused upon how to channel her newly emerging energies, and was occupied with questions as to whether she wanted to have a child or train for a new career. Her attention was again drawn into relationship work; she dialogued with and role-played parents and friends, and continued to address her inner critic in various forms. Through these explorations she was integrating more of her shadow, and in particular embodying aspects of herself that were powerful, strong, fun, and not so sensitive to others' perceptions and criticisms of her. Freeing herself from the dynamic of 'parenting' her parents by taking care of their needs, being seen by them for who she is, and being respected by others, were important issues during this phase of her work. She connected to her deep need to hear her father acknowledge that his affair with her cousin was wrong, and to understand how much it had hurt her; he continued to deny that he had done wrong, and in this he was also was denying her experience of pain. She needed him to apologize, without excuses, defence or denial.

Some sessions later we returned to her accidents, and went back to the fall in the hot-air balloon. As the balloon was landing, she went 'floppy', thinking that this was the best way to avoid injury. In fact she needed to brace herself and use her protective responses, but was unable to. As the balloon landed badly, her father had called and reached out towards her cousin in such a way that it became clear to Arlene and her mother that they were having an affair. Arlene fell, hurt herself, and went into shock; no one noticed this, her mother being preoccupied with the realization of her husband's affair. She walked off alone and wandered around the field where they had landed, cold and in shock, for some time. In the session we went back to the time of the trauma;

she went into the position and feeling her body remembered after the fall, and I held her, following her own directions, as she had needed to be held at that time, so that she could reconnect to her frozen feelings and begin to release them. Eventually she was able to call upon her protective responses and brace herself in a way that would have enabled her to avoid the fall and the injury; it was necessary for her to embody this response fully, so that patterns learnt at the time of the fall could be unravelled and new resources learned. After this she looked present, clear, and grounded. It was as if part of her had remained up in the balloon all this time; now she felt as if she had come down and was clearly on the earth again.

Following this work Arlene felt open and quite vulnerable for a while. Again, bodywork that was nourishing, containing, and focused on balancing sympathetic and parasympathetic activity was used. We also explored the equilibrium responses that should have protected her from the fall in the balloon, but were inactive at the time, probably because the fear engendered by the earlier falls was inhibiting them. We were now about two years into our work together, and Arlene was asking more and more to be shown ways that she could work with the body processes on her own at home. In this way she was integrating resources and slowly preparing herself to end therapy. She was able to say that she loved her body now, and expressed feeling more content with being who she is and enjoying the simple things in life, rather than striving and pushing herself to do something 'important' in the future. I see this as identifying more with the feminine way of creating a meaningful present, in contrast to the masculine heroic mode of forging a new path into the future. She was accepting the woman she is, and realizing that what had been stopping her from feeling this contentment with the simple moments of life was a fear of being like her mother; she felt her mother had been a fool for accepting her father's affairs, and not demanding more from him.

Arlene was beginning to reflect on her process in therapy, and recognized that the relationship with her father was central to her work; while she felt closer to being able to forgive him and let go, she knew there was still some more work to do. Continuing difficulties in her relationship with her husband had led her to see that perhaps she had married a man who was, in some ways, like her father; she wanted Mark to change and be more emotionally available and committed to the marriage, but she began to see that perhaps, in marrying such a man, she was still trying to get the unconditional love and the attention she felt she had never received from her father. As a child she had felt her father had little time for the family, giving her the sense that his life was more important and interesting than hers; this led her to undervalue herself and her own life, and to struggle to emulate him in order to get his attention and praise. This eventually led to her illness. Being ill or having problems was also a way of getting his attention, but this kept her almost constantly ill or in crisis. She was jealous of his grandchildren who seemed to receive the quality attention she felt she had never received.

Eventually she was able to own her jealousy and hatred of Sandra, her cousin, who she felt was privileged to the 'one to one attention' that she did not have. Sandra had also received the sexual love that was forbidden between Arlene and her father, but which was nevertheless tantalizingly and confusingly present. As a child Arlene had felt special to her father but she later lost this feeling when he withdrew from her during her adolescence. Being made to feel special to him, then losing this privileged place in his world, made Arlene vulnerable to the inappropriate attentions of men in positions of power and authority, such as the therapist mentioned earlier. Unable to resist the restoration of the feeling of specialness to a father figure, Arlene was unable to say 'no', and her boundaries were easily violated. When she learned of her father's affair with Sandra, that her cousin had usurped the special and privileged place that she had once held, she felt he could not possibly love her if he could do something like this to her. She came to equate not receiving emotional support, or being let down by someone, with not being loved. Owning her jealousy and hatred was clearly hard, but it was a powerful and important act, and seemed to enable further resolution of the central issue with her father.

Ending therapy

During this period Arlene had also been working hard on her relationship with her husband; we explored their conflicts and the stuck place they had come to in many ways, using dialogue, role-play, and embodied enactment to understand the issues more clearly. She had been able to discriminate her projections, and take responsibility for her own patterns and the conflicts with her father; her personal therapy seemed almost complete, but there were still problems in their relationship. He seemed to be 'married to his job', which left her feeling lonely, neglected, and taken for granted, and her attempts to address this situation tended to drive him further away; thus a vicious cycle had been established and they could not get free of it. Eventually Mark agreed to her request to enter couple's therapy together, and this coincided with the ending phase of our work together.

The therapy seemed to be progressing well. Mark began to connect to his own feelings, and to take more responsibility for the relationship, and this allowed Arlene to let go of struggling and to connect to an underlying sadness at the loss of an old dream for their life together. She was viewing both herself and the relationship more realistically. She also felt stronger and knew that, even though there would still be difficulties at times, 'strong winds would no longer blow her over'.

In the ending phase of our work, bodywork again became important. Arlene was taking back more and more of her own authority in this and other relationships, and was able to know with some clarity what she needed to address, at the same time as being able to surrender to her process through somatic work. She focused upon gaining resources that she could use at home, both in terms of somatic work, in which she was now quite experienced, and strategies for dealing with difficult emotions and relationship problems. Although she had been doing some part-time work and had participated in some women's workshops, yoga classes, writing and other creative activities, she was still not clear about the direction of her life. Gradually she came to acknowledge that healing her relationship with her husband, and being a wife and homemaker were the most important things for her at the moment. It was difficult to own this; it did not seem 'politically correct' or fashionable to want these traditional values, and her inner critic kept telling her this was not enough. But in fact it marked a great degree of commitment to herself, and understanding of her own wishes and values, to be able to stand up against inner and outer pressures and acknowledge that which was true for her. Now that she was her own person, accepting a more traditionally female role than she was used to aspiring to no longer meant becoming like her mother, or accepting her mother's fate and resignation. And as she grew in self-confidence Arlene was also beginning to receive the respect from others that she longed for.

In a session just a short while before her therapy was to end, we followed a process of active imagination with an image that had emerged. She saw herself trying to climb a wall, which surrounded a castle and garden. Seeing a ladder nearby, she realized she did not have to struggle with the impossible task of climbing the wall – she could use the ladder instead. She came to the top of the wall and was very happy to see birds and insects flying between the two worlds; the world within the wall and that without were connected by their movement – the two worlds were essentially one. She had seen this castle and wall in her imagination years ago, but at that time she was too afraid to go out. Now the place felt too small, and she was curious to step outside. She went out through the gate and found it felt safe and pleasant to walk around the outside of her castle walls. She saw many people and places in the distance, and was curious about them; she knew she could go there, but did not need to at the moment. Instead she sat by a tree at the main gate, trusting that there was something out there for her, and that one day she would make the long journey to discover it – she would travel with her 'wise woman' on a motor-bike! Eventually she went into the castle and met the male and female housekeepers who looked after it, and watched over what came in and went out through the gates – they were both housekeepers and gatekeepers, guardians and caretakers of her inner world.

When she had first encountered this image some years previously, her father had been inside the castle walls with her. This made her feel both protected, and also imprisoned and afraid, feelings that clearly expressed the ambiguity and confusion in her relationship with him. Now he was no longer there; it was wholly her own space, and she was now her own self. She could protect her boundaries and choose who entered her space; she could also venture out into the wider world without fear, and had come to understand how the inner and outer worlds are not separate but are intrinsically connected parts of the whole of experience.

Arlene still suffered from some physical symptoms, and had to be mindful of her limitations and stress levels, but she had developed many resources to process her feelings, accept and transform disturbing body symptoms, and support herself in relationships. Finally she needed to own her own authority and wisdom, and other qualities that she had projected onto me as her therapist. She described the core of her work as 'to be able to know what is true for me, and trust my inner voice'. Another image in the penultimate session reassured her that she was now empowered to do this. She was looking for a way to remember the feeling of wellbeing she had now, to support herself at times when things were difficult, and entered a visualization process. She saw her 'wise woman' who gave her a key. It was the 'master key' that could open many doors. Behind some of the doors would be light; behind others would be dark and threatening things. Both were present, but she could choose when to open and close the doors. She was taking back projections onto wise and helpful figures, both internal and external, and including her therapist, and now held the key by which she could master her own inner life.

The week before Arlene's last session of therapy seemed to reflect the paradoxical nature of her life. Her grandfather had died during the previous week, and at the funeral in a few days time she would meet her cousin Sandra for the first time since learning of the affair with her father. It was unfortunate that we would not be meeting after this, but we both felt she was now prepared to meet this challenge, as well as carry the double grief of losing her grandfather and her therapist. A new phase of her journey was beginning, where she would be challenged to integrate all she had learnt at a deeper level. At the same time, during the week Arlene had gone shopping and treated herself by buying clothes and special oils and perfumes, as she was going to a friend's wedding - the themes of death and marriage again coinciding. It was as if she were now truly ready for her own wedding, her inner marriage, and was adorning herself in celebration of her womanhood. I was reminded of Psyche's journey to the underworld to receive Persephone's beauty ointment before her divine marriage to the god Eros (Johnson, 1977: 23-4). Arlene had come to know and value herself as a woman, and to accept herself as a being of both spirit and matter; now she was marking this moment with a symbolic act reminiscent of the initiatory myths of antiquity.

Concluding words

Our body is our homes and ground. It is the vehicles through which we learn and grow, communicate and express ourselves in the world. From the subtlest of molecular exchanges within the cells of the body, to the most intricate of dance or acrobatic movements, the body is a universe of experience, constantly changing, evolving, and transforming from moment to moment. Most of these processes occur beyond the reach of consciousness and the verbal realm, but nevertheless they are determined by a wisdom far beyond the capacity of our reasoning alone. Cellular intelligence, the wisdom of the body, is intimately connected to the conscious and unconscious processes of mind and emotions. The body can reveal the secret, hidden, or forgotten areas of experience embedded within it, and as we learn to listen to the body in its constantly transforming expressions, we learn to know ourselves more deeply. Body and mind inseparable, the bodymind, becomes the playground for our adventure into self-knowledge and self-discovery, when we approach it with a willingness to listen and to surrender to that which is beyond the rational, the obvious, and the mundane.

In order to befriend our world and live in peace with it in all its diversity, we must first befriend ourselves. This entails acceptance of all that within us that feels alien or unacceptable - our problems, our negative emotions, our sickness, our disappointments and limitations. So often the unacceptable parts of us are somatized, and the body responds by becoming ill, developing pain, or refusing to perform as we would like it to. By paying attention to these symptoms, we can source back to the origins of the problem and gain insight into what needs to change, be let go of, embraced, or healed. Treating the body as an alien object deepens the rift between our conscious life and the source of life, leaving us feeling lost, ungrounded, anxious, and angry with the way things are. To return to our source and regain the feelings of wellbeing, trust, and love, we need to cultivate a conscious relationship with the whole of who we are - body, feelings, mind, and spirit.

We have explored how a holistic approach to therapy, embracing body and spirit as well as mind and feelings, can help to nurture our growth towards wholeness and the full embodiment and expression of our authentic self. I now dedicate this work to you, the reader, in the hope that something within it will have touched you, encouraged you, informed or inspired you on your own path.

Appendix 1: developmental movement patterns

Pattern	Body coordination, species, age
1 Cellular breathing	Expansion and contraction of each cell of body in internal respiration. Integrates and aligns physical body. The original one-cell (ovum). One-celled organisms, for example amoeba. Present throughout life from conception – underlies breathing and all life processes. Mind of 'being'.
2 Navel radiation	Integrates the extremities of the body into the centre, through the navel. Starfish. Present in utero.
3 Mouthing	Head rocks on lower jaw; nursing action of infant. Hydra, sea squirt. Prebirth and birth; dominant during early infancy.
4 Prespinal	Integrated movement between head and torso, to tail; spinal movements initated in 'soft spine' of spinal cord or organs. Lancelet amphioxus. Underlies spinal patterns; prebirth, birth and early infancy. Transition to 'doing' mind.

5 Spinal yield and push from head	Integration of spine from head to tail; spinal movements. Inch worm, caterpillar.
6 Spinal yield and push from tail	Prebirth, birth, early infancy.
7 Spinal reach and pull from head	Movement of spine through space, led by head or tail; enables child to change levels.
8 Spinal reach and pull from tail	Fish. Birth, early infancy. Initiation first from mouth – other senses develop in first few months.
9 Homologous yield and push from upper extremities	Both arms/hands together push the body backwards; then both feet/knees push the body forwards.
10 Homologous yield and push from lower extremities	Rabbit, kangaroo; other mammals, for example, horse, dog, when running at speed. From upper – birth to 3 months. From lower – 3 to 5 months.
11 Homologous reach and pull from upper extremities	Both arms reach forwards and pull the body through the space in front; then both legs reach backwards and pull the body through the space behind. Fingers and toes initiate.
12 Homologous reach and pull from lower extremities	Frog leaping, squirrel; other mammals when running at speed. 5 to 7 months.
13 Homolateral yield and push from upper extremities	Belly crawling; right arm pushes back into right leg, elongating right side and flexing left. This prepares for push from left foot through to left hand, and movement forwards.
14 Homolateral yield and push from lower extremities	Alternate sides initiate and elongate. Amphibians and reptiles, for example lizard, alligator. Some mammals, for example, camel, elephant. Others revert to this pattern when trotting at moderate pace. From upper – 5 to 6 months. From lower – 6 to 8 months.

15 Contralateral reach and pull from upper extremities	Cross crawling on hands and knees, walking, running, and so forth.
16 Contralateral reach and pull from lower extremities	Fingers of one hand reach forwards to pull opposite leg through and move forwards. Toes reach backwards to pull opposite arm and crawl backwards. Most mammals when walking. Humans. 'Brachiation' pattern of primates (for example, apes) involves reach and pull through hands. From upper – 7 to 9 months. From lower – 9 to 11 months. From about 1 year onwards contralateral walking and running gradually develops.

All patterns, once developed and integrated, continue to be refined and strengthened throughout childhood and adult life. They are, under normal circumstances, present throughout the whole of life. Ages given are approximate times a pattern fully emerges and temporarily dominates. Individuals may vary greatly in this timing, and also in the actual movements they make within each basic patterning; however the natural order of the unfolding of the sequence of patterns is universal.

(This chart is taken from *Wisdom of the Body Moving*, Linda Hartley, pp. 84-5.)

Appendix 2: inner body dialogue

(Please note that this exercise should not be used in a professional context with clients unless training in this kind of work has been received. However, if you wish to explore it yourself, you might like to ask a friend to put the questions to you and guide you from one stage to the next; or you could make a tape recording of them.)

Exercise to explore the inner body dialogue

First sit or lie down comfortably and spend a little time relaxing and becoming aware of the different sensations in your body. Then gently touch your body in the area to be explored and focus your awareness into the tissues needing attention. Begin to explore with questions such as:

1. What do you feel there? There may be sensations, images, feelings, sounds, memories; notice and describe them in as much detail as possible.
2. What do you feel towards this part of your body, or the image, voice, or feeling that you connect to there? What are your thoughts and attitudes towards it? Can you identify any belief systems associated with it? Be open and receptive to whatever arises.
3. Begin to dialogue with it, saying what you are thinking and feeling to this part, or to the image which represents it. You might also want to ask it questions, such as: What or who are you? What is your function? What do you want? Why are you in this condition? What do you need? Find your own questions, and listen inwardly and receptively for the responses.
4. You may then wish to go a step further and identify with this part of yourself. First check carefully whether this feels right. If it does, then imagine taking on all of its qualities, its shape, posture, movement, voice, energy, and so forth. Breath by breath, gradually absorb it into you, until you feel you have become it. Physically embodying the part can often be more powerful and effective than simply imagining that you identify with it, so try this out if you wish, moving and speaking as this 'character'.

5. As this part, or the image representing it, dialogue back to yourself, again expressing your feelings, attitudes, your desires and needs Feel free to express yourself in any way, including movement and sound.

6. When this feels complete, disidentify from the part and come back to being yourself; physically changing your posture or place will help you to do this. Then witness any changes you see or feel towards this part of you now. The process of identifying with and disidentifying from the part or image can be repeated several times, if necessary, until the dialogue feels complete.

7. To ground and integrate the experience, take time to talk (or write some notes, if you are exploring this exercise on your own) about what happened and what it means for you in your life. Are there any new insights, new attitudes or beliefs to be integrated? Are there new choices to be made? Is there something you now understand that you need to do or to receive, as a result of what you have learned and felt during this exercise? Be specific about how, where, and with whom these things can be integrated into your life.

8. Writing, drawing, singing, clay sculpting, or dancing are some of the creative ways you can both witness and record your experiences, and embody them more fully. For example, through dance and movement energetic shifts can occur that facilitate the integration of change at physiological as well as cognitive levels so that new awareness and choices can be supported in a natural and organic way. So if you wish to, find a creative way to express what you are feeling now, and any important experiences that occurred during the inner body dialogue.

(Please note that if you contact feelings that you need to explore in more depth during this exercise it may be advisable to seek the help of a qualified therapist to help you to look at the issues that have arisen.)

Appendix 3: myalgic encephalomyelitis (ME)

Sadly there are many within the medical profession and amongst the general public who still view the disease myalgic encephalomyelitis (ME), or chronic fatigue syndrome (CFS), as 'all in the mind', despite ample scientific research that proves otherwise. (Many research and clinical papers on ME have been published in standard medical journals but are infrequently read by doctors. These papers have been collected into one volume by Byron Hyde of the Nightingale Research Foundation, Canada – see Hyde, 1992.) The onset of the illness is frequently associated with a viral infection, compounded by immuno-depressive agents such as secondary viruses, recent immunization, steroid treatment, hormonal disturbances, excess exercise, and emotional, mental, or other stress factors. The disease process continues long after the activity of the virus ceases; it is now understood that:

> . . . during multiplication of the causal virus, a number of incomplete defective variants are produced which can evade the normal immune defences. Thus, patients have to suffer a prolonged struggle for supremacy between a normal, if overactive, immune system and an abnormal, defective virus. (National ME Centre, 1993: 17)

Myalgic encephalomyelitis is considered to be primarily a neurological and immunological disease; inflammation of brain tissue and the occurrence of lesions in areas of the brain coincide with disturbances in a variety of neurological functions and other body systems. The muscles, liver, heart, endocrine, and lymphatic glands are all commonly affected.

At Lynden Hill Clinic in Berkshire, treatment for ME is based upon a belief that accidents which injure the spine are also causative factors in the onset of the illness. So far I know of no research that looks specifically at the relationship between the onset of ME and post-traumatic stress disorder, but most of the people I have encountered who suffer from this disease have experienced a significant physical or emotional trauma or bereavement, either early in life or soon before the onset of the disease, which has not been resolved. Peter Levine, who has worked in the field of stress and trauma therapy for 30 years, believes that ME occurs as a result of unresolved trauma (Levine, 1997: 149, 165). Certainly it is now generally agreed that a period of mental stress precedes the onset of the illness; this weakens immune system responses, and causes widespread dysfunction of the neuroendocrine system. Digestion, metabolism, cognitive and neuromuscular functioning are all adversely affected as the person spirals into a state of increasing physiological imbalance and exhaustion from which they cannot recover, without specialized help and extensive lifestyle changes.

Research by Dr David Smith at University College Hospital, London, suggests that a deficiency in neurotransmitter substances is responsible for the wide range of debilitating symptoms present in ME patients (Smith, 1995: 24-7); neurotransmitters are the chemical messengers that transmit electrical stimuli from one neuron to another across the synapses between cells. This deficiency is global in ME, affecting every area of the brain, the central and peripheral nervous system, and thus a multitude of functions. He believes that the neurotransmitters are damaged because holes form in the blood-brain barrier. Blood plasma is toxic to neural tissue; to prevent the diffusion of the larger toxic protein molecules and blood plasma into the nervous system, fine membranous sheaths coat all neurons and blood vessels entering the brain – this is known as the blood-brain barrier. In ME, these membranes are damaged and blood plasma leaks into the brain, effectively poisoning it and causing damage to the neurotransmitters and their receptor sites.

As described earlier in the book, imbalanced activity of the autonomic nervous system can result from stress of all kinds, and affects the healthy functioning of the immune system. The brain has its own independent immune system, distinct from but closely linked to the immune system of the body and it is most likely that the brain's immune system will be adversely affected by stress, as the body's immune system is. Dr Smith believes that mental stress can reduce the brain's ability to control the immune system response. He hypothesizes:

> Thus, instead of your immune system making a swift but appropriate response to the virus it produces a volcanic, uncontrolled pathological process. It doesn't have to be a particular ME virus, or glandular fever or Epstein Barr virus or enterovirus; it can be any virus that is capable of triggering your immune system. As the immune response is wildly out of control, instead of just the normal slight malaise and headache that you experience with flu, there is actual damage to the blood-brain barrier to such a proportion that one becomes clinically ill . . . The blood-brain barrier damage and the immune response persists and this produces the functional disorder of Post Viral Syndrome. (Smith, 1995: 35-6)

At Harley Health Clinics in London, Ian Hyams takes a very broad and integrative approach to the treatment of ME. Using highly sensitive diagnostic procedures, imbalances in neurological, nutritive, endocrine, and immune functions can be assessed and individual programmes of treatment devised. Lifestyle management, together with conventional and nutritional medicine, offer a comprehensive multilayered approach to treatment, which aims to restore biochemical, physiological balance and health. Dr Hyams agrees that ME is an 'immune activation illness'; he believes there is a genetic predisposition, and onset of the disease may be triggerd by viral infection or toxicity, with stress playing a major role. He states:

> There is no single beneficial treatment to control this illness. It is a complex illness, with many symptoms which seem to mainly revolve around the immunology and neurology systems . . .
>
> We apply an *integrated pyramid approach* to treatment which aims at trying to correct the whole pathogenesis of the illness . . . In brief, our integrated pyramid approach to treatment involves the following levels: . . . lifestyle management programme . . . neurological medication . . . scientifically-based nutritional supplementation . . . [regulation of] the function of the gastrointestinal tract . . . hormone function . . . immune modulation approaches. [Transcript of interview with Hyams, published by Action for ME.]

In traditional Tibetan medicine it is thought that there are three sources of disease: external agents, such as viruses, bacteria, and environmental toxins; internal causes, such as the way our thoughts, emotions, and attitudes affect our health; and karmic causes, which could be thought of as genetic disposition in modern medical language, that which we bring with us into life. Myalgic encephalomyelitis seems to have both causes and symptoms in all three of these areas, and so healing needs to address all levels – biochemical and physiological imbalances, psychological and emotional disturbances, and a spiritual approach to healing the deeper issues of the individual's life.

Appendix 4: professional associations

Association for Dance Movement Therapy (ADMT) UK
c/o Quaker Meeting House
Wedmore Vale
Bedminster
Bristol BS3 5HX
UK

Association of Humanistic Psychology Practitioners (AHPP)
BCM AHPP
London WC1N 3XX
UK
Tel: 08457 660326

Authentic Movement Institute
PO Box 11410
Oakland
CA 94611-0410
USA
Tel: 510 237-7297

Body-Mind Centering® Association, Inc.
16 Center Street,
Suite 530
Northampton
MA 01060
USA
Tel: 413 582-3617

British Complementary Medicine Association
PO Box 5122
Bournemouth BH8 0WG
UK
Tel: 0845 345-5977

British Holistic Medical Association (BHMA)
59 Lansdowne Place
Hove
East Sussex BN3 1FL
UK
Tel: 01273 725951

European Association for Body-Psychotherapy (EABP)
Leidsestraat 106–108/2,
1017 PG Amsterdam
The Netherlands
Tel: 0031 20-330-2703
www.eabp.org

International Somatic Movement Education & Therapy Association (ISMETA)
PO Box 547
Hadley
MA 01035
USA
Tel: 212 229-7666

The Somatics Society
1516 Grant Avenue
Suite 212
Novato
CA 94945
USA
Tel: 415 892-0617

United Kingdom Conference for Psychotherapy (UKCP)
167–169 Great Portland Street
London W1N 5FB
UK
Tel: 020 7436-3002

References

Aalberse M (1994) Projective identification and organic transference. Energy and Character 25(1): 59-76.

Adler J (1987) Who is the witness? Contact Quarterly. Winter 1987. Reprinted in Pallaro P (ed.) (1999) Authentic Movement. London and Philadelphia: Jessica Kingsley Publishers.

Adler J (1991) Body and soul. Paper presented at The American Dance Therapy Association 26th Annual Conference. Reprinted in Pallaro P (ed.) (1999) Authentic Movement. London and Philadelphia: Jessica Kingsley Publishers.

Adler J (1994) The collective body. Paper presented at the First International Clinical Conference in Berlin on Dance/Movement Therapy. Reprinted in Pallaro P (ed.) (1999) Authentic Movement. London and Philadelphia: Jessica Kingsley Publishers.

Ansbacher EH and Ansbacher R (1956)The Individual Psychology of Alfred Adler. New York: Basic Books.

Assagioli R (1975) Psychosynthesis. Wellingborough: Turnstone Press.

Assagioli R (1984) The Act of Will. Wellingborough: Turnstone Press.

Badcock C (1988) Essential Freud. Oxford: Blackwell.

Bailey A (1975) Esoteric Healing. New York: Lucis.

Baumgartner MU (1995) Too much 'HIV' research, not enough AIDS-research: an introduction to the work of Prof Alfred Hässig. Continuum 3(4): 6-8.

Beringer E (1995) Interview with Ilse Middendorf. In Johnson DH (ed.) Bone, Breath, and Gesture – Practices of Embodiment. Berkeley CA: North Atlantic Books.

Boadella D (ed.) (1976) In the Wake of Reich. 2 edn. London: Coventure.

Boadella D (1980) Transference. Transcript of talk given at the Boyesen Centre, London, November.

Boadella D (1987) Lifestreams. London: Routledge & Kegan Paul.

Boadella D (1988) Biosynthesis. In Rowan J, Dryden W (eds) Innovative Therapy in Britain. Open University Press.

Bohm D (1980) Wholeness and the Implicate Order. London: Routledge & Kegan Paul.

Bowlby J (1997-8) Attachment and Loss (Trilogy). London: Pimlico.

Boyesen G (1976) The Primary Personality and its Relationship to the Streamings. In Boadella D (ed.) In the Wake of Reich. 2 edn. London: Coventure.

Brennan BA (1988) Hands of Light. New York: Bantam Books.

Brennan BA (1993) Light Emerging. New York: Bantam Books.

Brown JAC (1961) Freud and the Post-Freudians. London: Penguin Books.

Brown S (1993) Healing through the human energy field: Barbara Brennan in interview. Caduceus. 21: 16-19.

Capra F (1975) The Tao of Physics. Berkeley: Shambhala.

Capra F (1982) The Turning Point. New York: Simon & Schuster.

Chodorow J (1977) Dance Therapy and the Transcendent Function. Paper presented at First Regional Congress of the International Association for Social Psychiatry, Santa Barbara CA. 1977; and First International Conference of the American Dance Therapy Association, Toronto, Canada. 1977. Reprinted in Pallaro P (ed.) (1999) Authentic Movement. London and Philadelphia: Jessica Kingsley Publishers.

Chodorow J (1991) Dance Therapy and Depth Psychology – The Moving Imagination. London and New York: Routledge.

Chodorow J (1994) Body, Psyche, and the Emotions. Paper presented at the First International Clinical Conference in Berlin on Dance/Movement Therapy at the Nervenklinik Spandau: The Language of Movement: Application of Dance/ Movement Therapy in Psychiatric Settings.

Christ C, Plaistow J (eds) (1989) Weaving the Visions. San Francisco: Harper.

Cohen BB (1993) Sensing, Feeling and Action. Northampton MA: Contact Editions.

Comparetti AM (1980) Pattern Analysis of Normal and Abnormal Development: The Fetus, the Newborn, the Child. University of North Carolina.

Conger JP (1988) Jung and Reich: The Body as Shadow. Berkeley CA: North Atlantic Books.

Davis W (1989) Transference. Energy and Character (April): 10–21.

Davis M, Wallbridge D (1983) Boundary and Space. Harmondsworth: Penguin Books.

Dowd I (1991) The use of intentional touch. Contact Quarterly (Winter): 21–9.

Dychtwald K (1977) Bodymind. New York: Tarcher/Putnam.

Eiden B (1998) The use of touch in psychotherapy. Self and Society 26(2): 3–8.

Eiden B (1999) Reich's legacy. Counselling News (January): 12–14.

Eliade M (1972) Shamanism. New York: Routledge & Kegan Paul/Bollingen Foundation, Princeton University Press.

Eliade M (1975) Rites and Symbols of Initiation. New York: Harper & Row.

Estes CP (1992) Women Who Run with the Wolves. London: Rider.

Firman J (1991) 'I' and Self: Revisioning Psychosynthesis. Palo Alto CA: Firman.

Ford CW (1989) Where Healing Waters Meet – Touching Mind and Emotion through the Body. Barrytown, New York: Station Hill Press.

Frosh S (1987) The Politics of Psychoanalysis. New Haven/London: Yale University Press.

Gardner L (1972) Deprivation dwarfism. Scientific American (July): 76–82.

Geissinger A (1998) Toward the unknown: an interview with Janet Adler. A Moving Journal (Fall-Winter): 4–10.

Gerber R (1988, 1996) Vibrational Medicine. Santa Fe: Bear & Co.

Goldenberg NR (1989) Archetypal Theory and the Separation of Mind and Body. In Christ C, Plaistow J (eds) Weaving the Visions. San Francisco: Harper.

Grof S (1985) Beyond the Brain. New York: Suny.

Grof S (1988) The Adventure of Self-discovery. New York: Suny.

Hanna T (1970) Bodies in Revolt. Novato CA: Freeperson Press.

Hanna T (1994) Three elements of somatology. Somatics 1(4) (Spring/Summer): 4–9.

Hardy J (1987) A Psychology with a Soul. London: Penguin/Arkana.

Hartley L (1995) Wisdom of the Body Moving – An Introduction to Body-Mind Centering. Berkeley CA: North Atlantic Books.

Hässig, A, Wen-Xi L, Stampfli K (1996) Stress-induced suppression of the cellular immune reactions: on the neuroendocrine control of the immune system. Medical Hypotheses 46: 551–5.

Hughes JM (1989) Reshaping the Psychoanalytic Domain. Berkeley CA: University of California Press.

Hunter M, Struve J (1998) The Ethical Use of Touch in Psychotherapy. Thousand Oaks CA: Sage.

Hyde B (1992) ME: Collected Papers. The Nightingale Research Foundation, Canada.

James G (1995) New perspectives on homoeopathy: like cures like. Continuum 3(4) (November/December): 10–13.

Janov A (1975) Primal Man. New York: Cromwell.

Johnson R (1977) She. New York: Harper & Row.

Johnson DH (1995) (ed.) Bone, Breath, and Gesture – Practices of Embodiment. Berkeley CA: North Atlantic Books.

Johnson DH, Grand IJ (eds) (1998) The Body in Psychotherapy. Berkeley CA: North Atlantic Books.

Jourard SM (1994) Somatic disclosure and perception of the soma. In Lowman M, Jourard A, Jourard M (eds) Sidney M. Jourard: Selected Writings. Berkeley CA: Round Right Press.

Juhan D (1987) Job's Body – A Handbook for Bodywork. Barrytown, New York: Station Hill Press.

Jung CG (1933) Modern Man in Search of a Soul. New York: Harvest.

Jung CG (1968) Mandalas. Bollingen Series XX, CW 9. Princeton NJ: Princeton University Press.

Jung CG (1969) The Structure and Dynamics of the Psyche. Bollingen Series XX, CW 8. Princeton NJ: Princeton University Press.

Jung CG (1972) On the psychology of the unconscious. In Two Essays on Analytical Psychology. Bollingen Series XX, CW 7. Princeton NJ: Princeton University Press.

Jung CG (1976) Psychological Typology. Bollingen Series XX, CW 6. Princeton NJ: Princeton University Press.

Jung CG (1980) The Archetypes and the Collective Unconscious. Bollingen Series XX, CW 9. Princeton NJ: Princeton University Press.

Keleman S (1975) Your Body Speaks Its Mind. Berkeley CA. Center Press.

Keleman S (1976) Bio-energetic concepts of grounding. In Boadella D (ed.) In the Wake of Reich. London: Coventure.

Keleman S (1985) Emotional Anatomy. Berkeley CA: Center Press.

Kestenberg JS, Buelte A (1977) Prevention, infant therapy and the treatment of adults. 2: Mutual holding and holding-oneself-up. International Journal of Psychoanalytic Psychotherapy 6: 369–96.

Kurtz R (1990) Body-Centred Psychotherapy – The Hakomi Method. Mendocino CA: Life Rhythm Publications.

Kurtz R, Prestera H (1976) The Body Reveals. New York: Harper & Row.

Laban R (1974) The Language of Movement. Boston: Plays Inc.

Leadbeater CW (1927) The Chakras. Wheaton IL: The Theosophical Publishing House.

LeDoux J (1998) The Emotional Brain. London: Weidenfeld & Nicolson.

Leonard LS (1986) On the Way to the Wedding. Boston and London: Shambhala.

Levine P (1997) Waking the Tiger – Healing Trauma. Berkeley CA: North Atlantic Books.

Lewis P (1986) Theoretical Approaches in Dance-Movement Therapy. Dubuque: Kendall/ Hunt.

Lewis P (1994) Depth Psychotherapy in Dance-Movement Therapy. Paper presented at the First International Clinical Conference in Berlin on Dance/Movement Therapy.

Liang TT (1977) T'ai Chi Ch'uan for Health and Self-Defense. New York: Vintage Books.

Lovelock J (1991) Gaia. London and Stroud: Gaia Books Limited.

Lowen A (1971) The Language of the Body. New York: Collier Books.

Lowen A (1976a) Bioenergetics. Harmondsworth: Penguin Books.

Lowen A (1976b) Bio-energetic analysis: a development of Reichian therapy. In Boadella D (ed.) In the Wake of Reich. 2 edn. London: Coventure.

Mcneely DA (1987) Touching – Body Therapy and Depth Psychology. Toronto: Inner City Books.

Martin P (1998) The Sickening Mind – Brain, Behaviour, Immunity and Disease. London: Flamingo.

Mayland E (1995) The Rosen method. In Johnson DH (ed.) Bone, Breath, and Gesture – Practices of Embodiment. Berkeley CA: North Atlantic Books.

Meier CA (1989) Healing Dream and Ritual – Ancient Incubation and Modern Psychotherapy. Einsiedeln: Daimon Verlag.

Mills M, Cohen BB (1979) Developmental Movement Therapy. Amherst MA: School for Body-Mind Centering.

Mindell A (1982) Dreambody – The Body's Role in Revealing the Self. New York: Penguin/Arkana.

Mindell A (1989a) River's Way. New York: Penguin/Arkana.

Mindell A (1989b) Working with the Dreaming Body. New York: Penguin/Arkana.

Mindell A (1991) City Shadows. New York: Penguin/Arkana.

Mindell A (1992) The Dreambody in Relationships. New York: Penguin/Arkana.

Mindell A (1993) The Shaman's Body. San Francisco: Harper.

Montagu A (1971) Touching – The Human Significance of the Skin. New York: Harper & Row.

Moss R (1986) The Black Butterfly. Berkeley CA: Celestial Arts.

Myss C (1997) Anatomy of the Spirit. London/New York: Bantam Books.

National ME Centre (1993) What's New? ME research, 2nd Millenium BC – 1993. Romford: National ME Centre.

Northrup C (1995) Women's Bodies, Women's Wisdom. London: Piatkus.

Oschman JL (2000) Energy Medicine: The Scientific Basis. London: Churchill Livingstone.

Pallaro P (ed.) (1999) Authentic Movement. London and Philadelphia: Jessica Kingsley Publishers.

Pert CB (1986) Neuropeptides: the emotions and bodymind. Advances 3(3) (Summer): 13-18.

Pert CB (1999) Molecules of Emotion. London: Pocket Books. Simon & Schuster.

Pierrakos J (1990) Core Energetics. Mendocino CA: Life Rhythm.

Piontelli A (1992) From Fetus to Child. London and New York: Tavistock/Routledge.

Ratcliffe M (1995) AIDS babies? Continuum 3(3) (September/October): 11-13.

Reich W (1970) The Function of the Orgasm. New York: Meridian.

Reich W (1973) Cosmic Superimposition. New York: Farrar, Straus & Giroux.

Rossi EL (1986) The Psychobiology of Mind-Body Healing. New York and London: WW Norton & Co.

Rothschild B (2000) The Body Remembers: The Psychophysiology of Trauma and Trauma Treatment. New York and London: W.W. Norton & Co.

Rowan J (1985) Listening as a four-level activity. British Journal of Psychotherapy 1(4): 274-85.

Rowan J (1988) Primal Integration Therapy. In Rowan J, DrydenW (eds) Innovative Therapy in Britain. Open University Press.

Rowan J, Dryden W (eds) (1988) Innovative Therapy in Britain. Buckingham and Bristol: Open University Press.

Russell P (1988) The Awakening Earth. New York: Penguin/Arkana.

Schore, A (1994) Affect Regulation and the Origin of the Self. Hove: Lawrence Erlbaum.

Scott Peck M (1978) The Road Less Traveled. New York: Simon & Schuster.

Sharaf MR (1976) Reich and the Bio-Social Revolution. In Boadella D (ed.) In the Wake of Reich. 2 edn. London: Coventure.

Sheldrake R (1988) The Presence of the Past. London: Collins.

Siegel EV (1984) Dance Therapy: Mirror of our Selves. New York: Human Sciences Press.

Siegel EV (1994) Psychoanalytic Dancetherapy: Bridge between Psyche and Soma. Paper presented at the First International Clinical Conference in Berlin on Dance/Movement Therapy at the Nervenklinik Spandau: The Language of Movement: Application of Dance/Movement Therapy in Psychiatric Settings.

Simonton OC, Matthews-Simonton S, Creighton JL (1980) Getting Well Again. New York: Bantam Books.

Smith DG (1995) Understanding Post Viral Fatigue Syndrome – Its Treatment and Management. London: University College Hospital.

Smith FF (1986) Inner Bridges – A Guide to Energy Movement and Body Structure. Atlanta GA: Humanics New Age.

Soth M (1999a) The body in counselling. Counselling News (January): 15–17.

Soth M (1999b) Relating to and with the Objectified Body. London: Chiron Centre Publications.

Southwell C and staff of the Gerda Boyesen International Institute (1988) The Gerda Boyesen method: biodynamic therapy. In Rowan J, Dryden W (eds) Innovative Therapy in Britain. Buckingham and Bristol: Open University Press.

Stattman J (1988) Organic transference. Energy and Character.19(1) (April): 27–41.

Stern DN (1985) The Interpersonal World of the Infant. New York: Basic Books.

Storr A (1983) Jung – Selected Writings. London: Fontana.

Stromsted T (1994–5) Re-inhabiting the female body. Somatics (Fall/Winter) 10(1): 18–27.

Van der Kolk B (1994) The body keeps the score: memory and the evolving psychobiology of posttraumatic stress. Harvard Review of Psychiatry: 253–65.

Van der Kolk B, Van der Hart O (1989) Pierre Janet and the breakdown of adaptation in psychological trauma. American Journal of Psychiatry 146: 1530–40.

Van der Kolk B, Van der Hart O (1991) The intrusive past: the flexibility of memory and the engraving of trauma. American Imago 48: 425–51.

Whitehouse M (1958) The Tao of the Body. Paper presented to the Analytical Psychology Club of Los Angeles. Reprinted in Pallaro P (ed.) (1999) Authentic Movement. London and Philadelphia: Jessica Kingsley Publishers.

Whitehouse M (1963) Physical Movement and Personality. Paper presented to the Analytical Psychology Club of Los Angeles. Reprinted in Pallaro P (ed.) (1999) Authentic Movement. London and Philadelphia: Jessica Kingsley Publishers.

Wilber K (1979) No Boundary. Boston and London: Shambhala.

Wilber K (1980) The Atman Project. Wheaten, Illinois: The Theosophical Publishing House.

Wilber K (2000) Integral Psychology. Boston and London: Shambhala.

Wolf JM (ed.) (1968) Temple Fay, MD – Progenitor of the Doman-Delacato Treatment Procedures. Springfield, Illinois: Charles C. Thomas Publications Inc.

Woodman M (1982) Addiction to Perfection. Toronto: Inner City Books.

Woodman M (1985) The Pregnant Virgin. Toronto: Inner City Books.

Woodman M (1990) The Ravaged Bridegroom. Toronto: Inner City Books.

Index

30359786R10162

Made in the USA
San Bernardino, CA
12 February 2016